The solution-focused helper

Ethics and practice in health and social care

Trish Walsh

Open University Press

Open University Press
McGraw-Hill Education
McGraw-Hill House
Shoppenhangers Road
Maidenhead
Berkshire
England
SL6 2QL

email: enquiries@openup.co.uk
world wide web: www.openup.co.uk

and Two Penn Plaza, New York, NY 10121-2289, USA

First published 2010

A catalogue record of this book is available from the British Library

ISBN-13: 978-0-33-522884-3 (pb) 978-0-33-522883-6 (hb)
ISBN-10: 0335228844 (pb) 0335228836 (hb)

Library of Congress Cataloging-in-Publication Data
CIP data applied for

Typeset by RefineCatch Limited, Bungay, Suffolk
Printed in the UK by Bell & Bain Ltd, Glasgow

Fictitious names of companies, products, people, characters and/or data that may be used herein (in case studies or in examples) are not intended to represent any real individual, company, product or event.

Mixed Sources
Product group from well-managed
forests and other controlled sources
www.fsc.org   Cert no. TT-COC-002769
© 1996 Forest Stewardship Council

The *McGraw·Hill* Companies

The solution-focused
helper

Praise for this book

"Walsh's book is a conceptualization of the solution-focused helper that presupposes familiarity with a solution-focused outlook and its skills. Her SF helper would possess the combination of personal qualities and professional knowledge and skills needed to ethically practice in public health and social welfare settings that demand public accountability. Her book is not only thorough, thoughtful and clearly written, it is also timely because as solution-focused practice applications with their parallel knowledge bases continue to multiply, the questions Walsh addresses so competently are cutting edge for adopting a solution-focused approach to practice in human services."

Peter De Jong, Solution-focused Therapist, Trainer, and Consultant,
Emeritus Professor of Social Work, Calvin College, USA.

"Authoritative, accessible and engaging. Trish Walsh's book will prove invaluable for anyone wanting a more in-depth discussion of the value and uses of solution-focused approaches in health and social care."

Nigel Parton, NSPCC Professor, School of Human and Health Sciences,
University of Huddersfield, UK.

Contents

Dedicated to Dave, Tom, and Jessica Willow

Acknowledgements

I am grateful to the many practitioners in health and social care settings who shared with me their interest in solution-focused helping, their stories of experimentation in practice, and their reflections on its place in their work. In particular, I would like to thank Bernie Price, Elinor Jenkins and their colleagues (Martina Nash, Louise Donegan, Stephanie O'Brien, Jenny Duggan, and Ann-Marie Jones) in Temple Street Children's Hospital in Dublin; Martina Doyle and her colleagues in Brothers of Charity Services for Intellectual Disability in Waterford City; Bernie Cullinane, community development worker with the Health Service Executive and her colleagues (especially Fiona Martin) who worked on the Six Steps Programme in Tallaght, Dublin 24; Dr Regina McQuillan, Consultant in Palliative Medicine, St. Francis Hospice, Dublin; and Ann Moroney of Access Ireland Refugee Integration Project, Dublin. A special thanks to Dave Willow for help in drafting Chapter 2. Thanks are also due to all my colleagues in the School of Social Work and Social Policy in Trinity College Dublin, and in particular to Fiona Clarke for her help in obtaining permissions for copyright material, Ruth Torode for her feedback on chapters, and the Research Committee of the College for the grant awarded to assist with the development of this book. In addition, the assistance of both the reviewers of my initial book proposal and staff at Open University Press including Rachel Gear, Melanie Havelock, Jack Fray, and Katharine Morton was invaluable. Finally, thanks to those who gave assistance in helping me track down relevant articles and books (including Andrew Turnell, Susan Gray, Marilyn Bonjean, Lisa Edwards, Keith Brownlee, and Jeffrey Guterman) and the authors and publishers who gave permission for me to reprint copyright material. If any necessary permissions were overlooked please accept my apologies, and the matter will be rectified once contact is made.

Introduction

It is a hazardous enterprise to attempt to accurately date the 'arrival' of an innovation. In the case of therapeutic innovations, is it the date on which a team or individual worker makes a breakthrough in understanding or action? Is it the date on which a presentation is made to a conference, or an article published in a journal read by peers? Is it the moment when colleagues or peers try this innovation out for themselves, and decide, 'yes, this is new, this is interesting, this is useful?' Or is it when someone acts as intermediary, when they invite or sponsor innovators to present their work to a new audience in a different region or country? Depending on who you are, and how you have heard of this innovation, it can be any one of these moments.

For workers in the helping professions in North America, the 'News of a Difference' (Bateson, 1972), which was solution-focused therapy (SFT), arrived earlier than it did for those of us in Europe. Through a range of professional networks, conferences, and publications, the news of SFT spread beyond the American therapy community from the late 1980s. In Diffusion of Innovation Theory (Rogers, 1995), some individuals are seen to act as enthusiastic innovators and influential product champions, introducing new ideas into local social systems (including professional networks). Chris Iveson and the team now known as Brief (brieftherapy.org.uk) acted as early product champions for SFT in the late 1980s, being centrally involved in introducing the model itself and the developers of the approach, Insoo Kim Berg and Steve de Shazer, to English audiences.

Despite local differences, for all of us the process of engagement with an innovation appears to be the same (Rogers, 1995; Smale, 1996). We learn and pick up new ideas through a range of communication channels involving some of the following: doing, reading, listening, watching, thinking, trying out, seeing what happens, reflecting on what has happened. Or we do not learn if we decide to reject the idea, if we decide that this particular idea is not 'News of a Difference' (as an early American newsletter for SFT was entitled); or that it is not useful, or that it does not have advantages over our established ways of working, or that it is incompatible with our way of working or thinking. Whatever new skill it is – driving a car, assessing a situation, interviewing a client, offering therapeutic interventions to clients/patients – we all go through different stages of learning: from hearing about to deciding to try out by experimenting (if we think this new idea might be useful), and then depending on how that experiment goes and is reflected upon, deciding on whether to persist and learn this innovation, or not. We may go through this cycle only once, or we may go through it many times. This is how the diffusion of innovation is theorized (Rogers, 1995) and also how the learning cycle is conceptualized (Kolb, 1984).

All of us as helpers, when faced with an innovation, have to engage in a process of meaning-making, of weighing up this new idea against our existing ones, in the process of deciding whether it is something we are going to make an effort to learn, try out, and then use in our work. Because it is about change (and changing our own practice), taking in new ideas and learning changed patterns of behaving or thinking can be as difficult for us as experienced helpers as it can be for those we are working with. It may indeed be easier for novice helpers, as they do not have established patterns that need to be disrupted if new ideas are to take root and be developed.

The innovation under consideration here is solution-focused therapy (de Shazer et al., 1986; Miller et al., 1996; Lipchik, 2002; O'Connell and Palmer, 2003; Macdonald, 2007). Some readers may baulk at the notion of SFT as an innovation, maintaining that it is now mainstream, part of a strengths-based family of therapeutic approaches. That is true, but in part because there has been a paradigm shift in the helping professions since the 1980s (when SFT was conceived in its original form), a paradigm shift that will be considered more fully in Chapter 1. Solution-focused therapy is, to all intents and purposes, now mainstream in many (but not all) fields of practice, although not universally liked, as will be described later. What popularity it possesses has come about not just because it fits with a new mood, a new emphasis on resilience and strengths; it has also arguably come about because it has been found to be useful and relevant by many practitioners across a range of helping professions worldwide. Unlike other practice frameworks, SFT has yet to be adopted and disseminated on national and organizational levels; unlike, for example, cognitive behavioural therapy promoted as part of the NHS strategy Improving Access to Psychological Therapies (www.iapt.nhs.uk). Given the absence of organizational promotion, it is quite intriguing how persistent the appeal of SFT has been for the last twenty years. It raises the question: Is there something unique and different about SFT that accounts for its appeal? And if so, what is the nature of that appeal? To answer this question, we need first to heed Howe's recommendations to consider the relationship between a particular practice, the times in which it lives or dies, and the context in which it does well. The comings and goings of different methods will then seem less random as we discover that methods are shaped by, and themselves shape, the ideological currents of our time.

(Howe, 1991: 148)

In Part One of this book, straddling three chapters, the relationship between SFT, the time in which it developed, and the context within which it continues to do well will be considered. In Chapter 1, solution-focused therapy's roots in and connections to family therapy, brief therapy, and especially strategic family therapy are considered. Some possible reasons why SFT fared so well in the field of family therapy are suggested. The initial formulation of SFT (de Shazer et al., 1986) as a variant of strategic therapy is described, followed by a summary of how its originators subsequently developed their thinking, ultimately allying themselves to a social constructionist/constructivist philosophy and distancing themselves (somewhat) from a strategic therapy allegiance. I consider shifting epistemologies within the helping professions that created the space and a language with which to articulate and build SFT. In the latter part of Chapter 1, the question of what value (and risks) SFT may pose for helping professions is considered in the light of critiques and concerns voiced.

This is followed in Chapter 2 by an articulation and consideration of some of the value dimensions of the helping enterprise particular to public services, the pragmatics of public service provision in health and social care in these uncertain times, and current thinking on the specific organizational, moral, and ethical responsibilities of practitioners within such services. This is not to imply that ethical considerations are absent from the existing literature on SFT; far from it, rather the case is made that there are moral issues specific to public service settings that warrant specific consideration and emphasis.

In Chapter 3, a revised formulation of SFT is offered, based both on ethical considerations and empirical studies. I develop the concept of the solution-focused helper as a practitioner who remains mindful of context, role and responsibilities, and ethical dimensions of practice; also a practitioner who acknowledges explicitly the parallel (and multiple) knowledge bases on which he or she draws, and who understands the importance of hope as an underlying condition for active helpful engagement with clients. This is not an attempt to claim a drastically different model – rather it is to build on existing knowledge of and research into the particular contours of practice that health and social care professionals find themselves in.

All three chapters that form Part One are informed by doctoral research carried out with over fifty practitioners in health and social care settings in Ireland (Walsh, 2002), as well as related case studies (Walsh, 1997) that specifically examined the adjustments needed for ethical applications in public social service settings as well as other work that suggests that practitioners fall into different patterns of usage of this practice model (Pichot and Dolan, 2003). These suggest that any assessment of its value needs to move beyond the impact on clients and problems to also encompass its impact on the helper. In so doing, it relates back to de Shazer's approach to research – that of ecosystemic epistemology (Keeney, 1979; Keeney and Sprenkle, 1982) – which includes the person and actions of the helper as well as the process of helping in the equation when considering the value of an intervention. It will take us beyond the narrow confines of the current preoccupation with a hierarchy of standards in evidence-based practice focused primarily on independently assessed outcomes (valid as this is) to a more holistic consideration of the helping process, one that affirms the social constructionist basis of encounters between helper and client and that explicitly addresses the mind-set of the helper as an important component of the helping process.

In Part Two, five chapters consider the use and limitations of SFT in different practice contexts, ones which I consider have not yet been as fully represented in the literature as those relating to child welfare, education, and mental health contexts. The five chapters consist of:

Chapter 4   The solution-focused helper working across cultures in a globalized world

Chapter 5   The solution-focused helper working across the lifespan in learning disability services

Chapter 6   The solution-focused helper working in primary, acute, and specialist health care services

Chapter 7   The solution-focused helper working with older people and in end-of-life care

Chapter 8   The solution-focused helper working in community development and with groups

Throughout the book, the terms *therapist, helper,* and *practitioner* are used interchangeably, with the former term used extensively in Part One, where it is most appropriate as I relate how the SFT model developed; in Part Two, I rely more on the terms *helper* and *practitioner* in recognition of the fact that many of those who may view themselves as solution-focused helpers in public services may not consider themselves therapists as such. The term the *solution-focused helper* is used to denote the importance of the individual helper in his or her own specific context and to move the focus beyond that of the therapeutic approach itself.

The aim of the book is to address the need for practitioners to remain articulate about the forms of theory that they draw on in their practice, and to consider further the ethical dimensions of their practice in these times of increased public accountability, while inviting them to consider the possibilities offered by a solution-focused framework. I present a form of solution-focused helping that integrates qualities required of the practitioner (an active change-agent orientation to practice and a hopeful stance), qualities in the environment of practice that require attention (issues of organizational context, role, and mandate), and dimensions of practice that require explicit attention to meet the demands for public accountability (ethics, evidence, and parallel knowledge bases). The book is best suited to those who have already completed basic courses in solution-focused thinking and techniques – that is, are familiar with the core concepts and principles. Existing texts such as those by de Jong and Berg (2008) and O'Connell and Palmer (2003) cover the core principles and techniques, as do courses by reputable trainers such as **Brief** in London.

PART 1
The case for change

1 Solution-focused therapy: twenty years on

The emergence of solution-focused therapy in the 1980s: context and antecedents

Solution-focused therapy (SFT) was developed in an American clinical family therapy setting in the 1980s, a particular context and time when family therapists had some specific challenges to contend with. The initial target audience for its dissemination was the community of American family therapists, peers of de Shazer, Berg, and their team in Milwaukee. Three factors that both provided a receptive context for the development of SFT and also acted as antecedents to its development are: (1) the field of family therapy itself; (2) the increasingly convincing case for brief approaches; and (3) the existence of brief strategic therapy.

The field of family therapy itself

A review of the evolution of family therapy up to the 1980s indicates a dynamic and ever-changing expansion of ideas focused on a family orientation. Cybernetics (the study of control and regulatory systems), family systems theories, and Bateson's work on communication were influential in shaping the new therapy. Gregory Bateson, John Weakland, Jay Haley, Virginia Satir, and other members of the Mental Research Institute in California were significant early innovators in family therapy, as were Salvador Minuchin (associated with structural family therapy) and Monica McGoldrick and Betty Carter (associated with the changing family life cycle and developmental stage therapy) on the east coast of the USA. European theorists of note – including prominent teams from the UK, Ireland, and Italy – also emerged during this time.

An ever-increasing range of approaches in the 1970s widened the popularity and influence of family therapy primarily through individual, charismatic, and gifted therapists who became international celebrities. These were the valued communication channels of the time, long before information technology had such an impact on the dissemination of ideas and information. As the field expanded, attempts to classify different approaches met with varying degrees of success, with one author by the mid-1980s admitting defeat: 'It is said there are as many ways of practising family therapy as there are workers in the field' (Burnham, 1986: 62). By the late 1980s, not only was there a plethora of family therapy models but also concern that claims for its effectiveness were overstated.

By the early 1990s, family therapy was assailed by a wider range of criticisms. Feminist critiques, such as those of Hare-Mustin (1978, 1987) and Pilalis and Anderton (1986), identified a blindness to gender difference in systems theory and the low status and lack of attention paid to traditional female roles of caretaking and nurturing as issues of concern. Consumer studies, such as that of Howe (1989), were indicating that: clients did not feel understood by family therapists on their own terms; sessions were dominated by therapists who set the agenda; and clients felt powerless and disliked videotaping and live supervision. Howe came to the conclusion that systemic family therapy was unable to understand the significance of individual personal experience, banishing the subjectivity of the user and preventing a genuine dialogue taking place between the user and their therapists. In their searching review and critique of family therapy, Reimers and Treacher (1995) found that: first, (at that time) claims for most models were not supported by empirical findings (with the exception of behavioural and psycho-educational models); second, many of the major theorists of the time did not demonstrate any commitment either to validating their results or exploring the service-user's subjective experience; and third, there were problems with theory development and dissemination. The family therapy movement itself was charged with being:

> disproportionately shaped by the influence of charismatic leaders performing (literally) as showmen at important conferences and workshops . . . apparently highly effective interventions are demonstrated by skilful practitioners who are excellent showmen. Failures are typically not shared and there is usually little attention paid to research findings. Many of the presenters of such workshops actually earn their living from their presentations so there is often an in-built marketing factor which militates against presenters being objective about their own successes and failures.
>
> (Reimers and Treacher, 1995: 24–25)

The conclusion Reimers and Treacher reached was that if family therapy was to fulfil its potential as an ethical and effective practice, more attention had to be paid to the user's perspective and less to a fascination with versions of systems theory, which rendered the user (and individual subjective experience) invisible.

The increasingly convincing case for brief approaches

An important debate in family therapy (and indeed individual therapy) at the time also focused on the relative benefits and disadvantages of short-term versus long-term approaches. This is a subject of enduring interest not only to practitioners but also to policy-makers and public service managers responsible for the ethical and efficient use of resources. In the early twentieth century, Freud and collaborators such as Sandor Ferenczi initially practised psychotherapy in brief and concise forms (Budman, 2002). In the mid-1950s, family therapists were using brief treatment approaches, although these were not formalized into models for practice until the late 1970s (Erickson, 1954; Haley, 1973). Long-term work was seen to be expensive, demanding for practitioners and clients, and risked creating problems of dependency. There were also fears that long-term therapy could become directionless. Motivation was thought to be highest at the initial crisis point of seeking help or in the first few sessions. Research results indicated that clients not only preferred brief interventions but also generally tended to stay in therapy for between six and ten sessions (Reid and Shyne, 1969; Garfield and Bergin, 1978; Koss, 1979). It was also shown that those receiving brief interventions (six to eight sessions) achieved significantly more positive change than those receiving an open-ended service (Reid and Epstein, 1972), and that changes made in short-term treatments were at least as durable as those in longer-term interventions (Reid and Shyne, 1969; Fisher, 1984). As the issue of cost-effectiveness became more compelling, the case for favouring brief therapies and interventions grew (Barker, 1995). The increasing focus on short-term interventions has not been without its critics however. Some have linked the growth of short-term focused interventions to an increasing emphasis on 'surface' over 'depth' (Howe, 1996) in helping methods; others (Stevenson, 1998) have raised concerns about the appropriateness of short-term targeted interventions with particular problems such as chronic child neglect. Some of Stevenson's concerns mirror those of Howe regarding the lack of attention paid to meaning and causal theories in the rush to be brief:

> The need to find meaning in the behaviour of neglectful parents is a prerequisite for effective work with them ... Why cannot a parent control or protect their children? Why do some parents live in utter squalor and discomfort?
>
> (Stevenson, 1998: 113)

Advocates for SFT, as a therapy that initially not only carried but promoted the label of a brief form of intervention at a time in the 1980s when such approaches were in particular vogue, probably contributed to the notion that all problems could be solved in the short term and so played into the hands of North American health insurers and service providers who at the time introduced restrictions on lengths of treatment. The introduction of 'Managed Care' by health insurers in the USA at the time was seen to be particularly detrimental. Although the initial emphasis on brevity had these unintended consequences, it is important also to recognize that for de Shazer the central point was that professionals should not overstay their welcome in clients' lives, and should seek to help clients make necessary changes as speedily and as efficiently as possible. Nor was the emphasis on brief interventions embraced by all SFT advocates. Lipchik (1994) specifically criticized this element of the early practice model. Although the central notion that formal helping interventions should be, wherever possible, brief, effective, and efficient, these critiques remind us of the risks of a rush to be brief, the heterogeneity of 'problems', and the complexity of processes of change.

The existence of brief strategic therapy

Brief strategic approaches are the true precursors to SFT. Strategic therapy has been defined as a combination of 'a communication systems approach, the use of paradox and the strategic wizardry of Milton Erickson' (Guerin, 1976: 20). While this is a somewhat dated definition, it is the most useful for the purpose of comparison here. Erickson's work as a psychiatrist and therapist in the 1940s and 1950s was 'uncommon' for the time, especially when viewed against the prevailing psychodynamic orthodoxy, in particular his use of paradoxical injunctions and the use of metaphor in communication (Haley, 1973). The Mental Research Institute (MRI) founded by Don Jackson in Palo Alto, California in 1959, brought together some of the original members of Gregory Bateson's communication project team, such as Haley and Weakland, and incorporated ideas from Erickson's uncommon techniques to establish the MRI Brief Therapy Project. Their approach was outlined in two major publications in 1974: a book entitled *Change: Principles of Problem Formation and Problem Resolution* (Watzlawick et al., 1974) and a paper in the journal *Family Process*, 'Brief therapy: focused problem resolution' (Weakland et al., 1974). Defining brief therapy as (i) focusing on observable behavioural interaction in the present and (ii) involving deliberate interventions to alter the ongoing system, the MRI group claimed a new conceptualization of the nature of problems as well as their resolution. Brief therapy in this mould was characterized by the absence of any 'elaborate theory of personality or dysfunction' and relied instead on simple diagnostic formulations that would allow therapists to intervene as briefly and effectively as possible (Cade and O'Hanlon, 1993: 5). It was based on the premise that the types of problems people need help with persist only if they are maintained by ongoing behaviour by themselves and others (in other words, 'stuck' patterns of behaviour or thinking), and that the problematic behaviour or thinking is not in itself a symptom of a deeper systemic dysfunction thus obviating the need to engage in self-exploration or focus intensively on the past. The role of the therapist becomes that of an active agent of change (and more of this later) whose aim is to intervene 'to alter poorly functioning patterns of interaction as powerfully, effectively and efficiently as possible' (Weakland et al., 1974: 145). Cade and O'Hanlon (1993) describe brief therapy as concentrating on promoting change rather than promoting growth, understanding or insight; where the role adopted by the helper is one of agent of change; which uses the term *interactional* rather than systemic; and focuses on 'observable phenomena, is pragmatic and related to the belief that problems are produced and maintained 1. by the constructs through which difficulties are viewed, and 2. by repetitive behavioral sequences (both personal and interpersonal) surrounding them . . . (which can) . . . include the constructs and inputs of therapists' (Cade and O'Hanlon, 1993: 5).

In summary, the context of American family therapy at the time that SFT emerged from Milwaukee in the 1980s was one where established methods of family therapy were considered by some to be over-technical and anti-humanistic, overly popularized by high-profile charismatic leaders in public performances, under-developed in terms of evidence of effectiveness, and lacking in service-users' perspectives. Despite valid concerns about the growing dominance of brief methods of interventions (and what that indicated about broader changes in social conditions where health insurers and service providers were limiting budgets for psychological therapies), there has been an enduring interest in them to the point now when brief therapies are the type most commonly offered (Macdonald, 2007). Brief therapy as it emerged from the MRI group offered a template for a short-term intervention with a pragmatic focus on problem resolution. Strategic therapies had fallen into disrepute primarily because of concerns about the ethics of some techniques, such as paradoxical injunctions (Carr, 1995). This, then, was the context within which SFT found favour.

Given the range of criticisms that family therapy was attracting at the time, the appeal of SFT is understandable: operating from principles that emphasize the client as a person of resources, it questions the assumption that the therapist/helper knows best, redefining the role of the therapist/helper as facilitator and collaborator rather than all-powerful expert.

The emergence of solution-focused therapy

Solution-focused therapy is attributed to Steve de Shazer, Insoo Kim Berg, and their colleagues at the Brief Family Therapy Center (BFTC) in Milwaukee,

Wisconsin (de Shazer, 1985, 1988, 1991; de Shazer et al., 1986). The original team at BFTC also included Eve Lipchik, Elam Nunnally, Wallace Gingerich, and Michelle Weiner-Davis. That the development of the model was a collaborative exercise centring primarily on the partnership of de Shazer and Berg (but with other team members contributing a significant role) is evident from subsequent publications and presentations. While this chapter will continue to refer to the model as 'de Shazer's' (because he authored most of the seminal publications in the 1980s and 1990s from the BFTC), it is in my view more accurate to view de Shazer and Berg as joint developers of SFT but with others deserving credit for their role as members of the original clinic team. The later publications by de Shazer and Berg prior to their deaths in September 2005 and January 2007, respectively, reflect more accurately the central role Berg played in the refinement of the model across a range of practice settings (Berg and Kelly, 2000; Berg and Dolan, 2001; Berg and de Jong, 2002; Berg and Steiner, 2003). As subsequent publications by Lipchik (2002), Weiner-Davis (O'Hanlon and Weiner-Davis, 2003), and other members of the original team make clear, they too have a legitimate claim to the increasingly broad church of solution-focused approaches.

After years of experimentation on different pathways through the therapeutic process, always focused on a pragmatic search for 'what works', and informed by close observation and review of bona fide therapy sessions, de Shazer and Berg made their conceptual advance in the early to mid-1980s. Both have always acknowledged the influence of other theorists and model-builders, in particular Gregory Bateson, Milton Erickson, and John Weakland (de Shazer et al., 2007). De Shazer also saw his development of the solution-focused model as a *progression* of the MRI approach:

> We have chosen a title similar to Weakland, Fisch, Watzlawick and Bodin's classic paper, 'Brief Therapy: Focused Problem Resolution' to emphasize our view that there is a conceptual relationship and a developmental connection between the points of view expressed in the two papers.
>
> (de Shazer et al., 1986: 207)

In the early publications, the roots of the SFT approach in strategic therapy were obvious not only in de Shazer's conceptualization of problems, the change process, and an intervention model (de Shazer, 1985, 1988; de Shazer et al., 1986), but also in his adoption of many features of the MRI approach, including:

- *reframing* (defined as changing 'the conceptual and/or emotional setting or viewpoint in relation to which a situation is experienced and to place it in another frame which fits the "facts" of the same situation equally or even better, and thereby changes its whole meaning'; Watzlawick et al., 1974: 95);

- the use of *tasks*; and
- the depiction of different *levels of commitment to change.*

The connections between Erickson's formulation of strategic therapy, the bridge of the MRI brief therapy model, and de Shazer's starting point for SFT are clearly shown when mapped as in Box 1.1.

While incorporating these components, de Shazer also departed from the MRI model in several significant ways:

- the use of compliments and the active elicitation of exceptions and strengths;
- the emphasis on the development of a cooperative relationship; and
- the shift from task to process.

Solution-focused therapy, as initially developed, consisted of a formulaic,

---

Box 1.1 Conceptual linkages between Erickson and de Shazer

Erickson's 12 'uncommon techniques'	De Shazer's 7 corresponding interventions
Encouraging resistance	Resistance – the family's unique way of cooperating
Communicating in metaphor	Constructing metaphors using client's phraseology
Encouraging a relapse	Prediction of setbacks/emphasis change as non-linear
Emphasizing the positive	Clients viewed as doing their best; use of compliments
Seeding ideas	Possible solutions suggested as 'clues'
Amplifying a deviation	Exceptions – elicit, amplify, reinforce
Avoiding self-exploration	Concrete goals and future focus/avoid problem-focus

Amnesia and the control of information
Awakening and disengagement
Providing a worse alternative
Encouraging a response by frustrating it
The use of space and position

Erickson's uncommon strategies expanded from Haley (1973). Many also present in MRI work.

staged practice model for a clinic-based session (de Shazer et al., 1986) in a deliberate and conscious replication of the 1974 MRI model. De Shazer's 1985 and 1988 books developed the theory behind the main concepts in the model, while his two later books in 1991 and 1994 developed the philosophical foundation of his theories of therapy and in particular his reconceptualization of therapy as a language-game, as he was increasingly influenced by Wittgenstein's work on the philosophy of language. The final posthumous publication (de Shazer et al., 2007) provides a useful insight into their (de Shazer and Berg) thinking some twenty years on. While they restate many of the core concepts of the approach, they also highlight new aspects – for example, the role of the therapist/helper is now acknowledged as being located within a hierarchical relationship, not one of equality with clients.

There follows a quick summary of SFT as originally developed before we consider its subsequent linkage with social constructionism and postmodernism.

Core principles of solution-focused therapy

De Shazer et al. (1986: 208) describe the key to SFT as: 'Utilising what clients bring with them to help them meet their needs in such a way that they can make satisfactory lives for themselves'. The main principles underlying the approach are:

1   Problems develop and are maintained in the context of human interactions. Individuals possess 'unique attributes, resources, limits, beliefs, values, experiences and sometimes difficulties, and they continually learn and develop different ways of interacting with each other' (p. 208). Solutions lie in 'changing interactions in the context of the unique constraints of the situation' (p. 208).
2   The aim is to get clients doing something different, 'by changing their interactive behaviour and/or their interpretations of behaviour or situations so that a solution (a resolution of their complaint) can be achieved' (p. 208).
3   Clients are viewed as experts on their own lives. De Shazer subscribes to Erickson's belief that individuals have a reservoir of wisdom learned and forgotten but still available. The task of the practitioner is to facilitate the client in making contact with forgotten or unnoticed wisdom.
4   'Resistance' is viewed not as a label to be affixed to particular clients (usually deemed to be uncooperative), but as 'the client's way of letting us know how to help them' (p. 209). The key to cooperation is 'to connect the present to the future (ignoring the past, except for

past successes) . . . point out to the client what we think they are already doing that is useful and/or good for them, and then – once they know we are on their side – we can make suggestions for something new that they might do which is, or at least might be, good for them' (p. 209).

5   The meanings attributed to particular behaviours are seen to be of significance, especially in relation to the detrimental effects of labelling. The meaning that any behaviour is given depends on perception and perspective. Reframing is therefore proposed as a way in which 'new and beneficial meaning(s) can be constructed for at least some aspect of the client's complaint' (p. 209).

6   Goals should be small and achievable, since only a small change 'can lead to profound and far reaching differences in the behavior of all persons involved' (p. 209). The bigger the goal identified or the bigger the desired change, the more difficult it is to either establish a cooperative relationship or to achieve success. De Shazer (1991) subsequently articulated more fully the qualities of well-formed goals (reproduced later in this chapter). One small change in one part of an interactional system leads to changes in the system as a whole. Individual change can trigger interactional change.

7   Perhaps most controversially, de Shazer initially insisted that solution-construction did not require a detailed knowledge of the problem pattern: 'How will we know when the problem is solved? . . . Details of the client's complaints and an explanation of how the trouble is maintained can be useful for the therapist and client for building rapport and for constructing interventions. But for an intervention message to successfully fit, it is not necessary to have detailed descriptions of the complaint. It is not even necessary to construct a rigorous explanation of how the trouble is maintained' (p. 209). This stance was unsustainable in practice and the SFT model clearly incorporates a stage of quite detailed problem exploration prior to action.

The 1986 clinical model of de Shazer et al.

It is worth noting the different stages in the helping process as initially formulated:

1   *Pre-session change.* On the basis that asking for help in itself is a new behaviour (and that this change in itself can lead spontaneously to other changes), and one that the self-referring client can take full credit for, the client is given a task when making an appointment:

'Between now and the time when we meet, can you look out and note any changes or differences (in the problem)?'

2 *Problem-free talk* (building rapport and locating strengths). In this phase of the interview, the worker is encouraged to connect with the person, find out a bit more about them beyond the parameters of the problems, and note what the client does well, what adversity they have overcome, and what strengths they display. The practitioner starts to listen with a constructive ear (Lipchik, 1991) for the strengths that the client brings and ways they have already developed to deal with adversity.

3 *Statement of the problem pattern.* Although de Shazer maintained that for an intervention message to fit successfully it is not necessary to have a detailed picture of the problem, in practice some exploration of the problem pattern almost always takes place. The point de Shazer was emphasizing is that detailed explanations of problem patterns may not necessarily lead to solutions, as problem patterns and solution patterns may be dissimilar. An experimental trial by Macdonald (2007) and his team in Scotland in omitting to ask for any information about 'the problem' resulted in negative feedback from clients and this approach was abandoned.

4 *Exploration of solution patterns.* This takes place by eliciting and amplifying exceptions to the complaint and successful attempts to diminish its effects, and by eliciting and amplifying successful behaviour and thoughts in other areas of life. The focus is on interactional processes, which either maintain a problem pattern or interrupt it. The search for exceptions (through the use of such questions as, 'tell me about the times when it doesn't happen/when it's less bad/when you say "no"') is seen to be an intervention in itself, as it implicitly lets the client know that there are times when they are being effective, and therefore reframes them as competent rather than powerless in the face of the problem. It can therefore provide some hope for clients that problems can be solved or alleviated or that they can be competent and resilient in the face of problems. The importance of language in the careful framing of questions is implicit in this approach. Exceptions are amplified by the worker as they will help 'to create the expectation that a future is possible which does not include the problem' (de Shazer et al., 1986: 210).

5 *Goal-setting* is emphasized as crucial, so that both worker and client will know when it is time to terminate contact. This phase is also important because the essence of SFT is to convey to the client that change is not only possible but inevitable. Goal-setting also provides a clear focus for therapy, and facilitates evaluation of progress and outcome. Two techniques most associated with SFT – The Miracle

Question and Scaling Questions – are actively used to determine progress towards well-articulated goals. De Shazer later elaborated on the characteristics of well-formed goals as outlined in Box 1.2.

6   *The small steps of change.* Once specific, observable goals are co-constructed along the lines suggested above, small steps of change can be mapped out. De Shazer sees this as an intervention in itself, in that the more time spent in a session on 'change talk', with the focus being on the absence of the complaint and what will replace it, the more it creates the expectation that change is not only possible but inevitable.

7   *The 'break' and the message/homework.* A planned interruption in the session when the practitioner devises the message to be delivered to the client at the end of the session. What is emphasized is the importance of the 'fit' (i.e. the relevance) of the message. The task for the practitioner is to devise a message that shows a client that their situation is understood and that acknowledges them (compliments) while also flagging up possible solutions that the client may find acceptable (clues). Compliments are designed to establish a 'yes set' (Erickson and Rossi, 1979) of agreement from the client so that he or she would be more receptive to the clues or directions put forward. However, positive feedback has since been built into the fabric of the session by many practitioners as an important challenge to the view of self as powerless or at fault. De Shazer initially developed a series of formulaic tasks to be given in homework but these are not too commonly used in practice now.

This, then, is the essence of the SFT model as it was initially developed in 1986 and, as already noted, disseminated in an influential journal (*Family Process*) to peers in family therapy settings. The emphasis was on a minimalist prescription

---

Box 1.2   Characteristics of well-formed goals (de Shazer, 1991: 112)

'Workable goals tend to have the following general characteristics:

1   Small rather than large;
2   salient to clients;
3   described in specific, concrete, behavioural terms;
4   achievable within the practical contexts of clients' lives;
5   perceived by the clients as involving their "hard work";
6   described as the start of something and not as the end of something;
7   described as involving new behaviours rather than the absence or cessation of existing behaviours.'

for therapy with the development of a single session model. Only as SFT became known and popularized outside of clinical therapy settings did its adaptability and versatility become more evident and the focus move beyond the initial session. Initially adopted by family therapists, the model began to attract a more general interest from those in the helping professions from the end of the 1980s onwards. It has since been modified for work in various settings, with diverse client groups and types of problems, across the globe – from Asia to continental Europe, North America to the Antipodes. The last published work outlining the core approach from de Shazer and Berg (de Shazer et al., 2007) reiterates the major interventions of the approach and illustrates how they have retained a consistency since 1986. They are outlined in Box 1.3 later in this chapter.

Is solution-focused therapy a strategic form of therapy?

Both in 1986 and in subsequent publications, de Shazer explicitly conceptualized his SFT model as a derivative of but different from the Mental Research Institute (MRI) model of brief strategic therapy. That SFT is both strategic and complementary to the MRI model was a view expressed by members of the MRI team: 'At a specific level, I do not think the use of the term "strategy" necessarily implies a contest between therapist and client; indeed I would propose that de Shazer carries on his therapeutic conversations strategically' (Weakland, 1991: viii). Some analysts agree that the SFT and MRI models are more similar than different (Cade and O'Hanlon, 1993; Shoham et al., 1995) and that the SFT model is a strategic approach (Weakland, 1991; Shoham et al., 1995) or at least consistent with strategic approaches (Gale and Long, 1996): 'We focus primarily on attempted solutions that do not work and maintain the problem; de Shazer and his followers, in our view, have the inverse emphasis. The two are complementary' (Weakland and Fisch, 1992: 317).

While solution-focused techniques may be used strategically, the innovations de Shazer introduced are in my view sufficient to locate it outside the realm of brief strategic approaches. These include:

1   The emphasis given to the concept of future-focused 'solutions' as opposed to resolution of the problem.
2   The reformulation of the therapist–client relationship as a co-constructivist and collaborative relationship, albeit with the more recent caveat that solution-focused helpers 'accept that there is a hierarchy in the therapeutic arrangement, but this hierarchy tends to be more egalitarian and democratic than authoritarian' (de Shazer et al., 2007: 3–4).
3   The focus on process rather than interventions and the emphasis

placed on alternative possibilities and meanings that the therapist offers the client through the construction of solution-focused conversations. By 1985 de Shazer saw therapeutic change as 'an interactive process involving both client and therapist' (de Shazer, 1985: 65). Despite this, the approach does make use of particular techniques, mainly through a particular form of questioning.

4   The view of clients as essentially cooperative and as experts on their own lives. From his earliest writings, de Shazer was interested in how the most effective relationship could be developed between therapist and client and he began to note the differences in levels of cooperation that were elicited by various strategies, such as the use of compliments. In his 1982 model, the contact with families began with what was termed the 'prelude', where the therapist tries 'to build a non-threatening relationship with the whole family and to learn something about how the whole family sees the world' (de Shazer, 1982: 27).

5   The abandonment of the need for a team approach. By 1985 de Shazer viewed the team as dispensable: 'A team is not necessary for working this way' (de Shazer, 1985: 19).

6   The rejection of task-setting as a central feature of therapy: 'Accepting non-performance as a message about the client's way of doing things allowed us to develop a cooperating relationship with clients which might not include task assignments. This was a shock to us because we had assumed that tasks were almost always necessary to achieve behavioural change' (de Shazer, 1985: 21).

7   The emphasis on meaning and on the client's subjective experience, beliefs, and values.

8   The importance of language, particularly the craft of constructing useful questions and utilizing the client's own terminology in describing both problem and preferred futures.

Specific techniques, such as the Miracle Question, the identification of exceptions, and the use of scaling are arguably strategic in origin. In its initial conceptualization, the SFT model was highly prescriptive in its six-stage formula. Despite this, de Shazer can be said to have fundamentally altered the balance of power in the therapeutic relationship away from a strategic stance by suggesting that therapists should start from a viewpoint of seeing the client rather than the therapist as holding the key to the solution. The role of the therapist in the SFT model became one of a facilitator who helps the client 'discover' forgotten wisdom and who does so through a firm focus on the future and the concept of goal-setting through the detailed description of a preferred reality, an element of the approach not previously centre-stage in therapeutic endeavours and still very distinctive in solution-focused helping.

One answer to the question of whether SFT is strategic or not has to be: 'it depends'. And it depends on how SFT is interpreted and practised by individual practitioners. In the hands of one it could be highly strategic, whereas in the hands of another not at all strategic. It is in the practising of SFT that its true shape emerges, and that is conditional on qualities related to the practitioner as much as to the model itself; related to ways of thinking as much as ways of being. The issue of whether SFT is a strategic form of therapy might have continued to be debated if there had not been a wider paradigm shift (Kuhn, 1970) that created a change in thinking about how therapeutic endeavours work. By the 1990s, there was a new grouping of social constructionist strengths-based models of practice, influenced by advances in developmental psychopathology, in particular the construct of resilience (Rutter, 1987, 1990; Luthar, 2000), the development of the strengths perspective in social work (Saleebey, 1992, 1997, 2001), the emergence of concepts of learned optimism and hope in psychology (Seligman, 1991; Snyder and Lopez, 2002), as well as the less helpful generalization of a positive psychology movement (of which more later). Here SFT found a new home.

Constructivism, postmodernism, and social constructionism

That SFT is of a new generation of social constructionist models is now generally accepted. The interrelated ideas of social constructionism, constructivism, and postmodernism deserve some consideration with respect to their influence on the field of therapy.

Social constructionism views 'ideas, concepts and memories arising from social interchange and mediated through language' (Hoffman, 1990: 8), and as applied to therapy draws on the work of authors such as Kenneth Gergen and Michael Foucault. Wetchler (1996) proposed that four approaches, one of which is SFT, fit this category, being 'based on the concept that reality is an intersubjective phenomenon, constructed in conversation among people' (p. 129), identifiable by their adherence to four principles:

1   *That reality is constructed in conversation*, and that what we perceive as 'real' is often due to dominant beliefs within ourselves and society as we view the world through the lens of a succession of stories – personal and gendered but also influenced by community, class, and culture. As the concept of the 'self' is itself socially constructed, therapists do not have any special insights into individual or family life but are instead participants in constructing a reality with their clients.

2 *The systems metaphor for describing families is rejected.* The ability of therapists to objectively 'diagnose' families is challenged and so the systems metaphor that encourages therapists to take an objective stance is also rejected: 'The concept of systems originally was used as a metaphor for describing families. Over time therapists began to view families as actually possessing those concepts' (Wetchler, 1996: 131).

3 *Therapist expertise holds no more prominence than client expertise.* Drawing on work by Foucault, narrative therapists such as Michael White highlighted the issue of how psychological knowledge and diagnosis often reproduce dominant cultural values that serve to marginalize the wisdom of those who are socially excluded and viewed as outsiders. By reframing the therapeutic encounter as one to which each participant brings his or her own expertise, therapy is seen to become more ethically and morally sound: 'By placing therapist knowledge above client knowledge, we not only further objectify and demean our clients, but we also close the door to new and possibly unique ways of viewing and solving client problems' (Wetchler, 1996: 131–132).

4 *Therapy is co-constructed between therapist and client.* A balancing of therapist knowledge with client knowledge leads to therapy becoming less hierarchical: 'The role of the therapist becomes one of opening doors for clients to explore new meanings in their lives. This means engaging them in a slightly different conversation than the ones they usually have around the problem' (Wetchler, 1996: 132). Through this new dialogue, clients develop different ways of viewing their situation, and hence new ways of overcoming their difficulties.

As we shall explore further in Chapter 3 and the subsequent chapters on specific practice settings, this assertion has to be tempered with recognition of the role and responsibilities of workers in different contexts.

Constructivist ideas were introduced into the brief strategic field primarily through Watzlawick's (1984, 1990) work, followed by specific features in family therapy journals in the later 1980s (Efran et al., 1988; Leupnitz, 1988). Constructivism has been defined as

> an epistemological paradigm that has its roots in the writings of the Greek Skeptics . . . Constructivists view knowledge as actively constructed by the individual, and although not denying an ontological reality, 'deny' the human experience the possibility of acquiring a 'true representation' of reality.
>
> (Gale and Long, 1996: 13)

'The Inverted Reality' (Watzlawick, 1984) drew together contributions from a number of constructivist philosophers, of whom the radical constructivist, Von Glaserfeld, appears to have had most impact on both the MRI and the Milwaukee team (de Shazer, 1988, 1991). These ideas were introduced into the wider field of family therapy through the work of the Milan associates, especially Boscolo and Cecchin (Boscolo et al., 1987), and informed by the constructivist school of Maturana and Varela (1987). Constructivism has been viewed as most useful in its scepticism about the concept of truth: 'When families, or families and professionals, are engaged in battles over "truth", a constructivist frame that incorporates many different truths is invaluable' (Burck and Daniel, 1995: 26). Taken in isolation, constructivism can be blind to potential ethical and moral issues in relation to what is observed; and if it leads to a privileging of subjective reality, risks minimizing or ignoring issues of oppression or abuses of power within and outside the therapeutic process.

Constructivist ideas brought about three important shifts in systemic thinking: the emphasis given to the functioning of the individual within the group and not exclusively to the collective phenomena of the system; greater attention was paid to the *meaning* that one person has for another and the cognitive, emotional, and relationship factors that bind them together; and the recognition that the presence of an observer changes the context of the observations and therefore modifies the nature of the information gathered (Reder et al., 1993: 26). Constructionism, on the other hand, 'based on the concept that reality is an intersubjective phenomenon, constructed in conversation among people' (Piercy et al., 1996: 129), is more grounded in a philosophy of community and relatedness.

Another important theoretical influence on de Shazer, which he incorporated more fully in his later publications, was *postmodern* philosophy. This had a broad impact on family therapy in its ability to provide 'a framework within which to address differences and challenge polarities ... while postmodernist ideas seem to reflect well the experiences of fragmentation and saturation that many individuals live in the modern world' (Burck and Daniel, 1995: 29–30). Postmodernism could be problematic if it was interpreted as according all narratives equal status, and ignoring context: 'i.e. our society, which neither confers equal validity and status on all views, nor provides the resources for all views to become established in practice' (Burck and Daniel, 1995: 30). Solution-focused therapy is frequently categorized as one of three postmodern therapies (along with narrative therapy and collaborative language therapies) distinguishable by an attempt to minimize an authoritarian stance in favour of a more collaborative approach. Subsequently, integrated models drawing on different postmodern approaches have been developed, particularly in social work. Parton and O'Byrne (2000) outline a social constructionist framework for social work practice that incorporates both solution-focused and narrative concepts and techniques. Their constructive approach 'emphasises process, plurality of both knowledge and voice, possibility and the relational quality of knowledge ... An ability to work with ambiguity and uncertainty both in terms of process and outcomes is key' (Parton and O'Byrne, 2000: 184).

De Shazer can be said to have taken a postmodern stance on helping when he asserted that problems exist when clients acknowledge that there is a problem to be addressed; and problems are resolved when clients' evaluations indicate that this is the case. This stance created some formidable distance between de Shazer and the evidence-based practice community, who distrust client feedback and evaluation as a sole source of knowledge.

Since the 1990s, the social constructionist paradigm has become more rather than less influential (McNamee and Gergen, 1992; Carr, 1995; Witkin and Saleebey, 2007). The effect it has had on brief therapists, some of whom started off using pure strategic models, is described thus:

> We are now less certain, less audaciously tactical, less wedded to over-simplistic models, and far less impressed with our own cleverness. We have become more concerned with the resourcefulness of our clients and with avoiding approaches that disempower, either overtly or covertly. We have become more concerned with the development of a cooperative approach.
>
> (Cade and O'Hanlon, 1993: xii)

Although the metaphor of a conversation may now be frequently used to denote therapeutic encounters, to signal the changes towards a more equal relationship between client and practitioner, and to indicate that both have contributions to make, there is a limit to how far the metaphor can be taken if the practitioner is also to fulfil his or her professional and ethical obligation to offer some expertise in how problems may be solved or solutions constructed. This point has now been acknowledged quite explicitly by de Shazer in a significant shift:

> SFBT therapists *accept that there is a hierarchy in the therapeutic arrangement*, but this hierarchy tends to be more egalitarian and democratic than authoritarian ... The therapist's role is viewed as trying to expand rather than limit options ... SFBT therapists lead the session, but they do so in a gentle way, leading from one step behind.
>
> (de Shazer et al., 2007: 3–4, my emphasis)

In accepting that therapists use influence to help people change and use particular interventions to help them to do so, brief therapists implicitly restrict the extent to which the metaphor of 'conversation' can be used to depict the therapeutic encounter. The issue of how influence is used (and experienced) in work with vulnerable people is as much a preoccupation for frontline workers in health and social care settings as it is for therapists explicitly designated to carry out psychological change-work. The development of anti-oppressive and anti-discriminatory frameworks for practice in health and social care (Dominelli, 1988; Thompson, 1993, 1998, 2003) evolved from a concern about how workers sometimes use their power in an oppressive manner. In considering the adaptations to the approach required for ethical practice beyond the clinic walls, such concerns will need not only to be recognized but will be addressed in Part Two.

Solution-focused therapy: a moving target

Solution-focused therapy is acknowledged by many as being one approach that has been adopted and applied in tremendously diverse ways, so that: 'Any description of solution-focused therapy by outsiders will be, at best, a partial snapshot of a moving target' (Shoham et al., 1995: 151–152). This theme was not only accepted by de Shazer but elaborated upon:

> We believe that it is useful to think about solution-focused therapy as a rumor. It is a series of stories that circulate within and through therapist communities. The stories are versions of the solution-focused rumor . . . *Our goal is not to offer the final, definitive and only credible story* about solution-focused therapy. We recognize that rumors belong to whole communities. No particular story-teller 'owns' a rumor.
> (Miller and de Shazer, 1998: 368, my emphasis)

That SFT continues to evolve is evident from the post-1986 publications of de Shazer and Berg and others. A more fitting description for this 'moving target' may be as a minimalist formula that is underpinned by a number of principles developed by other skilled therapists and which uses some simple strategic interventions, but does so within a social constructionist perspective and with a strong dose of hopefulness at its core. That it is indeed a hybrid is more proudly acknowledged by its originators now as they emphasize its inductive and practice-based origins: 'SFBT is not theory based but was pragmatically developed. One can clearly see the roots of SFBT in the early work of the Mental Research Institute in Palo Alto and of Milton H. Erickson; in Wittgensteinian philosophy; and in Buddhist thought' (de Shazer et al., 2007: 1).

Also of relevance is the increasing emphasis placed in recent years on the precise construction of questions and communication patterns. Payne (1997) places SFT in the category of practice models based on social communication theory. Kim and Franklin describe it as using

> carefully posed questions that purposefully use communication tools from communication science that change perception through co-

constructive language, combined with collaborative goal setting, and the use of solution-building techniques that occur between therapist and client . . . *These carefully constructed communication processes are believed to be key components to helping client's change.* Solutions emerge in perceptions and interactions between people and problems are not to be solved solely by the therapist but rather solutions are co-constructed with the client(s).

(Kim and Franklin, 2009: 464, my emphasis)

As the model remains dynamic, it is more accurate to refer to the 'family' of solution-focused approaches, which are themselves increasingly seen to belong to a larger grouping (or 'community') of collaborative, language-based approaches. These are part of a generation of approaches to change-work based on the epistemology of social constructionism and premised on the philosophical position that the therapist is not an omniscient expert but a facilitator to the client seeking change.

While de Shazer launched his model in 1986 as a complete 'prescription' for therapy, this status is debatable. Modifications made since then both by the originators and those who have applied it in various settings suggest that most

---

Box 1.3   Therapeutic principles (de Shazer et al., 2007)

1   Positive, collegial, solution-focused stance – positive, respectful, and hopeful
2   A search for previous solutions
3   Questions versus directives or interpretations
4   Present and future focused questions versus past-oriented focus
5   Compliments
6   Gentle nudging to do more of what is working

'The therapist's role is viewed as trying to expand rather than limit options' (p. 4).

Underlying beliefs
1   The future is both created and negotiable: 'With strong social constructionist support, this tenet suggests that the future is a hopeful place, where people are the architects of their own destiny' (p. 3).
2   No problems happen all of the time – there are always exceptions to be utilized, and the three main principles are: 'If it ain't broke, don't fix it'; 'If it's not working, do something different'; and 'If it works, do more of it'.
3   The language of solution development is different from that needed to describe a problem: 'The language of solutions is usually more positive, hopeful and future-focused, and suggests the transience of problems' (p. 3).

commonly it is used as an approach consisting of three elements – a belief system, a set of principles, and an array of techniques – which are versatile and flexible and have proven adaptable across a range of problems and client groups and capable of being integrated with other approaches such as psycho-educational and cognitive-behavioural programmes.

Examples of the range of the approach include: residential child care in Australia (Durrant, 1993), groupwork with paediatric nurses in the UK (Goldberg and Szyndler, 1994), social work in child psychiatry in Ireland and the UK (Wheeler, 1995; Sharry, 1996), mature social work students in the USA (Baker and Steiner, 1995), adolescent and adult substance abusers (Berg and Gallagher, 1991; Berg and Miller, 1992b, 1995), Home Based Services for children and families (Berg, 1994), child psychiatry in Finland (Furman and Ahola, 1992), community care social work in Ireland (Walsh, 1995, 1997), generic social work practice in Finland and the USA (Sundman, 1997; Maple, 1998), counselling practice in the USA (Littrell, 1998), fostering social work (Houston, 2000), groupwork in Ireland (Sharry, 2001), child protection in Australia (Turnell and Edwards, 1999), child protection in the USA (Berg and Kelly, 2000; de Jong and Berg, 2001; Antle et al., 2009), and social work practice teaching in the UK (Bucknell, 2000). There are also texts that act as instruction manuals for the development of solution-focused skills (e.g. de Jong and Berg, 2008). This list is not exhaustive – and is supplemented by more detailed accounts of the literature relating to specific practice contexts in Chapters 4–8 – but it does demonstrate the extent of its appeal. Against this a range of concerns and criticisms has been voiced about the approach.

Critiques of solution-focused and brief methods

Some authors have taken issue with brief methods of treatment, others with cognitive approaches, and others with SFT itself. The more general critiques will be explored first and followed by those specifically concerned with SFT.

General concerns

Some British social work theorists deplore the rise of brief, focused methods of intervention linking them to the rise of a radical liberal perspective: 'Clients arrive, in effect, without a history; their past is no longer of interest. It is their present and future performance which matters' (Howe, 1996: 88–89). Howe believes that little attention is then paid to the construction and understanding of the client's narrative:

> Work is short-term, time-limited and 'brief' ... There is no

accumulated wisdom because there are no psychological or sociological theoretical frameworks in which to order and store it. Each
new encounter simply triggers a fresh set of transactions, negotiations
and agreements.

(Howe, 1996: 90–91)

Howe maintains that this preoccupation with 'surface' rather than 'depth' prevents workers from understanding and appreciating the non-rational and
distressed behaviours of people under stress and that this inhibits their ability
to respond appropriately. Like Stevenson (1998), his concern is for those problems and client situations that he believes are not amenable to minimalist
interventions. Taken in isolation, the original article by de Shazer et al. (1986)
that launched SFT might give the impression that it uses the concept of 'solutions' to trick clients into thinking differently about their problems without
any sensitivity or consideration for their subjective experience, and is narrowly
focused on minimalist outcomes as Howe worries. If this were how it was practised, it would raise major issues. The notion of persuading people that things
are not as bad as they think clearly has to be tempered by an understanding of
both the salient factors in people's lives and of the need to express and process
negative and strong emotions. Of relevance here also is the critique of 'positive
thinking' recently issued by Ehrenreich (2010). In her book, entitled *Smile or
Die: How Positive Thinking Fooled America and the World*, she asserts that the
assumption underlying positive thinking is that you only need to think a
thing or desire it to make it happen. She describes this practice as immoral, as it
dupes people into thinking that they have control over aspects of their lives
when they are in fact powerless. She relates this to the existing practice in the
USA of hiring motivational speakers to 'counsel' people being made redundant
that this catastrophe in their lives is in fact a golden opportunity, as so persua-
sively conveyed by George Clooney as Ryan Bingham in the film *Up in the Air*.

As outlined earlier, many SFT practitioners emphasize the quality of the
relationship forged between worker and client, and focus on process. Lipchik
(1994) notes that the most obvious clinical error of all when using SFT is to
'focus on the technique and neglect the actual flesh-and-blood client sitting
with them . . . in general, the choice of techniques should be driven by how a
particular technique will serve and fit the client, not the therapist' (pp. 37–38).
Subsequent research on micro-communication (Beyebach and Carranza, 1997;
Tomori and Bavelas, 2007) confirms the importance of following the client's
lead in establishing an active engagement.

Research studies outlined in more detail in Chapter 3 indicate that SFT in
general is not normally used in a formulaic manner but has been most often
thoughtfully combined with other approaches, and sometimes 're-invented'
to meet the needs of specific clients or client groups. In Chapter 3, the extent
to which practitioners drawing on the SFT approach exercise sensitivity and

judgement in deciding when and how to use the approach will become more evident.

Political concerns

Objections to brief models of therapy have also been made on political grounds based on the legitimate fear that policy-makers and budget-holders ultimately restrict choice and therapists' professional autonomy by imposing restrictions on the length and type of treatment. The introduction of 'Managed Care' in the USA and the curtailment on length of treatment funded by private insurance companies in Ireland and the UK illustrate that these fears are justified. The issue centres not on dismissing the real benefits that brief methods can offer but on promoting a deeper analysis of the complex nature of many problems, which acknowledges that short-term active change-work is not always possible or appropriate. Again, although not obviously explicated, the SFT model does caution against presuming that all clients are ready (or able) to work towards change – de Shazer (following on from the MRI team) emphasized the importance of assessing whether a client was a 'customer' for change or in another category. If the latter, other activities are needed to motivate people towards more active problem-solving.

'Grand claims' concerns

Concern has been expressed about the indiscriminate acceptance of the SFT model by some social workers and social agencies, 'in spite of the dearth of empirical evidence for its claims to provide clients with more rapid and more enduring change than other treatment models' (Stalker et al., 1999: 468). These objections have been echoed in the addictions field about SFT advocates (Miller and Berg, 1995) promoting 'The Miracle Method' as a radically new approach to problem drinking. This claim is viewed as excessive given that (at that time)

> not a single scientific evaluation has yet been published to support the 'solution-focused' counselling method that it described . . . [and] Desperate and vulnerable people deserve, and have a right to expect, a higher standard of professional responsibility and accountability.
>
> (Miller, 2000: 1765)

Stalker's and Miller's objections to the approach stem from the exaggerated claims of some SFT proponents. That both critiques emanate from North America may reflect the lucrative and competitive nature of the therapy business there, but as British-based Edwards also notes:

> People in that sort of situation [with addiction problems] are, however, immensely vulnerable to the blandishments which may be offered by any treatment approach which is marketed with large claims for efficacy and carries a public relations message which connives with expectations of a magic cure.
>
> (Edwards, 2000: 1749)

Clearly, there are issues involved in exaggerated claims: claiming *anything* as a 'miracle method' is unethical.

'Insensitivity' concerns

Fook critiqued the growing development of strengths perspectives throughout the 1990s, which she maintains do not take account of the differing realities, vulnerabilities, and challenges that individuals experience over their lifetimes:

> 'Progressive' models of practice assume an ideal of 'strength' towards which the healthy personality works. Such views, however, do not take into account the changing contexts and historical times which all people experience in the course of a lifetime. In this sense, practice models may be far out of touch with the experiences of service users.
>
> (Fook, 2000: 65)

The point she makes is that there is more complexity in human suffering than that allowed for in over-simplistic notions of solutions and strengths. In addition, the ideal of 'strength' may need to be more contextual than allowed for in generic models. Yet, complexity in appreciating unique suffering is also apparent in some SFT texts. As noted earlier, 'coping' questions are a central part of SFT developed to use where hope is missing or simple solution-work is not appropriate:

> Like all workers, we encounter clients who are feeling hopeless and seem able to talk only about how horrible their present is and how bleak their future looks. Sometimes these clients are experiencing an acute crisis that gives rise to their hopelessness, and at other times the hopelessness represents a persistent pattern of self-expression and relating to others. In both cases, coping questions can be helpful in uncovering client strengths.
>
> (de Jong and Miller, 1995: 733)

Feminist concerns

Dermer and colleagues' (1998) feminist critique of SFT starts from the premise that such critiques can 'identify gender and power imbalances and biases unintentionally perpetuated through therapy' (p. 240). Drawing on one of de Shazer's publications (1985) and comparing SFT to Leupnitz's (1988) model of feminist therapy, they conclude that SFT fails in certain respects but in others is congruent with feminist ideals. Dermer and colleagues' (1998) principal objections centre on:

(a) the concentration on behaviour change to the near exclusion of insight or explanation: a 'tendency to overlook larger contexts within which families operate' (p. 241);

(b) (the) adherence to notions of circularity leading to a rejection of the concept of blame as ever helpful. Making a distinction between 'non-productive blame' and 'other-angered blame' (the former obscures each individual's responsibility and the latter identifies limitations placed on subordinate groups by dominant groups) Dermer et al. assert that both feminism and solution-focused perspectives 'recognize that nonproductive blaming is not therapeutic, and both perspectives highlight responsibility . . . [they] agree on matters of personal responsibility but differ on the subject of blame' (p. 242);

(c) the relativist tendency inherent in SFT. By placing a great emphasis on client-determined goals, it can be charged with taking a position of absolute relativism leading to unethical practice if no stand is taken to challenge damaging or dangerous goals. This possibility risks leading to a lack of attention to pressures inherent in unequal power relations, a consequent failure to engage in any thorough pluralist analysis ('which examines the possibility that what is good for the family may not be what is good for an individual' p. 243); and

(d) the 'neutral' therapist as advocated in SFT is more likely to unwittingly collude with existing oppressions. Dermer et al. (1998) are particularly critical of the espousal of a neutral stance in domestic violence, which while condemning the violence itself will make no move to advocate a woman leaving a violent partner, or to side with a woman against a violent partner. Yet Lipchik (1991) defends the use of SFT in 'spouse abuse', asserting that her priority is always the prevention of further violence, that therapy stops if the commitment to ending violence is breached, and that while she focuses on solutions that are ethical and consistent with clients' own values, one of her own beliefs is that 'sociopolitical issues must be addressed in some way in all cases' (p. 63). The subsequent development of specific treatment programmes for spousal abuse (or domestic violence as it is more commonly known in the UK and Ireland), such as that by Milner and Singleton (2008), which adopt a solution-focused approach within a clear ethical framework, indicates that advances in the practice model are possible which retain the integrity of the approach as well as incorporating a clearer ethical position.

Where SFT and feminist therapy do converge is on the position of the therapist and the value base of the approach. The feminist aims to adopt a position that is enabling and that values purposive self-disclosure as a starting point for emphasizing difference, and in this respect is roughly similar to solution-focused therapists. Solution-focused therapy is seen to be most congruent with feminist therapy in relation to the role of the therapist and the nature of the therapeutic relationship. Both advocate a collaborative relationship, clear therapeutic goals, and attention to the power of language. Dermer et al. (1998) conclude that while SFT uses methods congruent with feminist therapy, it falls short of feminist principles in its lack of attention to inequality and gender relations. They are correct in their identification of the lack of structural or gendered analyses within the original SFT theory. This weakness has been acknowledged from an early stage of SFT's development by women therapists such as Lipchik (1991, 2002), Lethem (1994), and Dolan (1991), who have developed their SFT practices to include a more explicit ethical stance linked to feminist concerns.

The charge of being 'apolitical'

A key issue in the feminist critique is how overtly or explicitly political the therapy process should be. For Dermer et al. (1998), as feminist scholars, therapy is viewed as a *political* process, and 'as such, therapists should preserve their own beliefs while appreciating other positions' (p. 243). Neutrality is seen as an unacceptable position because 'failure to espouse one's own beliefs and values may unintentionally reinforce the status quo. Clients may interpret neutrality as agreement with their political and personal views' (p. 243). For de Shazer, on the other hand, it is unacceptable for the therapist to promote their own values and beliefs in sessions. He distinguishes between the goals of therapy and therapists' personal orientations:

> Therapists ask questions and make suggestions that are designed to help clients improve their lives . . . Therapists who fail at this job fail at therapy, no matter what else they may accomplish in the process . . . Therapists often use [certain] questions and answers to define therapy as a *cause*, and to assign different kinds of therapy to different causes. Stories about these issues are mostly told by therapists to other therapists. Thus, clients' concerns and influence on the therapy

process are often minimized in these stories. Understandably, most clients have little interest in them. Why should clients care about the intellectual, political and other causes with which their therapists are identified? Clients have their own problems.

(Miller and de Shazer, 1998: 367)

Power and influence concerns

The development of more gender-sensitive forms of SFT, such as those described above, suggest that it is possible to combine the broad concepts of solution-focused therapy with anti-oppressive practice and a more explicit ethical position as required for helping professions in public services. Yet the case remains that unless the practitioner comes to SFT with an already developed sensitivity to gender and power issues, he or she will not find a framework for anti-oppressive practice in the original theory. It is only in more recent conceptualizations (Turnell and Lipchik, 1999; Lipchik, 2002; Macdonald, 2007) that an explicit acknowledgement of the importance of relationship and context has been developed. Lipchik (2002), for example, outlines how she proposes 'a theory and basic assumptions for SFT that refutes the frequent accusation that SFT is formulaic and mechanical. It diverts emphasis from techniques to the therapist–client relationship . . . and to the use of emotions' (p. 9). Her concern relates to areas that suffered neglect in the over-emphasis on a minimalist approach to therapy; also to the isolation of language 'from the living human systems we are' (p. xiv). Being reductionist in the description of a practice model is one matter, but tied to this is the lack of an analysis of the use of power and influence in the practice models we adopt. This is a point that I consider requires further emphasis and clarification for ethical practice in public services and so warrants a separate section in Chapter 3.

Conclusions

The 'ideological currents' that accompanied solution-focused therapy's rise in popularity include:

1   Growing criticism of family therapy from feminists, clients, and others for its lack of attention to gender and power issues, the suggestion of 'dirty tricks' in strategic therapy, its lack of user-friendliness to consumers, and its lack of attention to outcome studies (Howe, 1989; Reimers and Treacher, 1995). Changes were needed if family therapy was to fulfil its potential as an ethical and effective practice.

2   The increasing importance of social constructionism and constructivism as epistemological influences in the postmodern era.

Solution-focused therapy is seen to fit the category of social con-structionist models of therapy, and also 'fits well in the present post-modern environment because of its emphasis on and belief in helping clients construct solutions that best fit their own lives' (Mills and Sprenkle, 1995: 371). Given the range of criticisms that family ther-apy was attracting at the time, the appeal of SFT is obvious: it oper-ates from principles that emphasize the client as a person of resources; it questions the assumption that the therapist knows best; and it redefines the role of the therapist as facilitator rather than expert.

3   The advent of managed care and budgetary restrictions to psycho-logical therapies. Not only in North America but also in Europe, there is increasing curtailment of treatment lengths that both pub-lic services and insurance companies will cover, mainly due to the need to curtail ever-escalating health care expenditure. All brief therapies, not only SFT, stood to gain from this restriction of choice, although narrative and solution-focused therapies were seen to have an advantage as 'postmodern approaches of established brevity' (Mills and Sprenkle, 1995: 375). Debates about resource-led as opposed to needs-led decision-making and the curtailment of therapist discretion need to continue, but within a wider context – that therapy in itself is a very lucrative market and one which, some argue, in itself can be disabling and disempowering in its neglect of natural healing and spontaneous recovery phenomena (Furedi, 2004; Saleebey, 2008). To some extent, the contested claims and debates about SFT point to a phenomenon known as the 'polit-ics of theory'. This suggests that 'proponents of particular approaches compete to achieve acceptance and status for their model' (Payne, 1997: 3).

The philosophy of SFT is primarily humanistic with the emphasis on the client's experience of the encounter and a strong belief in the potential of innate human resilience and resourcefulness. Solution-focused therapy shares with cognitive-behavioural therapy an emphasis on establishing small goals, use of scaling and self-assessment, the importance placed on the client's view of the problem, and recognition of the often-disabling effects of stuck patterns of negative thinking, including hopelessness. Solution-focused questions are proposed as specific tools that can be used to develop the strengths philosophy (Saleebey, 1992, 1997, 2001, 2005, 2008) on a micro-practice level – with individuals, couples, and families: 'It is hard to imagine a tighter fit between philosophy and practice than that between the strengths perspective and solution-focused interviewing questions' (de Jong and Miller, 1995: 735).

The most significant criticisms of SFT have been:

- of exaggerated claims for its effectiveness and the relative paucity of rigorous scientific studies to justify its superiority;
- of its omission of any structural or gender analysis of power relations within client systems and client–therapist systems and lack of attention to these in the therapy process;
- concerns about the assumption that brief therapies can resolve all difficulties;
- the danger of clients in need not being offered longer-term supports and interventions;
- the ethical problems that can arise if concepts of neutrality and pragmatism are taken too far without sufficient attention being paid to issues of influence and power; and
- the risks associated with a simplistic application of a positive psychology, which can in effect concentrate the focus on the individual experience, blame the client for wider societal ills that cause their problems, and imply that a simple cognitive shift can work miracles.

Some of the issues raised by these critiques can be addressed in the form of questions regarding practitioners' use of SFT:

- Do practitioners use it to the exclusion of other theories and models?
- Is adoption of the approach wholesale or selective?
- Do practitioners use it primarily in a time-limited and performance-focused way?
- Are clients' narratives ignored?
- Do workers try to use it to persuade clients that their troubles do not exist?

In Chapter 3, following an analysis of the ethical dimensions of practice in the helping professions in Chapter 2, an attempt is made to address these questions drawing on relevant research studies.

2 Ethics, public services, and practitioners' responsibilities

> Not even a modest degree of reflection, description or analysis of our social world is possible without considering what is good for people ... In other words, it is simply not possible to avoid ethical evaluations because, to paraphrase Aristotle, all human action is informed by ideas about what is good and bad and how we ought to act.
>
> (Bessant, 2009: 423)

Introduction

What does it mean to be a professional in public health and social care contexts? What responsibilities does the individual professional have and how are these mediated within employing organizations and organizational expectations? What maps do professionals have for guiding action in moral decision-making? How do these maps relate to the process of solution-focused helping? Friedson refers to the need for professionals to have 'soul':

> Occupations could be said to have soul when they act as something more than just a technical enterprise at the service of the state, employers and consumers ... [Soul] is represented by what I call institutional ethics, which is concerned with a technical craft's integrity of purpose.
>
> (Friedson, 2003: 172)

In this chapter, the ethical dimensions of professional practice will be considered, specifically as they relate to work in health and social care organizational contexts: 'Ethics is the branch of philosophy that considers the formation and operation of moral values' (Hugman, 2008: 442).

A distinction will be made between personal moral values (such as those guided by political and/or religious beliefs or beliefs about the natural and

human world) and those deriving either/or both from an occupational morality and/or legal, policy or organizational imperatives. Different conceptual
approaches to the study of ethics will be considered and distinctions drawn
between theories, principles, and codes. Given the relative merits and disadvantages of the main branches of ethical thinking, and the range of tasks
and responsibilities carried out by health and social care professionals, a case
will be made for a starting point of defining professional obligations (and
related ethical standards) in terms of role-based responsibilities (Rowson,
2006). Given the centrality of the caring role in health and social care, particular consideration will be given to relational ethics/the 'ethic of care' (Gilligan,
1982; Noddings, 1984; Meagher and Parton, 2004; Held, 2006; Holland, 2009).
In addition, given the importance of the concept of relationship across many
caring professions, the position will be taken that for the solution-focused
helper, effective ethical practice 'depends on an effective performance of
oneself in transactions with other selves' (Jones and Jordan, 1996: 261). In
other words, solution-focused helping involves the person of the helper and
their capacity to build the necessary relational bridges to engage with clients
and carers.

Referring to the range of issues with which social workers are traditionally
associated (such as poverty, adversity, social exclusion, abuse, addiction and
health problems), Hugman (2008: 442) asks: 'How could ethics not always
be at the forefront of our thinking?' Similarly in medical ethics there has
been a continuity of attention to moral issues from the days of Hippocrates
(Beauchamp and Childress, 2001). Historically, ethical dimensions to health
and social care work have been explicitly recognized through the development
of moral codes and principles of conduct for qualifying practitioners. For
example, teaching on ethics and values has been a core component of both
social work and medical education over time and qualifying practitioners are
expected to subscribe to specific standards. The development of a moral or
ethical code for professions is important, as it helps both to articulate and also
manage expectations both internally within the profession but also with other
stakeholders and the public. Developing an ethical base for health and social
care occupations also adds weight to claims for the status of 'profession' given
the important of ethical codes as a signifier of professional standing (Friedson,
1986), although some sociological models of professionalism do not subscribe
to this view (Abbott, 1988).

In an era when professional expertise itself is increasingly questioned, it is
salutary to review comments by Schön (1983, 1987) outlining some of the
tensions and contradictions inherent in the contract between professionals
and society: 'When professionals fail to recognize or respond to value conflicts,
when they violate their own ethical standards, fall short of self-created expectations for expert performance, or seem blind to public problems they have
helped to create, they are increasingly subject to expressions of disapproval

and dissatisfaction' (Schön, 1987: 7), thus leading to a situation where professionals themselves 'argue that it is impossible to meet heightened societal expectations for their performance in an environment that combines increased turbulence with increasing regulation of professional activity' (ibid.). These were pressures identified over thirty years ago; consider how public expectations and disillusionment with the performance of public bodies and professionals have expanded exponentially since.

For many professional groups, the starting point for the development of ethical standards is a set of principles, often centred round specific values. Historically, the Hippocratic Oath provided the first statement of a moral code for doctors, traditionally an oath sworn by newly qualified doctors on graduation. Although it still exists in some forms across the globe, it has also been supplemented and/or modified in more recent times. In the aftermath of the Second World War, the Declaration of Geneva (1948) developed by the World Medical Association provided an explicit statement of doctors' commitment to humanitarian goals and modernized many of the central concepts of the Hippocratic Oath. The more recent Helsinki Declaration (2000) also developed by the World Medical Association provides specific ethical guidance for the area of medical research.

Although many of the values of social work can be traced back to Victorian times both in the USA and UK, Biestek's Principles are instantly recognizable as the starting point for defining some of the parameters of the casework relationship between social worker and client. The seven principles are individualization, purposeful expression of feelings, controlled emotional involvement, acceptance, non-judgemental attitude, self-determination, and confidentiality (Biestek, 1961). Sometimes mistakenly depicted as ethical principles, they are more accurately described as principles that have a moral dimension but which are formulated specifically for a particular form of practice – that of individual casework relationships (Banks, 2006; Hugman, 2008).

Historical accounts of the development of ethical theory, principles, and codes for social work demonstrate how these were (and are) influenced by wider social, economic, political, and cultural trends, as well as organizational and occupational changes (Reamer, 2001; Banks, 2006; Hugman, 2008). They do not remain static over time, although core concepts such as fairness/justice and respect for autonomy tend to prevail.

In this chapter, as well as outlining the differences between different levels of ethics theory, I consider the range of organizational settings for health and social care and the impact this has on practice before moving to frameworks for ethical practice that might be useful to the solution-focused helper. But first, what are professional ethics and how do they differ from personal ethics?

Concepts and definitions

All of us gain some understanding of what is considered 'right' and 'wrong', 'good' and 'bad' as children when parents, teachers, religious educators, and carers attempt to instil moral codes and values through demonstration, exhortation, and instruction on what we should and shouldn't do. Depending on the particular cultural context within which one is located, different sources of moral guidance may be involved, such as religious teachings, family values, culturally specific local customs, and practice and legal parameters. These are commonly referred to as personal values and need to be distinguished from occupational or professional values.

Values can be defined as a set of beliefs (either for or against) held by individuals and/or groups in which an emotional investment has been made. In short, the values that we hold matter to us. There may be a hierarchy in the values we hold, which proves useful when values may conflict with each other in specific situations. Over time, as individuals we develop our own personal set of values, which are not necessarily shared collectively; over time, too, our value base may change. Personal values often reflect the influence of religion, culture, family, and peer group influences, as well as personal experiences.

The terms *morals* (from the Latin word for 'customs' or mores) and *ethics* [from the Greek root (*ethicos*) referring to both the concept of ethos (or defining character or characteristics) and that of common practices and customs] are used interchangeably here to mean a theory or set of principles commonly used to distinguish between right and wrong actions. Moral codes or frameworks can derive from a range of sources but usually they have more of a social element being shared and agreed within communities and groups. The term can be used both to denote an actual set of beliefs or values as expressed in action (descriptive), or an ideal set to which one should aspire (normative). Morals are not universal laws or rules and may vary considerably across cultures and times, although most centre on notions of doing most good and least harm.

Morality/ethics: a framework

Ethics are distinguished from values in being derived from a process of reasoned argument and social consensus rather than merely being inherited or habitual beliefs. It is important also to bear in mind the distinction between theories *about* ethics (meta-ethics) and theories *of* ethics (normative ethics). Our concern here is with the latter – the 'ought' rather than the 'is', or in Socrates' phrase, with the question of how we should live. Ethical standards require some form of justification and explication, while values often just *are*. One approach to normative ethics is offered by a framework that distinguishes between *theory, principle,* and *code/rules.* Needless to say, in adopting such a framework we must acknowledge that precise boundary distinctions are open to debate.

Beauchamp and Childress (2001) argue that a theory must satisfy the following criteria or conditions: clarity, coherence, completeness, simplicity, and explanatory power. It must also be possible to *justify* one's belief in a theory and for it to be capable of implementation (i.e. to be normative and not merely descriptive). It can be added that moral theories derive from or imply a belief or set of beliefs about the nature of existence and, most specifically, human nature and the role of social structures in encouraging 'the good life'. The most familiar example in the Judaeo-Christian tradition commonly known as 'divine command' argues that God is both creator of life and the originator of all concepts of right and wrong as revealed through the Bible, Koran or related human prophecy. While Socrates (as described in Plato's *Euthyphro* dialogue) identified an inherent flaw in this account long before the Christian era – if God's will and moral goodness are identical, it is impossible to identify the good as anything other than what He orders however outrageous; if they are not identical, then God must be accountable to some external and pre-existing standard – it is worth bearing in mind that this theoretical world-view still underlies the moral belief system of a substantial part of humanity.

The debate around secular accounts of moral theory has tended to centre on utilitarianism and deontological or Kantian ethics. The former, developed by Bentham and Mill in England, focuses on consequences or outcomes and argues that moral judgement should be based on *actions*, to the extent that they enhance or reduce the sum of human happiness or well-being. The latter (developed by the German moral philosopher Kant) looks at intention rather than outcome, arguing that a universal morality is based on rules that we could consistently will to be universal laws. It is beyond our remit to explore these traditions – both of which sprang from the European Enlightenment – more fully here, save to say that both are subject to a range of objections, with neither seeming to adequately 'fit' the reality of human experience. However, I will discuss further an alternative, or perhaps complementary, approach of *virtue ethics*, which is both more ancient and more modern than either of the above.

In contrast to these grand theories are codes, rules or laws, which tend to have an instructional or prescriptive purpose, and sometimes are used to narrowly define membership or attachment to a group or community. For example, the most familiar of these in the Judaeo-Christian tradition – the Ten Commandments – was not presented as a universal moral theory but as a 'condition of membership' of the tribe of Israel. While the parallels are hardly exact, professional codes of conduct and statute law may be similarly characterized. They may have a moral character and be informed by commonly held moral principles but adherence is generally required or expected rather than conditional.

In the fertile, if shifting, middle ground between theory and rule is the territory of moral *principle*, which is concerned with 'norms about right and wrong human conduct that are so widely shared that they can form stable (though usually incomplete) social consensus' (Beauchamp and Childress, 2001: 3). Principles are guidelines for action founded on shared assumptions (extending beyond any specific interest group or community), which also provide a framework for debate about ethical dilemmas. Such dilemmas are increasingly prevalent in health and social care fields in particular, often occasioned by technological advances or by value conflicts in democratic pluralist societies. Principles cannot be straightforwardly derived from moral theory any more than the technical skills of an engineer are directly and solely derived from mathematical or scientific theories. They owe something to theory but also to reflection on the kinds of decisions we commonly have to make in practical day-to-day circumstances. In the words of Sandel:

> If moral reflection is dialectical – if it moves back and forth between the judgments we make in concrete situations and the principles that inform those judgments – it needs opinions and convictions, however partial and untutored, as ground and grist.
>
> (Sandel, 2009: 29)

The English philosopher, W.D. Ross, who argued that no comprehensive moral theory fits all the facts of human experience, offers a list of commonly held principles (which he termed prima facie duties), which, he argued, derive from the kind of grounded reflection Sandel describes. He includes fidelity, gratitude, promoting justice, beneficence, and others in a list acknowledged to be unsystematic and incomplete. This kind of approach, sometimes referred to as 'common morality' (or even 'common sense morality'), offers a route into the discussion of professional ethics without being either mesmerized by theory or buried in a mass of detail.

Professional ethics

Professional ethics refers to a set of rules explicit to specific professional groups or contexts, such as codes of ethics that often relate to specific conducts that are permitted or proscribed. Beauchamp and Childress (2001) provide a useful summary of some defining concepts relating to health care professionals and professional morality.

Rowson (2006) usefully argues that the role of 'non-representative' professions (i.e. not representing any particular ideological perspective or interest

---

Box 2.1   The responsibilities of professionals (Beauchamp and Childress, 2001)

'In learned professions, such as medicine, nursing, and public health, the professional's background knowledge derives from closely supervised training, and the professional provides a service to others. Health care professions typically specify and enforce obligations for their members, thereby seeking to ensure that persons who enter into relationships with these professionals will find them competent and trustworthy. *The obligations that professions attempt to enforce are role obligations, that is, obligations determined by an accepted role.* Problems of professional ethics usually arise from conflicts over professional standards or conflicts between professional commitments and commitments of persons outside the profession. The rules of professional morality are vague, so that different interpretations emerge of the duties stated in these rules. To avoid moral confrontation and legal struggles, some professions codify their standards in order to reduce this vagueness.'

(Beauchamp and Childress, 2001: 6, my emphasis)

---

group, as opposed to ministers of religion, for example) in culturally complex (pluralist) societies is to achieve objectives – health, safe communities, education, welfare of children and older people, etc., for all members of society. Such broad objectives require similarly broadly based and consensual ethical standards. Only in this way can trust be obtained and sustained across society and over time. This is in accord with the view that professionals are expected to, and should, both be aware of and adhere to the kind of broad guiding principles alluded to above. Although professionals are subject to specific laws, codes, and regulatory requirements, it is the ability and willingness to go beyond such narrow confines and act, in some sense, as *moral agents*, together with a knowledge base and requisite set of skills that contribute to the definition of professionalism.

As noted above, the ethical standards of a profession are typically codified to a considerable level of detail, including such considerations as informed consent, confidentiality, and acting in the best interests of client/patient. There is often a dual focus in such codes and regulations: to safeguard the client and also to offer protection to the professional who may come into conflict with an employing/contracting body, with members of his/her own or other profession, with the client, or with members of the client's family. Such codes thus have a quasi-legal status and frequently are quoted when legal/ indemnity issues arise. Such codes also acknowledge that conflict *between* codified ethical requirements may occur and may need to be adjudicated by some external/regulatory body.

However, it is the broader 'middle level' principles that, while informing and often being cited in such prescriptive codes, are of particular interest to us as a focus for debate and reflection on the nature of ethical practice. Beauchamp and Childress (2001) adduce four such key principles in relation to medical ethics: justice, respect for patient autonomy, beneficence, and non-maleficence. While these inevitably are prone to conflict whenever a moral dilemma arises, the ethically informed professional must be able to reflect on such principles and then, using them, argue coherently for a morally justified course of action. Such a course of action generally involves assessing and ranking the 'rights' (that is, justifiable claims to which the principled professional must respond) of clients, patients, relatives, and the wider society, including the employing/contracting body. Similarly, Hinman's (2008) four principles for resolving moral conflicts while working across cultures (understanding, tolerance, standing up against evil, and fallibility) are equally likely to come into conflict with each other in real-life situations.

Take the example of a patient admitted to hospital with a medical complaint, which it is suspected originates from an infectious disease. Although reluctant at first, the patient eventually agrees to an infectious disease test. The patient dies before the test result is known, which turns out to be positive. Relatives arrive at the hospital and specifically ask the doctor involved if he had the named infectious disease. What should the doctor do? What sources of guidance are available? In the first instance, the doctor's representative legal body advises him that the duty of confidentiality to the patient persists after death. On the other hand, the doctor observes that the relatives have a claim, as do potential unidentified others in relation to the public health dimension. Should the claim of the deceased to confidentiality 'trump' these claims? Does it matter, in this context, that the patient is no longer alive and in a position to express a view?

Clearly, in principlist terms, there is a potential conflict between principles of patient autonomy and of beneficence and non-maleficence with regard to the welfare of those still alive. From the perspective of justice in society, is the wider principle of protecting privacy more important than the clinical harm and indeed emotional hurt that may accrue from doing so? The requirements of the law or of an insuring body may offer convenient protection in the short term, but the responsible professional, as in this case, will reflect on such issues.

Professional codes, like laws, must ultimately reflect ethical concerns and support good ethical practice, and for that reason need to be reviewed and revised from time to time. Indeed, as Rowson (2006) points out, rules of any kind will never be sufficiently detailed to account for every eventuality: 'the ethical obligation of mature people must include an element of judging for themselves what they ought to do in particular circumstances' (p. 49). Indeed, ethically sound judgement is central to the concept of *integrity*, which is essential if public trust is to be maintained.

Nor is integrity less relevant in the world of business and high finance. When the Enron Corporation became the largest bankruptcy in US corporate history in 2001 (more recently dwarfed by the demise of Lehman Brothers), the venerable accountancy firm Arthur Andersen was found to have turned a blind eye to Enron's essentially fraudulent financial practices in its audits. Arthur Andersen, which had previously shut down its once powerful 'ethical watchdog' committee, was denigrated in the USA in the aftermath of the Enron disaster. Its assets were intact but its reputation for integrity, as necessary to auditors as to health and social care professionals, was fatally damaged and no other corporate business would hire them.

Thus Rowson, in addition to advocating principles of justice, respect for autonomy, and seeking results that are most beneficial and least harmful to individuals and society (broadly in accord with Beauchamp and Childress's principles of medical ethics), further suggests that *integrity* should be an explicit professional principle – that is, 'acting in accord with the stated or implied values, undertakings and objectives of their profession' (Rowson, 2006: 48). Having already articulated a set of core principles to guide behaviour, is it necessary to include such a statement or should integrity be assumed? Would it have helped individuals working for Arthur Andersen, for example, or health and social care professionals who find themselves similarly pressured by their employing or contracting body to resist such pressures or is it only a form of words? This is something you can consider and decide for yourself.

Whatever you decide it should be noted that at the core of Rowson's argument, and of the specific linking of integrity with professional objectives, is the proposition that professional ethics is derived from the professional role, and in particular the functioning of that role in a pluralist society requiring standards of fairness and justice to all. This is also, of course, the very context in which professionals may be, in Schön's (1987) words, subject to expressions of disapproval and dissatisfaction because of the very difficulty of meeting professional standards in a culturally complex environment. It is in these very conditions that specific principle-based ethical approaches for working across cultures have been developed (Hinman, 2008). Warnock (2010) concurs, claiming that tolerance, for example, while being a virtue, can be overrated as a value. She believes that any notion that there is a shared morality across cultures is a form of imperialism and that when considering the morality of public policy decisions, the criterion against which such policies are to be judged according to other values such as expediency or economic value, '[t]hat there are many cultures in our society does not entail that there is no such thing as a common good. Such values as justice, honesty, respect for human lives, compassion, the love of learning – these are not culture-relative, it is in pursuit of such values that public policy should be formed' (Warnock, 2010: 2).

The organizational context

Professionals are usually employed by, or contracted to, organizations or institutions. With regard to health and social care professionals, it is useful to consider briefly the similarities and differences between organizations that are run directly by the state, those that are independent and contract their services to the state on a 'not-for profit' basis, and purely commercial organizations that employ such staff in a central or in subsidiary roles. In the first category, the state in some shape or form is both the employer and a significant 'stake-holder' in the outcomes and professional standards. Such will be the case for many hospitals and health care services, as well as services provided through the conduit of local authorities. The state also provides or contracts regulatory bodies and may, at a political level, be seen to be answerable for any problems or perceived shortcomings of the service, of which more below. Those in the second category, including organizations such as Barnardo's, independent hospital trusts, and voluntary organizations and charities, typically receive much of their funding from the state, possibly supplemented by charitable funds or some form of commercial income. Private medical or social care organizations working on a 'for-profit' basis will vary widely. In particular, there is a disparity between those with a primarily private customer base and those that, to varying extents, contract out services to the state on a fee per item or per service basis. Many (typically in the field of medical care) combine both approaches.

What these varying types of organization have in common is a govern-ance arrangement, usually consisting of a Board of Management whose make-up and responsibilities are set out in a constitution or similar document. As well as an expectation of sound financial management the Board will have responsibility for issues such as professional standards, and should have representation from the professions involved in service provision. The chief executive, while acting on behalf of the Board, is not usually a full member. The key principle, both ethically and managerially, is to ensure that the Board operates at arm's length from day-to-day activities, in the best interests of the organization and its clients. This requirement should ensure that maintaining and encouraging professional standards is enshrined in any governance arrangement. At times, it may also be a context for conflict between professional aims and standards and the aims of the organization. The professional, in his or her organizational role, should be aware of gov-ernance issues, however distant they may sometimes seem from day-to-day concerns.

Case example

In Ireland, many teaching hospitals were historically established by Catholic religious orders. Although many of these have recently conceded control to secular Boards of Management, in some adherence persists to a religious ethos as a requirement of practices in the hospital. In one instance, a clinical research study into cancer treatment required that participants did not become pregnant and was unable to proceed due to the Catholic ethos of the hospital, which was interpreted as needing to refuse use of contraception as a possible requirement. Due to the governance arrangements, the Board of Management through the hospital ethics committee had the final say in whether the proposed research project could proceed or not. They refused permission because of the conflict with the stated ethos of the hospital, which abided by the Catholic prohibition on use of artificial means of contraception.

Box 2.2 The professional in an organizational context: some questions to consider

---

- What is the make-up of the Board/Management structure and its stated aims?
- What mission statement exists for the service?
- What profession(s) are represented, what kind of expertise has a voice at board meetings?
- If it is a state-run or 'not-for-profit' voluntary organization, how is the voice of the service user represented?
- Are there potential conflicts of interest, e.g. staff members who are also Board members?
- Do you have any sense that the governance arrangement of your employing organization promotes your values and skills or presents obstacles?
- What records/minutes of meetings are available to staff and/or the general public?
- What ethical standards are contained in the constitution or terms of reference of the Board?
- Is there an explicit commitment to a religion or denomination?
- What protection do you have from your professional ethical code or the legal framework to support you in action you might take if needed, which conflicts with the organization's ethos?

Changing organizational, governmental, and societal conditions

Public and state-sponsored inquiries into unacceptable professional practices such as, for example, organ retention scandals in hospitals in the UK and Ireland; the HIV-infection of haemophiliacs and others receiving blood transfusions through the provision of contaminated blood products in the USA, UK, and Ireland; the abuse of children in institutions run by religious orders and the State; all have highlighted some of the processes and dynamics related to unchallengeable hierarchies, the abuse of power, outdated and unchallenged practices, cost-cutting and cost-saving measures, which enabled such practices to persist in climates where professional, religious, and managerial authority could not be questioned. We have more of an understanding now of the need for open, not closed, institutions; of the value of more inquiring and less compliant practitioners; of the absolute necessity for transparency, openness, and accountability in previously private and sacrosanct domains of professional practice. These cultural shifts manifest themselves in national governments taking a more proactive and central role in both the regulation of the professions and in opening up the processes of professional practice to closer scrutiny – in the passing of laws on freedom of information, on regulations changing the composition of many professional registration councils to ones where the public as opposed to professionals dominate, in decisions to make public inquiries into perceived or real malpractice and mistakes.

In addition, the media (or rather different sections within the media) has now become an important player in how the contract between public service professionals and citizens is negotiated. Sections of the media now play an active role in heading up campaigns for changes in public services and political decisions, lobbying for increased resources, and changes in policy. Furthermore, radical changes in information technologies continue to transform our communicative capabilities and have become another tool with which citizens can share information, network, and lobby. Social networking sites and tools such as Google, Facebook, and Twitter are new dimensions of the capacity of citizens to bypass professionals in their search for specialist knowledge and advice and in their ability to create instant pressure groups. This in itself also alters the contract between professionals and clients.

One recent example of the increased public gaze and changing organizational landscape for health and social care professionals has been the range of inquiries, professional practice investigations into doctors and social workers, and the dismissal of senior social service managers following the death of Baby P in Haringey, North London in 2008. In his subsequent review of the adequacy of child welfare services in England, Lord Laming (2009) spelt out the importance of inspection and regulation processes in ensuring standards of practice are maintained within organizational frameworks, and how positive practices can be unwittingly lost:

> The Inspection process [for child protection services] had not been as effective in scrutinising practice in safeguarding as it had been in education [following an amalgamation of children's services with education at a national level in England] . . . The development function that the Commission for Social Care Inspection provided for children's social care has been lost and not effectively replaced or expanded to support safeguarding child protection services across agencies.
>
> (Laming, 2009: 11)

In addition, he criticized the lack of oversight as to the quality of professional education for child protection workers: 'There is no rigorous regime in place to ensure that standards are being met by providers' (p. 51), following which he made an explicit recommendation that there should be a 'comprehensive inspection regime to raise the quality and consistency of social work degrees across higher education institutions' (p. 53). Lord Laming's comments demonstrate how explicitly national governments are now expected to actively regulate and oversee professionals in health and social care services, yet many such regimes are still failing to drive high standards of practice and education at an organizational level, leaving the individual worker somewhat isolated and vulnerable to extreme criticism when mistakes are made.

Hence, health and social care professionals now operate in an environment of increased complexity regarding their relationships with clients/patients and carers, the organizations within which they work, the governments and public bodies that most often fund their activities, the regulatory bodies that give them explicit licences to practise, and the wider public, who in addition to whatever (if any) direct contact they themselves have, gain their perception of the value and inadequacies of professionals' practice through media and communication channels.

In essence, a range of events in recent decades has led to a situation whereby the contract between professionals, the organizations within which such professionals frequently practise, and the clients/patients who are the recipients of their services has been under renegotiation, with health and social care professionals now answerable to registration councils, employers, inspection bodies, and sometimes the media, as well as to individual patient/clients and their carers.

Virtue ethics

As a background to this topic I will, as noted earlier, briefly consider the theoretical perspective offered by virtue ethics. This approach originated with Aristotle (c. 325 B.C.) and the question, what traits of character make a person good? This was not an idle debating point. The proposition is that the purpose of morality is to ensure 'right living', which itself corresponds to certain ways of behaving: behaviours that can be studied and learnt and are therefore amenable to reason. The need for characteristics such as courage, honesty, sympathy, and dependability emerges in the life of every person as part of their experience as a social and relational being (Aristotle indeed devoted a good part of his treatise on ethics to the topic of friendship). How we practise these and other core virtues is therefore a central concern of moral theory. In all cases, a balanced 'middle way' is advocated. This approach to morality was largely ignored by both the Christian and Enlightenment traditions, some of whose approaches were alluded to earlier. Their concern was no longer 'what makes a person good?' but 'what is the right thing to do in every case?', in each case seeking a source of authority in a deity or guiding principle. It is significant that one of the key voices in the reinvention of virtue ethics is the Irish philosopher Elizabeth Anscombe, who argued that the sources of authority that had been cited for so long in the western tradition as justifying duties and obligations could no longer be considered valid. Anscombe's (1958) seminal article led to a greater reconsideration of virtue as a valid topic for moral discussion. Concepts of impartial and universal moral prescriptions gave way to a recognition of the moral content of family relationships, friendship, neighbourliness, and so on. Indeed, some of the virtues – love and friendship, for example – presuppose that some relationships will take precedence over others. Virtue ethics has become of increased relevance to social work and social care professionals because in the face of a general trend towards more proceduralized and technical forms of practice, they locate the person of the helper as being at the centre of ethical action, in contrast to principle-based approaches:

> principles-based approaches to ethics (including professional ethics) places too much stress on actions (as opposed to the person doing the action), the rational and impartial nature of ethical decision-making and the universality of principles. Principles-based approaches ignore important features of the moral life and moral judgements, including the character, motives and emotions of the moral agent, the particular contexts in which judgements are made and the particular relationships and commitments people have to each other.
>
> (Banks, 2006: 54)

However, questions have also been raised about the heterogeneity of virtue ethicists, as well as diversity in how virtue is defined or established (Houston, 2003; Bessant, 2009). While welcoming the attention paid by academics to virtue ethics as an antidote to 'procedural rule-following, defensive practice and interventions lacking in reflexive awareness', Houston (2003) highlights the 'insufficient attention paid to the problem of how virtue is defined and established' (p. 819). Houston, like Rowson (2006) quoted earlier, locates ethical imperatives within contemporary societal conditions of cultural complexity. He draws on the work of philosopher Jurgen Habermas to suggest that the construction of virtue most apt for these uncertain times is one premised on an understanding that 'it is language and interaction that establish the virtuous character and act . . . Virtue is reframed, in this thinking, as an interactional and dialogical property' (Houston, 2003: 821). This leads to a new principle for moral decision-making:

> A valid moral decision is reached when those affected by it endorse it as the preferred way forward. In reaching this agreement, participants must accept the consequences of the decision for all concerned and its impact on everyone's interests . . . Thus, virtue is forged out of dialogue that is other centred, that moves dynamically beyond a simple marriage of convenience to an unremitting quest to empathize with perspectives that are different to my own.
>
> (Houston, 2003: 822–823)

The congruence of this process of decision-making with articulated values of the social professions is self-evident. Houston also articulates another important dimension – that of the need to develop processes that can quite consciously hold power in check. In so doing, he acknowledges the elephant in the room – the extent to which the enactment or performance of professional power can be oppressive and disempowering – a topic we will return to when considering the use of power and influence in therapeutic work.

In recent decades, virtue theory has been linked widely with a feminist approach to ethical theory, in particular with a critique of the male-dominated framework based on an adversarial model of conflict between various concepts and beliefs, especially those operating in the 'public' sphere of politics and academic debate. The 'private' sphere of family and other intimate relationships has rarely been allowed to figure seriously, and its values have not been promoted. As Rachels puts it:

> Virtue Theory sees being a moral person as having certain traits of character: being kind, generous, courageous, just, prudent and so on. Theories of obligation on the other hand emphasise impartial duty:

> They typically picture the moral agent as one who listens to reason,
> figures out the right thing to do, and does it.
>
> (Rachels, 1986: 172)

Rachels argues that virtue theory does have space for public as well as private virtues – indeed, for aspects of virtues that cover different spheres of experience. He goes on to suggest that virtue theory itself may best be considered as part of an overall theory of morality: 'The question then is whether such a total view can accommodate both an adequate conception of right action and a related conception of virtuous character in a way that does justice to both' (p. 190). He concludes that by taking the welfare of all humanity (and indeed other animal species) as a starting point, we do need to seek an approach that encompasses both the political and broader organizational spheres and the relational and private sphere that the feminist approach in particular addresses. In this context, I will go on to propose the importance of an ethic of care for health and social care professionals.

Relational ethics/the ethic of care

An alternative perspective to principles-based approaches such as those of Rowson (2006) and Beauchamp and Childress (2001), which emphasize the concept of justice, is offered by feminist approaches, such as the ethics of care, which focus more on interdependence as a feature of the human condition and the *relational* aspect of caring and helping as opposed to abstract concepts such as justice. Sometimes referred to as a form of virtue ethics, the ethics of care literature (Gilligan, 1982; Noddings, 1984, 2002; Tronto, 1993; Parton, 2003; Meagher and Parton, 2004; Holloway, 2006; Lloyd, 2006) goes beyond virtue ethics to include a specific focus on what kinds of qualities are required to help others locating the ethic of care within the context of connections forged between helper and client/patient in the caring or helping relationship. Noddings' work has been developed in relation to nursing and Parton, Holland, and Lloyd (among others) have related the ethic of care to social work. Empirical research by Juhila (2009) into the interpretative repertoires used by Finnish social welfare workers found that care considerations based on the ethic of care was cited most frequently.

Meagher and Parton (2004) describe the moral posture inherent in the ethic of care as follows: 'moral subjects should attend to others with compassion, responding to each person as unique and irreplaceable, and recognising each moral decision as taking place within a specific context' (p. 12). Holloway (2006) developed the concept to examine the capacity to care in both public and private spheres of life. She very usefully examines how organizational structures can damage and restrict the capacity to care, particularly when

---

Box 2.3   Tronto's (1993) ethics of care model

Attentiveness: noticing and understanding need; caring about the other(s) with the need.

Responsibility: taking responsibility for meeting need (dependent on individual and organizational roles and mandates).

Competence: to meet need, which relates both to individual skill and knowledge but also to availability or shortage of resources.

Responsiveness: incorporating an active elicitation of the client/patient viewpoint, beyond imagining or empathizing.

Integrity: refers to the holistic process from identification of need through to response(s) offered.

---

anxiety-reducing mechanisms such as splitting of tasks, routinization of response, and depersonalization of distress are introduced into the management of workloads and organizations, as initially identified by Menzies (1960) in her classic study of nursing in a London teaching hospital. The ethic of care as originally conceptualized by Gilligan (1982) denoted a singular moral voice that stems from (but is not restricted to) a female perspective on morality but which is now more commonly used in the plural to denote an approach to ethics in the health and care professions that emphasizes relationship, connection, communication, caring, and cooperation (Banks, 2006). Meagher and Parton (2004) suggest that the concept of caring has been lost in the changes to more technical, rule-bound approaches to practice in social work in which more attention appears to be paid to stakeholders such as government and employers rather than clients. They maintain that 'unless care is relocated at the centre of debates, policies and practices, the elements which can be seen to make social work and social care more generally distinctive will be lost' (Meagher and Parton, 2004: 4). In her work on the relevance of the concept for looked-after children in Britain, Holland (2009) emphasizes how care is both a practical activity as well as an ethical framework. She draws on Tronto's (1993) work to outline the main features of an ethic of care (see Box 2.3), noting also that 'care is a process and it can involve conflict. It is both particular and universal. It is present universally, but locally varies considerably' (Holland, 2009: 3). Holland locates many emerging practices within the field of looked-after children as being centred more on an ethic of justice rather than care (such as the promotion of gradual independence and self-reliance often at an earlier age than that of their peers not in state care), noting: 'The irony is that a group of young people who are identified as being in particular need of care are also the group required to move towards early self-reliance' (Holland, 2009: 4).

Lloyd (2006) relates the ethic of care to work with older people in culturally diverse societies and contemporary tensions in fields of health and social care, including the scarcity of resources, restrictions of their use, increased regulation, the imposition of a market economy in provision of care services, and the development of care management. Meagher and Parton (2004) highlight some of the risks of an over-reliance on 'care' as a governing concept, especially the danger of paternalism/maternalism. Lloyd (2006) thinks the real potency of the ethic of care lies in its potential as 'a form of political ethics, in which an enriched notion of social justice can be achieved through awareness of social practices and the ways in which these are influenced by power' (p. 1179).

While Gilligan (1982) and Noddings (1984) are seen to have made a strong case for a feminist-based ethic of care as an alternative to the then dominant ethic of justice, subsequent work has developed and applied the concept as a less oppositional or gender-specific approach but a broader perspective that can be incorporated with rights-based positions and that is now more influential in biomedical ethics (Beauchamp and Childress, 2008). For Holland (2009), relating it to 'looked-after children', an ethic of care needs to sit alongside an ethic of justice, so as to ensure that 'children who are looked after are enabled to form and sustain lasting care relationships, with formal carers and social workers and with their informal and family networks' (p. 16), echoing Rachels' (1986) point earlier. This seems a very apt point on which to end this review of ethics, highlighting as it does how the contextual conditions in which services operate, and the managerial imperatives imposed on them, can themselves create the conditions (such as staff and carer shortages, the targets culture, short-term solutions, and resource shortages) that can strip the work of its essential caring and relational dynamic.

Conclusions

Moral matters lie at the heart of health and social care work; at the intersection between individual need and state solution, private and public aspects of life. Technological and scientific advances throw up more complex dilemmas in bioethics. Changing formulations of our relationships as professionals with clients/patients and their carers (and the increasing emphasis on care in the community) result in shifting values regarding the right of the patient to autonomy *vis-à-vis* the needs of carers. While bioethics and social work ethics have developed along different lines, there is increasing evidence they are converging (Leathard and McLaren, 2007; Beauchamp and Childress, 2008; Cribb, 2008) as more attention is paid to the context within which services operate and the social and policy dimensions to these. Specific challenges for the future lie in articulating and implementing consistent ethical standards for interdisciplinary teams and inter-agency working, especially when workers are from diverse professional backgrounds (and in balancing the focus on professional moral codes with those of shifting and often ambiguous societal moral codes, and specifically those of clients/patients and their carers).

Some significant aspects of our engagement with moral dimensions to our work have been highlighted in this chapter. These include the importance of role and the development of professional ethics based on role responsibilities and obligations (Rowson, 2006), the centrality of relational care in many services for the vulnerable and ill (Meagher and Parton, 2004; Lloyd, 2006; Holland, 2009), the relevance of a virtue ethics based on communicative action (Houston, 2003), a recognition of the contextual nature of practice (Hugman, 2008), and the need to locate the person of the helper at the centre of moral action, responsible not for following rules alone but for thinking above and beyond this as a moral actor in their own right.

How, then, do we go about uniting these imperatives with the use of a solution-focused approach? To this, we now turn.

3 The solution-focused helper: a conceptual model for health and social care professions

Introduction

There are many fine textbooks that describe how the original model of solution-focused therapy has been adapted to fit within the specific contours of practice in a range of services. These have been most prevalent in mental health, education, and child welfare (e.g. Berg, 1994; Rhodes and Ajmal, 1995; Rowan and O'Hanlon, 1999; Turnell and Edwards, 1999; Berg and Kelly, 2000). In addition, a range of generic texts provides detailed guidance on the development of specific skills and interventions (O'Connell and Palmer, 2003; de Jong and Berg, 2008). A discernible pattern is now emerging of a wider adoption of solution-focused therapy (SFT) at organizational and regional levels in public services. For example, a model of solution-based casework for child welfare practice (Christensen and Todahl, 1998) has been adopted in the American state of Kentucky, where initial evaluations suggest promising results in the reduction of re-referrals of maltreatment (Antle et al., 2009). And there are reports of solution-focused DRM (differential response models in child welfare) practices being introduced at an organizational level across the UK and Ireland based on Signs of Safety (Turnell and Edwards, 1999).

I hope to contribute to the impressive existing literature on solution-focused helping in public services by providing a conceptual map of how the solution-focused helper can make sense of context and role, existing knowledge bases, ethical dimensions, and use of self in their work. The focus shifts from the therapeutic approach itself to the helper as a person who translates the approach according to their unique position. Based on research carried out with a range of practitioners in health and social care settings in Ireland (Walsh, 1997, 2002), as well as extensive training and consultancy work, it became increasingly evident that skilled practitioners perform a complex balancing act before deciding if – and then how – to use SFT in their work. These observations from practice are confirmed in a review of the research literature on SFT (see, for example, Macdonald, 2007). This process of sense-making

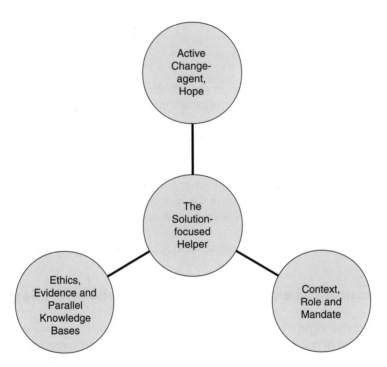

Figure 3.1   The components that make up the ethical solution-focused helper.

draws on several different dimensions of practice, the most important of which are: (i) concept of the self as helper; (ii) perceptions of context, role, and mandate; and (iii) perception of clients and their problems. In addition, skilled practitioners do not abandon everything they know in their rush to take up innovative ideas that appeal to them, rather most reflect on ethical implications and also continue to draw on parallel knowledge bases – theories and practice wisdom that they have already developed over time. Only if solution-focused therapy fits within their own personalized map of practice do they proceed to use it. So what, then, are the components that make up the ethical solution-focused helper? How might we conceptualize the ideal type?

The solution-focused helper:

- has a self-concept as active change-agent and an ability to offer hope;
- appreciates how the organizational context influences what is possible;
- is clear about his or her professional role and mandate (including what expectations clients will have);
- will continue to draw on parallel knowledge bases, including the evidence base for particular interventions;
- will remain ever-mindful of the ethical dimensions of practice and the tensions between professional values and organizational expectations.

Let us look at each of these components in turn.

Self-concept as an active change-agent who offers hope

To become an effective solution-focused helper, a certain approach to practice, and a self-concept as helper, is required. This I have termed an *active change-agent* orientation. Not all practitioners approach their work in this way. In my study of fifty-two practitioners from different settings (medical, child welfare, fostering, residential care, rehabilitation and convalescent units), four different self-concepts were evident across the group but the most successful adopters of solution-focused therapy had an active change-agent orientation. The other three were: *agency functionalist*, characterized by a more minimalist and rule-bound approach aiming only to fulfil their agency's expectations by carrying out tasks as required; *reactive agency functionalist*, characterized by a sense of being over-burdened and operating in circumstances of crisis and constant pressure, and aiming only to survive adverse conditions with no energy for creative strategies; and *a passive witness* orientation, characterized by an empathic caring approach to clients coupled with a belief that bearing testimony to clients' problems and distress, listening, and offering unconditional positive regard was the way to help clients deal with psychological distress.

The active change-agent is characterized by creativity, flexibility, and a willingness to consider how best to construct individualized programmes or approaches depending on client circumstances and need. The worker actively engages with each client, is willing to be flexible and creative in how best to do their work, and is comfortable adopting specific strategies to achieve client and agency goals. The active change-agent approach to work also embodies hope, and is neither too burdened herself to model hopefulness, nor too cynical about her work and potential to dismiss the possibility of change.

The importance of optimism/hope

> We hope because without hope we must despair. As such, the capacity to hope is a vital coping resource.
>
> (Lazarus, 1999: 675)

The successful adopters of solution-focused therapy in my 2002 study had an extra quality of optimism that distinguished them from the non-adopters. Whether the optimism was an innate aspect of their personality before exposure to SFT, or whether it was a *product* of exposure to SFT and/or successful experimentation, is an intriguing question but almost impossible to answer without further research. Seligman's (1998) work into 'learned helplessness' and 'learned optimism' suggests that while individuals might have natural leanings towards either a pessimistic or optimistic style of thinking, these are not fixed attributes but can be modified through cognitive restructuring. Is it possible that exposure to particular ideas and practice models can act as effective exercises in cognitive restructuring? Does solution-focused helping appeal because it has this quality? I would suggest that exposure to particular ideas, depending on the types of messages conveyed in the specific ideas, can raise levels of optimism and hopefulness temporarily but that other factors impinge on whether this shift is sustained.

Seligman maintains that there are three different dimensions to the explanatory styles of optimism or pessimism: permanence[1], pervasiveness[2], and personalization[3]. The *permanence* dimension determines how long a person gives up for following a setback or failure. Permanent explanations for bad events produce long-lasting helplessness and temporary explanations produce resilience. Universal explanations produce a *pervasive* helplessness across many situations and specific explanations help to limit helplessness. While *personalization*, and the extent to which blame is internalized, controls how you feel about yourself, permanence and pervasiveness control what you do – how long you are helpless and across how many areas of life. Hope is a product of two of these features – pervasiveness and permanence. 'Temporary causes limit helplessness in time, and specific causes limit helplessness to the original situation' (Seligman, 1998: 48).

Solution-focused therapy coincides quite remarkably with the features of a more optimistic style of reasoning. It concentrates on strategies to identify areas of life where the client is functioning well or adequately, highlights the exceptions to the problem when the client was in control rather than feeling controlled, and compliments the client on areas of their life that are going well and for which they can take credit. Problems are viewed as temporary phenomena and attention is focused on building concrete, specific goals that are realistic and achievable. The underlying message to practitioners is optimistic – clients have resources and strengths that helping professionals miss if they adopt completely pessimistic explanations for their difficulties. One implication of the findings of my study, in the light of Seligman's theory, is that explanatory theories that practitioners adopt, to make sense of the difficulties that clients present, affect their levels of hope and optimism. Contrast those theories premised on deterministic thinking (such as biological explanations) with those that focus on shifting (and shift-able) behavioural patterns and cognitive processes (such as cognitive behavioural therapy and SFT) and consider their connection to Seligman's theory: 'Finding temporary and specific causes for misfortunes is the art of hope . . . Finding permanent and universal causes for misfortune is the practice of despair' (Seligman, 1998: 48).

That participants on the training course who were the respondents in my research (Walsh, 2002) were struck by these ideas was obvious in the accounts of many. Hopeful, optimistic, positive were three of the most frequently cited qualities of SFT. What may have been less apparent to them was how important their own attributional theories might be in how they approach clients. Most of the respondents were at least temporarily buoyed up by the hope that the approach appeared to offer. They described feeling energized and positive towards their work and an underlying theme for some was the belief that this made a difference to clients, and possibly to outcomes.

There were some respondents in my study, especially newly qualified workers in child welfare services, who had little sense of agency that they could make a difference. One commented how: 'as an approach, I felt: oh, my God, this is too good to be true and nothing really works. Total pessimist – I'm just in the door and I'm a total pessimist'. Those who did not favour the approach cannot all be said to be less optimistic than the SFT advocates, merely that they did not accept that it could possibly make a difference to their practice and clients, and this is obviously a valid position. There were also those who indicated they were so stressed by conditions in the workplace that they lacked hope and interest, and for them a certain degree of pessimism may indeed have been functional. Some studies have highlighted the value of 'defensive pessimism', where 'anxious people lower their expectations and imagine the worst outcomes. This actually quells their anxiety, allowing them to then plan and act effectively' (*Psychotherapy Networker*, 2002).

> To hope is to believe that something positive, which does not presently apply to one's life, could still materialize, and so we yearn for it. Although desire (or motivation) is an essential feature, hope is much more than this because it requires the belief in the possibility of a favourable outcome, which gives hope a cognitive aspect and distinguishes it from the concept of motivation, *per se.*
>
> (Lazarus, 1999: 653).

More research is needed into the impact of a practitioner's level of hope on client outcomes. Although the concept itself has garnered considerable interest in recent years (Snyder, 2000; Eliott, 2005; Flaskas et al., 2007), it remains under-researched in the helping professions. An important caveat regarding the concept of hope is that its ethical use in interpersonal helping requires that it not degenerate into a blind and bland form of positive thinking of the form castigated by Enhrenreich (2010). Instead, it is best thought of as a form of hope bolstered by the practitioner's belief that he or she has strategies and assistance to offer that may make a difference, but that these will follow the client's lead.

Context, role and mandate

> Professional knowledge cannot be characterised in a manner that is independent of how it is learned and how it is used. It is through looking at the contexts of its acquisition and its use that its essential nature is revealed. Although many areas of professional knowledge are dependent on some understanding of relevant public codified knowledge found in books and journals, professional knowledge is constructed through experience and its nature depends on the cumulative acquisition, selection and interpretation of that experience.
>
> (Eraut, 1994: 19–20)

In my study, practitioners who were best able to draw on SFT and find ways of incorporating it into their work appreciated that their individual practice contexts offered both opportunities and some limitations. For example, those in multidisciplinary teaching hospitals or units actively drew on the stimulation and challenge of the competitiveness between different disciplines to improve their own practice and engage in continued professional development. They remained open to new ideas and keen to improvise on existing work practices. Working in pairs or in small study groups enabled them to build support, practise techniques, and review sessions.

Clarity about organizational role and mandate was also important but it was with hopefulness and a sense of vision that the practitioners looked beyond narrow organizational confines to identify the potential for solution-focused practices. For example, of the practitioners I interviewed who worked in child welfare services, those most likely to find a place for solution-focused helping in their work tended to describe their role as being more than child protection and tended to emphasize the preventative and positive aspects of their work. Those from medical settings similarly understood their role to include psychological change-work aimed at adapting in a hopeful way to chronic or debilitating illnesses. These hopeful practitioners also came from area teams that embodied a 'can-do' attitude of positive proactive work.

Associated with the need for clarity about role and mandate is the distinction that needs to be drawn (but which contains a rich potential for solution-focused work) between *agency goals* and *client goals*. As an ethical solution-focused helper, it appears you need to be both clear yourself and explicit with clients about what are the agency goals, and then negotiate how they can be addressed while also remaining true to the centrality of client-identified goals in the solution-focused model (Walsh, 2006).

An additional aspect to context is that of the culture of the agency or team in which you work. Is it an energetic, positive team? Or is it negative, demoralized, and lacking in energy? In my research, leaving aside those from voluntary or non-statutory settings, participants came from ten different area offices (as well as two specialist services). Broadly speaking, two different *cultures* of practice could be discerned. The first was one in which respondents displayed a generally high level of anxiety about the nature of the task, were preoccupied with bombardment rates and a sense of crisis and overload, appeared to lack support from managers, and felt too demoralized or lacking in confidence to experiment with a new approach however positive they were about the innovation itself. The second was one in which practitioners appeared to be less anxious and even hopeful about their core task, did not appear to be as concerned with managerial matters such as bombardment rates and waiting lists (and therefore more contained in themselves), and appeared to have both time and energy to move beyond a reactive form of casework to one in which they planned interventions and tried out different approaches (such as the innovation) in their work. The existence of area-based clusters of similar depictions of practice among the respondents strongly suggests differences in culture that are absorbed by practitioners as they become socialized into specific teams. Although the dominance of a reactive, crisis-driven conceptualization of practice where practitioners see themselves as victims of their work environment partially confirms this as a possible characterization specific to child protection settings, the concurrent presence of clusters of more hopeful, creative, and flexible workers in other locations simultaneously challenges it as the *only* form of practice possible in such settings. Furthermore, it demonstrates that possibilities for creative work exist in such settings and that work settings need to be analysed in more depth and across local areas and teams to make sense of these differences. That these different cultures were also linked with either patterns of successful experimentation and adoption of the innovation, or limited experimentation followed by abandonment, further strengthens the argument that different cultures of practice exist that can either facilitate or discourage creative and innovative practice in statutory settings. The team level factors of significance did include whether the line manager was supportive of experimentation and creative practice but only if the line manager was held in high regard and rated as someone who knew about such matters; otherwise, innovators turned to highly regarded peers, the 'old hands' on the team or in the office.

In both the literature on the transfer process (Reid and Barrington, 1994; Quinones, 1997) and on the diffusion of innovation process (Smale, 1998), the manager's role is emphasized: 'The role of the line manager is critical. The manager or team leader can either endorse, support and enhance any new learning, or oppose, block and otherwise extinguish any new development' (Smale, 1998: 206–207). But it has also been asserted that supervisors are not always the best supports for practitioners experimenting with new practices. Horwarth and Morrison have noted that:

> Many supervisors, in our experience, say that they are unable to address the developmental needs of staff as they feel they are no longer experts and familiar with current developments in particular areas of practice. It is not so much the practice expertise of the supervisor, rather it is the supervisory skills that are crucial for creating and sustaining a climate for learning.
>
> (Horwarth and Morrison, 1999: 158).

For the Irish practitioners in my study, line managers were not always present. Some, such as single-handed practitioners, those in voluntary organizations, and some in multidisciplinary teams, were not working within structures that included a line manager of the same profession. In such circumstances, practitioners appeared to become more self-reliant and autonomous and/or developed for themselves support groups and informal networks with which to support their practice. Several of the returnees on the training course who were single-handed social workers in voluntary or multidisciplinary settings used the second short course in SFT almost as a form of supervision and support for their use of the approach. For practitioners in single-disciplinary teams directed by a manager, variations existed in the role line managers either took or were expected to take in relation to the innovation. Some respondents referred to the views and/or levels of practical support and encouragement offered by line managers as something that they felt had affected their experimentation and adoption of SFT, but others did not see this as at all relevant. The accounts of the latter group indicated that they enjoyed a relatively high level of autonomy in deciding how to work with particular cases, but whether this was a conscious decision by managers to *give* free rein to practitioners whose practice they had confidence in, or a conscious decision by confident practitioners to *retain* control of the way in which they carried out their work, is unclear. Compton and Galaway (1994) refer to the possibility that team leaders may not share the concerns and priorities of the practitioners they manage. Several practitioners alluded to a perceived lack of interest or even disapproval on the part of managers regarding their experimentation with SFT. Although this did not appear to totally stifle practitioners' experimentation, it was perceived as a negative influence. The accounts of managers themselves who attended the short course indicate that they also varied in relation to their interpretation of their role in the post-training environment. Some, who rejected the innovation as being of any potential benefit, understandably did nothing to promote its use but *neither did they actively discourage it.* Some liked the innovation but felt inadequate in supporting practitioners implement an innovation that they themselves had not used in practice (or presumably come to own), but these managers similarly did not voice their approval for the method to peers. One other manager thought that interest in an innovation should stem from the team itself and not be suggested or imposed by managers, although he himself thought it could be of potential benefit. Several others who developed an enthusiasm for SFT took a more active role in either flagging up the innovation as a potential tool or by more actively supporting and coaching supervisees in using the approach. The very active role taken by line managers in one area combined with the high numbers of practitioners from this area who adopted the approach does lend support to the proposition that their influence can be critical but the findings from the study overall suggest that this is conditional.

Dynamics between practitioners and managers can vary enormously in that managers are not always looked to as role models or advisers on practice methods, nor do managers themselves always feel comfortable or competent in this role. Where managers and practitioners do share an enthusiasm for an innovation and where the manager feels comfortable and confident in a directive coaching role, the synergy created can be a powerful reinforcing influence for the experimenting practitioner.

Parallel knowledge bases

As will become clear in the following five chapters, in all settings there are solid existing knowledge bases about clients, problems, and the best ways of helping. These act as additional resources to the solution-focused helper, enabling him or her to draw on this practice and theory based wisdom. For example, if you are working in palliative and bereavement care, you will draw on existing research about when counselling interventions help and studies into what parents and relatives have said they would like from hospital services at end-of-life. In my study, practitioners both explicitly and implicitly demonstrated how their thinking and actions were influenced by pre-existing theories and beliefs. Theories of intervention at the individual level emanate from a range of philosophies and paradigms (behavioural, psychodynamic, systemic, and social constructionist to name a few). Early studies into social work practitioners' use of theory (Department of Health and Social Security, 1978; Curnock and Hardiker, 1979; Harrison, 1991) suggest that while practitioners may ally themselves to certain methods or frameworks, it is the exception rather than the rule for practitioners to adhere exclusively to one. Different approaches have been 'in vogue' over time in a process understood by examining the 'politics' of theory (Howe, 1992; Payne, 1997) but there is still a question-mark over the disparity between 'claimed' adherence to an approach and 'actual' use. Harrison (1991) queries whether adherence to one particular approach is even desirable, due to concerns that it leads to bias on the part of practitioners who stick to their preferred ideology rather than remaining responsive to diverse client and practice scenarios. It is now accepted that workers rely on knowledge from a range of sources to decide what to do 'in action', and typologies of knowledge (Payne, 1997; Drury-Hudson, 1999) have been developed. Fook and colleagues state this clearly:

> Experienced professional practice is . . . characterised by the ability to juggle and apply knowledge from a multitude of sources (personal and workplace experience, contextual knowledge, formal theory and popularised applications) in complex and changing situations in which there are no clear-cut solutions.
>
> (Fook et al., 2000: 148)

The findings from my study suggest that in the post-qualifying context, exposure to new approaches through short courses, followed by perceived benefit from practice experimentation, can result in practitioners expanding their repertoire of practice theories. In the views of many of the successful experimenters and adopters, the addition of SFT to their 'toolbox' enhanced their abilities to be effective in their work, as they developed skills as well as ideas from frameworks.

In addition, in the current climate of increased disillusionment with expert systems and questioning of standards of practice in a range of professions, attention has turned to the concept of continuing professional development and an examination of the various mechanisms that promote 'life-long learning'. Exposure to a new practice method can either affirm practitioners' pre-existing orientation to practice or, alternatively, challenge it. Either way, it signals that change is a possibility and offers participants a choice.

The evidence base for solution-focused therapy

Public accountability means that professionals now need to develop a strong evidence base for the interventions and help they offer clients and patients. There has been much debate in recent years about the concept of evidence-based practice and the complexity of applying traditional hierarchies of scientific evidence to interpersonal services. Macdonald (2007) suggests that in the light of studies reporting that identified common factors are more important in shaping constructive therapeutic interventions than any practice model alone (Hubble et al., 1999; Wampold, 2001), there is an increased tension with the demands for rigorously evaluated practice models. The problem with large-scale rigorous studies into a generic practice model such as SFT is that such studies require standardization and manualization of an approach followed by rigorous training so that individual differences do not confound results, and a rigid application with no deviations. These demands fly in the face of evidence for the need to remain responsive to client leads in therapeutic sessions (Beyebach and Carranza, 1997) and the core message of common factors research, which is that the quality of the therapeutic alliance as assessed by the client, and other factors such as the hope and expectancy generated in the therapy, are as important in determining outcome as practice models *per se*. Nonetheless, what if any evidence exists that SFT can help people change?

De Shazer and the team at the Brief Family Therapy Center (BFTC) in Milwaukee incorporated evaluation into their publications from their first article in 1986 including data on outcomes based on follow-up client feedback. Impressive as this may sound, it needs to be balanced by the recognition that in stubbornly sticking to the position that client feedback was the best form of evaluation possible, de Shazer can be said to have contributed to a delay in more systematic reviews and the inclusion of SFT in more rigorous controlled studies with independent objective measurements of change. Compared with other interventions such as motivational interviewing, which developed a manualized approach and a more rigorous research base (Miller and Rolnick, 2002; Rubak et al., 2005), SFT continued for some time to have a weaker evidence base. This has only started to change in recent years as more systematic reviews, meta-analyses, and randomized controlled studies have begun to appear in peer-reviewed journals and as standardized forms are developed or solution-based interventions are adopted on a programme- or region-wide basis (Antle et al., 2009).

Alasdair Macdonald, research coordinator of the European Brief Therapy Association, maintains a website listing many of the different studies (www. solutionsdoc.co.uk/sfb, accessed January 2010). In the first tranche of studies from 1986 to 2000, the evidence base remains weak but some of the individual findings are of significant clinical interest. These will be examined first.

Outcome studies, 1986–2000

At the BFTC in Milwaukee, outcome studies followed the Mental Research Institute formula and consisted primarily of client feedback. Clients were contacted by an independent evaluator some months after contact ended to ascertain levels of satisfaction with the outcomes of therapy. De Shazer defended this approach maintaining that since therapy usually starts with a client coming with a complaint, the only way of judging effectiveness is to ask the client if the complaint is still there. It also fits more comfortably with the constructivist paradigm to use the client's subjective experience to ascertain whether an intervention works as opposed to an externally devised and assessed instrument. Early results from the USA (de Shazer et al., 1986; Kiser, 1988; Kiser and Nunally, 1990) and the UK (George et al., 1990) indicate the approach enjoyed a similar, but not superior, rate of success to other established brief therapy methods (Budman and Gurman, 1988). Between 66 and 72 percent of respondents met their goals for treatment or made considerable progress towards them, in an average of four to six sessions. While direct comparisons with the Budman and Gurman assessment of brief therapies are problematic, due to the wide range of approaches contained under their definition of 'brief therapy', this way of working established an effectiveness at least similar to that of other short-term approaches.

One study by Wheeler (1995) on the use of the approach in child psychiatric social work in the UK used a different measurement, that of case outcomes in relation to the use of the method (i.e. were cases closed, referred on, or did clients stop attending?). An interesting result in this small survey was a significant difference in referral-on rates between cases seen not using the approach and those seen when using the approach. When using SFT, Wheeler's referral-on rate fell from 31 to 11 percent in a total sample of 73 cases. This suggests that the approach may impact *on the practitioner's* level of belief in client's competence.

In addition to individual empirical studies, in May 1997 the *Journal of Family Therapy* published five empirical studies of SFT. These studies were necessary for three different reasons: first, because SFT was the 'flavour of the month'; second, because it was presented as deceptively simple ('A simple formula incorporating the "Miracle Question", the use of rating scales, giving compliments and homework tasks (which seems to imply that anyone can do it), one suspects that there is more to it than appears at first sight'; Carpenter, 1997: 117); and third, because there was a paucity of studies that formally evaluated the model. These five studies are now outlined.

1. Macdonald's (1997) follow-up study of clients in an adult psychiatric clinic in Scotland was based on reports from thirty-six of the thirty-nine clients and from their general practitioners. The results indicated a 'good outcome rate' of 64 percent, approximately in line with a previous evaluation by the same author, and with estimates of the overall efficacy of other psychotherapies.

2. Zimmerman et al. (1997) researched the approach in couples work where solution-focused couples therapy was combined with 'psycho-educational' work. (A portion of the session teaching on 'myths that lead to relationship drain and guidelines for goal-setting . . . focusing on what works . . . pattern recognition and interruption strategies . . . evaluating pattern interruption failures . . . and planning for back sliding' (Zimmerman et al., 1997: 137.) Using a comparison group, their pre- and post-test scores indicated that treatment couples experienced some benefit from being involved in the solution-focused couple therapy groups, with significant changes in all four subscales used as a measurement instrument. Zimmerman et al. suggest that 'perhaps the positive focus and emphasis on strengths, skill-building and general "fellowship" of the couples groups contributed to this improvement' (p. 139).

3. Eakes et al. (1997) conducted a study of therapy with families, where one member had a diagnosis of schizophrenia and was receiving medication. Using a control group and experimental group design, they pre- and post-tested the ten participant families using an instrument that measured family roles and relationships. Their form of therapy combined solution-focused work with a reflecting team approach. They found significant differences between the groups in relation to expressiveness, active recreational orientation, moral-religious emphasis, and family incongruence. The first two of these scales showed positive increases after family-centred SFT, indicating a positive change towards more expressiveness and participation in social and recreational activities by the family members.

4. Beyebach and Carranza's (1997) study of dropout from solution-focused therapy in a clinic in Spain compared relational communication of sixteen sessions before dropout from therapy with relational communication

of sixteen sessions after which clients continued in therapy. Beyebach and Carranza's findings indicate that dropouts are not a homogeneous group, but more importantly their study 'provide[s] some empirical evidence to support the idea that therapists should promote supportive, harmonious and non-conflictual therapeutic conversations. A viable relationship is built, they suggest, on a close following of the client's lead rather than on strategizing' (Carpenter, 1997: 120).

5. Sundman's (1997) study in Finland involved an experimental group of social workers who received 'minimal' training in the approach (a combination of the SFT and MRI models), a well-matched comparison group of social workers (twenty-five in total), and some 382 of their clients. Outcomes were measured in a variety of ways: initial questionnaires about their work with the selected clients; tape-recordings of randomly chosen meetings; and follow-up questionnaires completed jointly by worker and client. Fifty-two percent of questionnaires were completed. Although there were no significant differences between the experimental and comparison groups in terms of goal achievement, the study indicated that clients who received the solution-focused intervention 'were more satisfied, more goal focused and more engaged in joint problem-solving with their social workers' (Carpenter, 1997: 119).

Several other small qualitative studies are important for what lessons they provide about the process of successful work. Using a one-group post-test design, Lee (1997) evaluated the use of SFT in a child mental health centre in Toronto. All families who received treatment from the solution-focused team within a three-year period (1990–1993) were included. Fifty-nine families agreed to participate in an independent study six months later. A 14-item questionnaire based on that used by the BFTC in Milwaukee was adopted and a sample of coding was cross-checked by two independent raters. Lee reported a 64.9 percent success rate ('success' being defined as either goals being met or partly met) for an average of 5.5 therapy sessions over a range of 3.9 months. This study confirmed the success rates of SFT as roughly equivalent to those of other brief therapies (but less than that initially claimed by de Shazer of between 72 and 80 percent). Lee suggests that this may in part be due to the differing experience of therapists at the two centres. That no differences were found when analysed for other variables suggests that the approach 'could work equally effectively with boys and girls of different age groups who live in diverse family constellations and have parents from different socio-economic strata' (Lee, 1997: 13). In relation to the process of helping she reported: 'being supported and validated' was the most frequently mentioned helpful element and she surmised that 'Rigid adherence to techniques can be perceived as the therapist's being inflexible, rigid, too positive, artificial and/or insensitive – all negatively related to goal attainment' (p. 14). Thus, forcing any approach on clients who are not responding is counter-productive. Other findings suggest that the nature of the presenting problem may have an important influence on goal attainment, with school-related issues and children's emotional regulation most positively connected with goal attainment. Lee suggests that these goals may be particularly amenable to change through small, concrete, behavioural steps. She poses the question of how clients who perceive their problems in more complex, global terms (such as family relationship problems) might be helped to think more in terms of concrete, small, and observable behaviours.

The implications of these early studies were as follows. First, in none of the studies did participants use the SFT model in its complete form; rather, they took aspects of it and adapted it to the specific context. This is important, as it has been confirmed in all the significant meta-analyses published subsequently (detailed below) as well as a number of naturalistic studies. In one, for example, SFT was combined with parent management training in a Sure Start programme (Brown and Dillenburger, 2004). The most commonly used aspects were: goal-setting; positive feedback; exception-finding; scaling; and in only one case (Macdonald) the Miracle Question. Lee (1997) describes the use of specific types of questions (exception, outcome, coping, relationship, and scaling questions) as the central component of SFT.

Second, both Macdonald and Lee looked specifically at socio-economic status as a variable, and found no significant variation in outcome for different social and occupational groups. This is important, as it differs from published outcome studies of other 'talking treatments', all of which are reported by McKeown et al. (2001) to have shown greater benefit for those of higher socio-economic status: 'Numerous studies suggest that lower socio-economic groups are less likely to use therapy and more likely to drop out of therapy, possibly because the client – and the therapist – have low expectations of a successful outcome' (p. 25). This raises the possibility that solution-focused brief therapy is potentially of more use with people of different socio-economic groups (and in Lee's study from a range of ages, educational backgrounds, and family types) than other forms of therapy. For one rather sceptical critic, it indicates: 'The potential benefits of SFBT for poor people with significant problems' (Carpenter, 1997: 118).

Third, although there were no differences in outcome in Sundman's Finnish study, there *were* significant differences in the clients' reported experience of social work contact between those who received a solution-focused contact and those who did not. The workers involved received minimal training in what the researcher termed solution-focused 'ideas', which emphasized goals, exceptions, and positive feedback, although the short training course provided some skills development. The SFT clients were more satisfied, more goal-focused, and more engaged in joint problem-solving with their social workers, which indicated that a collaborative relationship had been developed. And these clients were not at the 'soft' end of the problem spectrum – being either child welfare 'cases' or single men with serious addiction, mental health, and housing issues. What was *not* examined was what effect the training and use of SFT had on the perceptions or attitudes of the workers.

Fourth, although an inferred result rather than a directly stated one, Wheeler's drop in referral-on rates when using SFT suggests that using the approach may alter *practitioners'* perception of the coping abilities of their clients and their hopefulness regarding the possibilities of sustained change.

The development of a more rigorous evidence base, 2000–2009

Alasdair Macdonald's review of the research evidence, dated April 2009 (www.solutionsdoc.co.uk) identifies a total of eighty relevant studies, two meta-analyses, nine randomized controlled trials, and twenty-seven comparison studies. His summary concludes that of the nine random trials, six showed the benefit of SFT over existing methods; and of twenty-seven comparison studies, twenty-one favoured SFT. In addition, 'Effectiveness data are available from more than 2,800 cases with a success rate exceeding 60%; requiring an average of 3–5 sessions of therapy time' (Macdonald, www.solutionsdoc.co.uk).

Meta-analyses

Of the two meta-analyses identified by Macdonald, one American study (Kim, 2006) used hierarchical linear modelling software to synthesize the findings of twenty-two primary outcome studies, with the aim of calculating an overall effect size estimate. The twenty-two primary outcomes studies included some of those cited above; for all of them, Kim examined how many of the seven core components of the practice model [as specified by de Shazer and Berg (1997), and consisting of use of the miracle question; scaling questions, a consulting break, and delivery of a set of compliments to client; assignment of homework tasks; looking for strengths and solutions; goal-setting; and looking for exceptions to the problem] were present, and interestingly this varied from one to seven with ten studies using three components, and only one each at the ends of the continuum of one only or all seven. Kim concluded that

> SFBT appears to be effective with internalizing behaviour problems such as depression, anxiety, self-concept and self-esteem but does not appear to be as effective with externalizing behaviour problems such as hyperactivity, conduct problems, or aggression or family and relationship problems.

(Kim, 2006: 113)

Limitations of the analysis include the small number and variable quality of studies included, small sample sizes, as well as studies that were rated as poorly controlled.

The second meta-analysis cited by Macdonald is that of a Dutch study (Stams et al., 2006) with an English abstract. The original article in Dutch was inaccessible, so I am reliant on Macdonald's summary:

> 21 studies, many factors examined. Small to moderate effect; better than no treatment; as good as other treatments. Best results for personal behaviour change, adults, residential/group settings. Recent studies show strongest effects. Shorter than other therapies; respects client autonomy.
>
> (Macdonald, www.solutionsdoc.co.uk)

Systematic reviews

The three reviews identified consist of two generic reviews (Gingerich and Eisengart, 2000; Corcoran and Pillai, 2009) and one focused on outcomes for SFT in schools (Kim and Franklin, 2009). The earliest (Gingerich and Eisengart) reviewed fifteen controlled outcome studies to assess the extent to which SFBT had received empirical support:

> Five studies were well-controlled and all showed positive outcomes – four found SFBT to be better than no treatment or standard institutional services; and one found SFBT to be comparable to a known intervention . . . Findings from the remaining 10 studies, which we considered moderately or poorly controlled, were consistent with a hypothesis of SFBT effectiveness. We conclude that the 15 studies provide preliminary support for the efficacy of SFBT but do not permit a definitive conclusion.
>
> (Gingerich and Eisengart, 2000: 477)

In addition, the authors highlight two issues for future research – one was the wide variation in form of SFBT used. Similar to Kim (2006), they used a seven-component model of SFBT. They suggested that the area of greatest need was in providing a definitive practice model and detailed manuals for practice implementation. On the one hand they suggested that the range they found did lend itself to the belief that SFBT is widely applicable, but on the other hand: 'efficacy can only be established if the intervention is clearly and specifically proceduralized so that it can be implemented consistently by different investigators across research sites' (p. 486). Hence the continued difficulty in validating SFT according to the standards required for standardization and manualization.

Corcoran and Pillai (2009) reviewed ten studies that fitted their criteria (experimental or quasi-experimental; published studies in English; they excluded interventions that used only aspects of the approach or those that combined it with other interventions). They concluded that 'about 50% of the studies can be viewed as showing improvement over alternative conditions or no-treatment control' (p. 240). Because of the diversity of problems and populations in the studies reviewed (those with moderate to high effect sizes ranged from a telephone crisis hot line to orthopaedic rehabilitation, parents experiencing conflict with adolescents to Hispanic children of incarcerated parents), no definitive conclusions could be drawn on the efficacy of the solution-focused model *per se*.

Kim and Franklin (2009) reviewed the evidence on SFBT in schools, an important arena of practice given its widespread use throughout the school system not only in the USA but also in the UK. Again, the seven-component model of SFBT was used (with the criteria being that at least one of these seven components was present, and the authors defined their work as solution-focused), and only primary studies using experimental designs that examined the effectiveness of SFBT in either a school setting or with students in the USA were reviewed. The seven studies finally included in this review consisted of one experimental design, six quasi-experimental designs, and one single-case design. Sample size ranged from seven to eighty-six students spanning elementary to high school grades. Several used group work interventions, others individual sessions. The conclusion of this review was that of mixed results:

> Positive outcomes suggested that solution-focused therapy can be beneficial in helping students reduce the intensity of their negative feelings, manage their conduct problems, improve academic outcomes like credits earned, and positively impact externalizing behavioural problems and substance use . . . In one study it was also found that SFBT had equivalent results for impacting behavioural change as cognitive-behavioral therapy and had better therapy outcomes for engaging clients and retaining them in the therapy process. Effect sizes calculated by the authors in the individual studies and also for this systematic review study showed that SFBT had medium and some large effect sizes. On the other hand negative outcomes suggested that SFBT was not successful in raising GPA or improving attendance rates of students . . . SFBT was also not successful at impacting the self-esteem of students . . . [in] two studies.
>
> (Kim and Franklin, 2009: 468)

They conclude that although SFBT was promising in the school setting, and achieved significant changes on a range of outcome measures pertinent to school-based practitioners in a relatively short space of time (eight or fewer sessions), more systematic studies were needed to build its evidence base for school-based practitioners.

Naturalistic studies
Macdonald identified more than eighty relevant studies worldwide that fitted into this category. Those that are of relevance to the applied areas of practice detailed in Chapters 4–8 are reported there.

Some tentative conclusions on the evidence base for SFT to date

The research studies reviewed indicate that SFT can be as successful in its outcomes as other brief therapies, and that it has been mined successfully by practitioners as a source of 'ideas' from which they can construct therapeutic interventions with clients but it does not provide a research basis for arguing that it is superior to other practice models if outcomes alone are the determining factor. It has demonstrated effectiveness rather than efficacy:

> Effectiveness data are available from 30 studies including more than 2,200 cases with a success rate exceeding 60 per cent and using an average of 3–5 sessions of therapy time . . . Solution-focused therapy is a realistic and practical approach to many problems in mental health and elsewhere. The model is cost-efficient and training is straightforward . . . It can claim to be the equal of other psychotherapies, while also taking less time and resources for treatment, reducing the strain placed on therapists and providing help for a number of groups and clients who have previously found it hard to obtain useful help from psychological therapies.
>
> (Macdonald, 2007: 113)

Some of the more subtle research findings suggest that use of the model may influence practitioners' levels of belief and hope in clients' abilities to change and also lead to a more cooperative relationship with clients. In the main, SFT stands out as an approach that is versatile, capable of being combined with other approaches, and most often adopted by practitioners in a selective manner. It appears to have particular strengths in providing practitioners who are sympathetic to a strengths-based philosophy with a set of interventions and a style of questioning that is consonant with this philosophy, and in being generalizable outside of the formal therapy settings. More research is required into the specific features of the approach that work with particular clients or problems. As long as practitioners remain aware of its limitations as reported in the research literature and practise it ethically, then it remains a valid practice model to experiment with and evaluate in health and social care settings. Some thoughts on how to practise it ethically are now outlined.

Ethical considerations specific to solution-focused therapy

As outlined in Chapter 1, the most significant risks relate to:

- the need to avoid exaggerated claims for its effectiveness;
- the need to include structural and gender analyses of power relations within client systems and client–therapist systems and attend to these;
- the need to avoid the notion that brief therapies can resolve all difficulties;
- the need to ensure that clients are offered longer-term supports and interventions where warranted;
- the need to ensure that adoption is not tokenistic and superficial in the form of a positive psychology ideology that can in effect concentrate the focus on the individual experience and imply that a simple cognitive shift can work miracles;
- the need to pay particular attention to the use of power and influence in the helping process, so that the potential for increasing cooperative relations with clients is then not used against their best interests. This risk needs more detailed consideration.

The originators of SFT no longer subscribe to a position of the therapist/ helper being on an equal footing with the client; instead, they acknowledge that it is a hierarchical relationship (de Shazer et al., 2007). The helper does have power, does use influence, and it is in how that influence is used that ethical issues can occur. Howe (1986) has elsewhere contended that 'the most insidious exercise of power is to prevent people from having grievances by shaping their perceptions, cognitions and preferences' (p.112). Using your power and influence to persuade people that they have no grievances is unethical, but is it so to use it to give some realistic hope to people who feel hopeless? Is it not valid to work with clients to promote their sense of competence and mastery as long as the goals are realistic and the work is undertaken with care?

In my research into practitioners' use of SFT, I found virtually all of them to be cautious and careful about which clients they used it with, in which practice scenarios, and to what extent. There were also a very small number whose accounts suggested that they did use it to maximize cooperation of clients in situations where this might not be in their best interests, for example persuading vulnerable parents (with mental health, learning difficulties or addiction problems) to cooperate with child protection assessments where the outcome might be the removal of their children, without making clear that this was a possibility. This *is* unethical, and it relates back to the need for absolute clarity about the distinction between agency goals and client goals.

These tensions should not preclude use of the approach with mandated clients but it does mean that a solution-focused helper in such contexts must be explicit and honest about their mandate:

> A worker with statutory responsibilities must be clear and honest with clients about concerns that exist and procedures that are followed, but this does not preclude creatively using a solution-focused approach, particularly where clients either refer themselves, or are willing to engage once referred.
>
> (Walsh, 1997: 72)

Conclusions

Without making the assumption that change is necessarily always a good thing, findings from my study indicate that although interest in SFT has been sustained for over 15 years, it neither risks taking over the world nor have practitioners abandoned their critical faculties in their assessment and adoption of the approach. The extent to which the practitioners in my study were cautious and took care in their use of SFT, even though they almost universally found the approach to be of strong appeal, is most evident. Their accounts of tailoring it to particular practice scenarios demonstrated the ability to 'transform' theoretical knowledge of the innovation into personalized knowledge (Eraut, 1994) through its use. The care and thought with which practitioners considered adoption should reassure educators and academics that the transfer of practice models to practice is recognized by most practitioners as a complex matter that they engage in both critically and reflectively. A duty of care to clients was evident throughout, without any evidence emerging that practitioners embrace new ideas in a completely ideological manner.

Following from the range of influences identified in my 2002 study and subsequent research, the solution-focused helper in health care and social care adopts a self-concept as 'active change-agent', adopts a position of hopefulness, remains articulate and engaged regarding ethics, evidence and parallel knowledge bases, and appreciates the influences of context, role and mandate on his or her work with clients/patients. Let us now turn to how this works in practice across different settings.

Notes

1   People who give up easily believe the causes of bad events that happen to them are permanent; people who resist helplessness believe the causes of bad events

are temporary. 'Failure makes everyone at least momentarily helpless . . . It hurts, but the hurt goes away – for some people . . . For others, the hurt lasts . . . They remain helpless for days or perhaps months, even after only small set-backs' (Seligman, 1998: 45).

2   'People who make universal explanations for their failures give up on every-thing when a failure strikes in one area. People who make specific explanations may become helpless in that one part of their lives yet march stalwartly on in the others . . . The optimist believes that bad events have specific causes while good events will enhance everything he does. The pessimist believes that bad events have universal causes and that good events are caused by specific factors' (Seligman, 1998: 47–48).

3   'When bad things happen, we can blame ourselves (internalise) or we can blame other people or circumstances (externalise). People who blame them-selves when they fail have low self-esteem as a consequence . . . People who blame external events do not lose self-esteem when bad events strike' (Seligman, 1998: 49).

PART 2
Solution-focused helping in practice

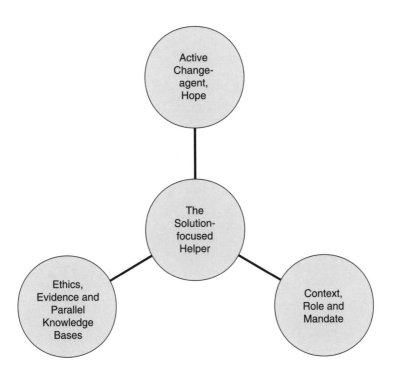

4 The solution-focused helper working across cultures in a globalized world

I note the obvious differences
   in the human family.
Some of us are serious,
   some thrive on comedy.

Some declare their lives are lived
   as true profundity,
And others claim they really live
   the real reality.

The variety of our skin tones
   can confuse, bemuse, delight,
brown and pink and beige and purple,
   tan and blue and white.

I've sailed upon the seven seas
   and stopped in every land,
I've seen the wonders of the world,
   yet not one common man [. . .].

I note the obvious differences
   between each sort and type,
But we are more alike, my friends,
   than we are unalike.

We are more alike, my friends,
   than we are unalike.
We are more alike, my friends,
   than we are unalike.
(edited version of *Human Family*, by Maya Angelou, 1990)

Box 4.1   Making assumptions and stereotypes: Berg's story told in an interview with Yalom

Berg: I went . . . for training in group therapy to work with a Vietnam vets group. We had a horrible case. One young man thought that the Viet Cong was coming after him. So he always slept with a shotgun under his pillow. And in the middle of the night, he shot his wife who was sleeping next to him. I thought, my God. I was a teenager when the Korean War started and was in the middle of it. So I had some experience of being in the middle of a war. I volunteered to work with these returning Vietnam vets because they would not go to VA hospitals. I organized this group . . .
Yalom: What did you do with these groups?
Berg: I didn't know what to do with them. So I made a videotape of a session and took it to . . . a supervision group. This very famous psychoanalytic supervisor was there. I showed him the tape and said, 'I need help. I don't know what to do for these people.' He turns to me and says, 'What is your countertransfer-ence issue?' I said, 'What? What are you talking about?' I was sort of shocked by this because I was asking for help. He said, 'These are veterans, these are people who shot and killed your kind of people.' I was just absolutely floored. Never expected something like that. To turn my plea for help, to turn it around and suddenly it became my problem, that it was my countertransference issue. I thought, 'You ass. My kind of people – I'm Korean! These are Vietnamese! You dumb ass.'

(Berg, 2003: www.psychotherapy.net/interview/Insoo_Kim_Berg)

Introduction

> International migration is a constant, not an aberration, in human history. Population movements have always accompanied demographic growth, technological change, political conflict and warfare.
> (Castles and Miller, 2009: 299)

Historically, the different waves of inward migration to Britain from the West Indies, India, and Pakistan, from the 1950s onwards, and the waves of outward migration from Ireland to Britain and North America from the nineteenth century, were the patterns and trends everyone was familiar with. Citizenship rights became an issue in the British discourse and a matter for public debate from the 1970s onwards, when different levels of rights were established for migrants from Commonwealth countries. Citizenship rights became an issue in Ireland also from the 1970s with Britain's membership of the European Union; initially a dormant issue but one that now exercises public debate following the radical changes to migration patterns experienced during the years of the economic boom in the 1990s. Given the established patterns of immigration into Britain from Ireland, India, Pakistan, and the West Indies, most workers will already be well versed in the dynamics of working across cultures and probably well supported within their agencies through Equality and Diversity – and Equal Opportunities – initiatives and policies. But globalization poses some intrinsic challenges to our traditional approaches and theories of migration and integration.

Castles and Miller (2009) describe contemporary international migration as part of a 'transnational revolution that is reshaping societies and politics across the globe' (p. 7). Several factors have contributed to this. For instance, international mobility in general has increased in the last two decades – due in part to what can be termed the 'Ryanair effect'. A combination of cheap airfares and multiple routes to more obscure local areas outside capital cities has not only led to an increase of people on the move but has also made it easier for people to travel long distances to work and retain a home life hundreds if not thousands of miles away: commuting on a level never previously envisaged (van der Klis and Karsten, 2009).

Binding directives promoting the free movement of labour across the European Union and intensive campaigns in recent years across the globe to recruit public service staff (especially education, health, and social care staff) in the light of chronic shortages in Europe and North America has facilitated this freer movement of workers beyond national and continental borders. It has also raised problematic ethical issues relating to the impact on developing countries of depriving them of their own highly trained professionals. Referring to the migration of social workers, Kasiram (2009: 648) notes that, 'The loss to high-income countries where better working conditions with upward mobility prospects exist, results in a critical brain drain that a low-income country like South Africa can ill afford'.

The ease with which people can now keep in contact (through mobile phones, text messaging, emails, and Skype technologies) enables family members to retain communicative and emotional relationships, although at a physical distance. As the proportion of women who migrate increases through the feminization of migration (Castles and Miller, 1993; Lutz, 2008), this also has significant implications on parenting practices and gender roles.

The ease of international travel has also had an impact on the distances that asylum-seekers can now travel in their quest for refuge. The ubiquity of modern telecommunications has created the global village where alluring images of life in the privileged developed countries is beamed into the most remote and materially impoverished corners of the world. When passage to the developed countries is seen as the only way out of a lifetime of grinding poverty, families will make great sacrifices to fund such endeavours. But not all have equal access.

> The inequality arising from globalization and social transformation is particularly evident with regard to migration. Differentiated migration regimes have been set up, to encourage the highly skilled to be mobile, while low-skilled workers and people fleeing persecution are excluded . . . in the globalized world mobility has become the most powerful and most coveted stratifying factor . . . The riches are global, the misery is local.
>
> (Bauman, 1998: 9 and 74, quoted in Castles and Miller, 2009: 57)

Alongside this increased ease of mobility has come an increase in people-trafficking as a lucrative trade. The sex and drug industries are in particular seen to be exploitative of both women and young people trafficked into countries for employment or enslavement, although it is hard to estimate with any accuracy the numbers involved precisely because these markets operate below the radar of regulated or supervised activities. A public debate continues in both Britain and Ireland, for example, in relation to the proportion of asylum-seeking children who may be trafficked.

Globalization, in short, has thrown up opportunities and challenges for both citizens of the world and service providers across the world. The modern globalized world has implications for how we work in health and social care services, both with patients and clients, but also within the workforce, with colleagues and fellow professionals. It also has implications for the types of communities we live in and the social networks and social supports we can and do develop. On the one hand, these changed conditions supposedly signal the cosmopolitan nature of contemporary society and could lead to the fallacy that human experience is becoming more generic and universal (and so services can become more generic and apply equally to all). On the other hand, there are particular tensions and sets of circumstances that play out only at the local level, that consist of unique situations and culturally specific difficulties – these call for individually tailored service responses that not only recognize and negotiate cultural and ethnic differences, but also work within the transitory and shifting frameworks of dual allegiances and responsibilities that characterize the experiences of many migrants today.

In this chapter, I explore first some of the general theoretical frameworks and principles that we can use to guide our work; then, some of the ethical dimensions of working across cultures before examining the use and limitations of solution-focused concepts and techniques in this context. The term 'ethnic and migrant groups' will be used to denote both those communities who have been part of our society for generations (such as West Indian and Pakistani in Britain; and Travellers in Ireland) and the newer communities of migrant groups who have become part of our societies in recent decades. In helping to make sense of individual experience and need within both communities, the broad solution-focused principle of eliciting the client's story and perspective and co-constructing solutions will be seen as a central intervention. But first, let us examine some of the macro policy dimensions that impact on our work at the micro level.

Macro issues: questions of citizenship and social policy

Migration has existed since time immemorial. As a consequence, throughout history nation-states have had to find ways of responding to increased ethnic diversity and population movements. Central to this process is the issue of citizenship: 'defining who is a citizen, how newcomers can become citizens, and what citizenship means' (Castles and Miller, 2009: 44). Different 'ideal' types of citizenship have emerged over time:

1   The *imperial model* – related to subject status of the same power or ruler – was formally in place in the UK until the Nationality Act of 1981. Castles and Miller (2009) note that this model 'helps to veil the actual dominance of a particular ethnic group or nationality over other subject peoples' (p. 44).

2   The *folk or ethnic model* – where the definition of inclusion is based on ethnicity (common descent, language, and culture) and involves excluding those groups and minorities that don't belong.

3   The *republican model* – defined on the basis of a constitution, legal framework, and the concept of citizenship, thus allowing for newcomers to become members once accepted as such under the legal and political process.

4   The *multicultural model* – similar to the republican model but with a pluralist dimension that allows continued adherence to cultural and ethnic norms (as long as they are permissible under national law). Prevalent in many Western countries for the latter part of the twentieth century but increasingly challenged since the attacks of 9/11 in the USA and 7/7 in the UK and increasing political focus on security and surveillance.

5   The *transnational model* – 'social and cultural identities of transnational communities transcend national boundaries, leading to multiple and differentiated forms of belonging . . . This corresponds with the fact that, through globalization, a great deal of political and economic power is shifting to transnational corporations and international agencies which are not currently open to democratic control' (Castles and Miller, 2009: 45).

Castles and Miller (2009) point out that the first four models, premised on membership of one nation-state, do not account for a new emerging form – the transnational. At the same time, they caution against the assumption that this will become the norm, citing the lack of research evidence and noting that the transnational pattern is not that adopted by the majority of migrants:

> Temporary labour migrants who sojourn abroad for a few years, send back remittances, communicate with their family at home and visit them occasionally are not necessarily 'transmigrants'. Nor are permanent migrants who leave forever, and simply retain loose contact with their homeland. The key defining feature is that transnational activities are a central part of a person's life. Where this can be shown empirically to apply to a group of migrants, one can appropriately speak of a transnational community.
>
> (Castles and Miller, 2009: 32–33)

Research into the Polish immigrant community in Ireland, for example, confirms that most plan to stay, citing significant social networks in Ireland as a strong pull factor (Krings et al., 2009).

Changes in national, European, and international law play a significant part in altering categories of citizenship. International human rights standards can influence conditions under which people are entitled to full citizenship or some citizenship rights in different nation-states, but as Castles and Miller point out, is dependent on the national ratification of such international treaties.

At a national level, immigrants who have been resident in either Ireland or Britain for a long period can apply to override the normal conditions for citizenship or for 'permission to remain': a particular status that confers specific rights termed 'quasi-citizenship' (which applies to millions of long-term residents in Europe, many born outside their country of residence). At a European level, directives on the free movement of labour within the European Union member states, on structures for the mutual recognition of professional qualifications, on free travel zones, and on the rationalization of third-level educational standards through the Bologna process continue the project of European integration, although it is not without its critics. In our local contexts, in Ireland and Britain, there is significant opposition to the European project and no consensus on how far the European project should extend.

In recent years, a range of events (including the 9/11 attacks on America, the wars in Iraq and Afghanistan, the varying national reactions to the Lisbon Treaty, and most recently the impact of the world banking and economic crisis) has thrown into sharper relief tensions between national, regional, and global policies on mobility and integration. Recent global events have also highlighted two other dimensions to the debate: first, that of the interconnectedness of economic, social, and political systems and events not only within but *beyond* individual nation-states and European borders; and second, the existing balances that are reordered when new entities are constructed. An example of the latter that is particularly pertinent to our work in social and health care services is the potential 'othering' of the non-European, which occurs, for example, through the construction of Europe-wide strategies for the management of asylum-seekers and refugees (as so-called 'Fortress Europe'); and through the privileging of European workers above workers from other parts of the world in the construction of the free movement of labour within Europe. Coming into sharper relief in recent times of economic uncertainty and recessionary conditions are tensions between migrant and local workers competing for increasingly scarce employment opportunities.

In conclusion, migration theory is an important foundational knowledge base that we can use to make sense of current patterns of migration and transnational movements that have an impact on our daily work (see Box 4.2).

Some facts and figures

Did you know that the Irish are the most populous foreign-born group in the UK? Or that Germans are the fourth most populous? In Ireland, the proportion of the population that was born outside the country now surpasses that in the UK (being over 10 percent at the 2002 census date compared with 8.3 percent). Becoming aware of such migration patterns and changing trends enables us to plan more effectively for changing needs in the communities we serve. It also allows us to counteract some of the urban myths that emerge related to rising anxieties about the scale and impact of immigration. Sriskandarajah and Road (2005) note that the proportion of British people who rate race and immigration as one of the key issues facing the country rocketed during the late 1990s and that now over 60 percent of the British population are thought to believe that there are too many immigrants in the country. However, they note that the policy issues for politicians are complex: 'understanding and managing increasingly complex flows of people; creating an efficient and responsive asylum system; meeting labor market needs where and when they arise; and, all the while, being seen to be in control of the system' (Sriskandarajah and Road, 2005: 2).

As workers and educators in the health and social care fields, it is important to start with a consideration of how we, as citizens as well as workers, absorb and make sense of the varying media coverage of migration trends because how we respond to the individual patient or client can be affected by wider popular media portrayals.

Box 4.2 Migration theory

- Migration and settlement are closely linked to other economic, political and cultural linkages being formed between different countries in an accelerating process of globalization;
- The migratory process has certain internal dynamics based on the social networks which are at its core . . . Thus the emergence of societies which are more diverse must be seen as an inevitable result of decisions to recruit foreign workers, or to permit immigration;
- Increasing numbers of international migrants maintain recurring and significant links in two or more places forming transnational communities which live across borders. This trend is facilitated by globalisation, both through improvements in transport and communication technology, and through diffusion of global cultural values;
- Most minorities are formed by a combination of other-definition and self-definition. Other-definition refers to various forms of exclusion and discrimination (or racism). Self-definition has a dual character. It includes assertion and recreation of ethnic identity, centred upon premigration cultural symbols and practices . . . Issues of culture, identity and community can take on great importance for the receiving society as a whole;
- [Relating to the significance of immigration for the nation-state] It seems likely that increasing ethnic diversity will contribute to changes in central political institutions, such as citizenship, and may affect the very nature of the nation-state;
- Distinctions need to be made between economically motivated migration and forced migration. Most forced migrants remain close to their country of origin, and 'onward migration is motivated both by the imperative of flight from violence, and by the hope of building a better life elsewhere' (p. 34) but open only to the privileged few with financial resources to fund onward travel.

(Castles & Miller, 2009, summarized from p. 33 and pp. 47–48)

Taking a personal inventory

First, let us look at 'popular' models that encapsulate general understandings and perceptions of other ethnic groups. Some migrant/ethnic commmunities appear to atttract more negative stereotyping than others, for example nomadic/semi-nomadic groups such as Irish Travellers and Eastern European Roma. Travellers and Roma tend to fare poorly on indices of health and social

Box 4.3   Countries of origin of foreign-born population in the UK, 2001

Countries of birth	Number	Percent of total foreign-born population
Ireland	533,205	10.9
India	467,634	9.6
Pakistan	321,167	6.6
Germany	266,136	5.4
USA	158,424	3.2
All other countries	3,150,005	64.3
Total	4,896,581	100.0

Source: United Kingdom National Statistics: http://www.statistics.gov.uk/
According to the UK Office of National Statistics, the foreign-born represented 8.3 percent (4,896,581) of the total UK population in 2001. (www.migrationinformation.org/DataHub/ Europe_map_cfm)

Box 4.4   Countries of origin of foreign-born population in Ireland, 2002

Countries of birth	Number	Percent of total foreign-born population
UK and Northern Ireland	248,515	62.1
USA	21,541	5.4
Nigeria	9225	2.3
Germany	8770	2.2
France	6794	1.7
All other countries	105,171	26.3
Total	400,016	100.0

Source: Central Statistics Office, Census 2002.
According to the Central Statistics Office, the foreign-born represented 10.4 percent (400,016) of the total population of Ireland in 2002. (www.migrationinformation.org/DataHub/ Europe_map_cfm)

well-being and appear to have particular difficulties in accessing and using health services (Peters et al., 2009).

The following typology (O'Connell, 1994, as developed in Torode, Walsh and Woods, 2001) is exemplified using Irish Travellers as the minority group:

1. The *liberal humanist* perspective views Travellers as individuals no different from anybody else. When this means that Travellers are equal citizens with the same needs and rights as everybody else it has a positive effect, but it can also be used to imply that Travellers have no distinct identity or culture in

a way that denies real cultural differences. In emphasizing the individual, the liberal humanist ignores or minimizes what can be significant collective differences in people's experiences. The liberal humanist perspective can be criticized: first, because identities are presumed to develop on an individual and personal level, which denies the social construction of identity; and second, because liberalism itself operates as an instrument of social control with differing identities offered varying degrees of acceptance within the dominant social order.

2. The *social pathology* perspective views members of minority groups as deviants. This model emphasizes individual deviation from a societal norm, where the oppressed are regarded as the pathology of the healthy society. Those viewed as social misfits are seen to be responsible themselves for their marginalization and discrimination, or they are viewed as 'victims' in need of charity. Personal inadequacy, a group-wide inability to function adequately or 'vice' are cited as factors in the marginalization process. The focus on deficits means that issues of economic injustice, power imbalances, exploitation, and oppression need not be explored. This leads to an avoidance of prejudice and allows for the expression of negative stereotypes and racism.

3. The *sub-culture of poverty* perspective views differences as emanating from economic poverty alone. This model holds that marginalized groups 'pass on values and attitudes from one generation to the next which perpetuate poverty' (O'Connell, 1994: 13). In the case of Travellers, these values and attitudes are perceived to privilege a present-time orientation and an inability to defer gratification, thus making them psychologically incapable of adapting to changing circumstances or new opportunities. The sub-culture of poverty acts to keep the members of that community passively tied into a different way of being. This model is unable to account for the significant differences in economic power and resources that can occur within particular populations such as Roma or Travellers, or the adaptability and ingenuity that is evident among different nomadic groups over time. Interventions are, like those of the liberal humanist and social pathology ones, focused on assimilating the members of the minority group into mainstream society, and ignoring or erasing difference.

4. The *idealist* perspective, in contrast to the above three, views those from minority groups as 'special' and 'exotic', as having some special innate qualities that mark them out as different from 'ordinary' people and as having a special status that needs to be protected. This model of 'cultural reductionism' ignores the oppression that minority groups suffer and does not acknowledge the effects of internalized oppression. Because of the 'special' label that is attached to the minority group, relationships are more likely to be patronizing rather than equal.

5. The *human rights* perspective defines minority groups according to

features that constitute a difference or grounds for discrimination under human rights legislation. Both differences in identity and experiences of oppression and discrimination are acknowledged as factors contributing to marginalization. Travellers, for instance, are regarded as a people with distinct characteristics (a long shared history, values, customs, lifestyle, and traditions associated with nomadism) and also as a minority group who share a history of oppression and discrimination. The main disadvantage of the emphasis on ethnicity is that it can lead to a perception from the dominant social order that those from ethnic groups are less equal, or less 'normal' and hence feed into a perception of 'the other'. This can develop into a mistaken assumption that ethnicity refers to some permanent essence attached to minorities that becomes deterministic. This needs to be counteracted by an emphasis on the difficulties of using one set of cultural norms – that of the dominant social order – to assess or judge the actions, behaviours, and beliefs of another group with their own set of cultural norms. The alternative – that minority groups take control of their own definitions and then engage in a dialogue with the dominant group about the cultural differences between them – is seen as preferable but does not obviate the ethical dilemmas that can occur regarding the dangers of cultural relativism.

What is also evident from the work of sociological theorists, as well as research statistics collected by government through census and surveys, is that migration patterns impact in a diverse number of ways on different countries, cities, towns, and regions. For social and health care workers in the remote rural location of Ballyhaunis, Co. Mayo in Ireland, for instance, the establishment of a specialist industry producing Halal meat mostly for export to the Middle East meant the arrival of several thousand Muslim workers into the area (and recruitment still continues on local job websites!). For the construction of the Olympic Village in Newham, East London for the Games in 2012, approximately 15,000 extra construction workers a year are needed, only 20 percent of whom it is estimated will come from the local area. As service providers, therefore, we need to be able to flexibly adapt our services (and draw down extra resources when required) to cater for specific communities that develop in our local contexts. We also need to

---

Box 4.5   Reflective exercise

Question 1: Which of these five perspectives, in your opinion, offers the least discriminating and most empowering perspective for understanding the experiences of minority groups? Why?

Question 2: Which two migrant groups or ethnic communities do you find present most challenges to your work and why?

be aware of the wider picture in relation to migration patterns in our area of work.

Parallel knowledge bases

Broadly speaking, there are four different perspectives of relevance to social and health care workers in their direct practice with ethnic minorities: anti-racism; anti-oppressive/anti-discriminatory practice; interculturalism/multi-culturalism; and human rights (Torode, Walsh and Woods, 2001). In many cases, individual agencies and/or workers adopt one or other of these broad frameworks as guidance for working across cultures.

Anti-racism

Dominelli defines racism as:

> a set of practices which assumes the inherent superiority of one 'race' over others and thereby the right to dominate . . . racism is about relations of dominance and subordination which are rooted in the 'othering' of others as a social process of exclusion in which particular personal attributes are identified as the basis for a racialised 'othering' to occur.
>
> (Dominelli, 1998: 39)

Hence in this discourse, concepts of power and domination and subordination are central. The political processes whereby dominant groups maintain their powerful position are not only acknowledged but seen to be of great import-ance in any understanding of, and action in, the field of practice. Dominelli (1988) constructed an anti-racist framework for practice that emphasized that racism occurs at three different levels: individual, institutional, and cultural. Thompson (1993, 1997, 2006) and Dalrymple and Burke (1995, 2007) also ana-lyse oppression using personal, cultural, and structural elements in the broader anti-oppressive practice framework. This perspective was developed primarily in the UK, where concepts of 'race', racism, and anti-racism characterized the debate about ethnic minorities in the British context in the latter part of the twentieth century. The British social and political context at the time was one in which there was an established pattern of immigration into Britain from the Commonwealth countries, so that by the 1980s when the debate about racism became central in the helping professions, this was reflecting an evident 'new racism' that was seen to have developed 'as the white Anglo-Saxon British response to Britain's declining socio-economic position and the existence of a substantial, settled, indigenous black population' (Dominelli, 1988: 9).

The anti-racist framework is, like all other theories, a product of its time. While certainly influential in the UK (in particular, challenging workers to acknowledge the oppressiveness of a colour-blind approach to work with ethnic minorities; the limitations of an individual focus in the face of structural inequalities; and the importance of understanding the effects of racism and discrimination on ethnic minorities), it also attracted critics who argued against what came to be seen as a 'politically correct' practice that concentrated too much on selective oppressions such as racism and sexism to the detriment of other wider oppressions such as poverty and inequality of opportunity. There have also been fears that too strong an emphasis on 'anti-racist awareness training' does not enable practitioners and students to de-construct their own attitudes and beliefs in a positive atmosphere, and may lead to negative attitudes going underground instead. The emphasis on 'black' as being the only category politically acceptable to encompass all minority groups has been criticized in particular. Constructing black/white as binary opposites 'constructs black people and white people as cultural and visual opposites rather than either as part of a continuum or as connected and/or differentiated by features other than 'race' (Tizard and Phoenix, 2002: 8). The anti-racist perspective has been subsumed by the more generic anti-discriminatory and anti-oppressive frameworks that evolved from it.

Anti-oppressive practice

A product of the 1990s, anti-discrimination/anti-oppressive practice (Thompson, 1993, 1997, 2006; Dalrymple and Burke, 1995, 2007) includes all forms of oppression in a generic anti-discriminatory framework. Oppression is defined as: 'inhuman or degrading treatment of individuals or groups; hardship and injustice brought about by the dominance of one group over another; the negative and demeaning exercise of power' (Thompson, 1993: 31). Anti-discrimination practice starts from the basis that any practice that ignores oppression and discrimination cannot be seen as good practice. The most distinctive feature of this approach is the primary focus on structural inequalities in society: linking personal, cultural, and societal levels. Various forms of oppression are seen to have an impact in terms of: alienation, isolation, marginalization; economic position and life-chances; confidence and self-esteem; and social expectations and career opportunities. One of the strengths of this perspective is that it emphasizes similarities and continuities between the various forms of oppression that clients/patients can experience and that workers need to develop awareness of and take action to counteract. Being a generic model also means that it is more likely to be incorporated through general principles for practice than the more specific theories, and it has proved to be an effective model for health and social care services (Thompson, 2003, 2006). Payne (1997) outlined difficulties associated with this approach:

specifically, that it derives from a particular and basically structural analysis that is not without controversy; that the view of the interaction between various oppressions as complex can present practical and ideological problems as agencies or workers may specialize in ways that makes it impossible for them to accord equal weight to all oppressions; and finally that clients/patients may resist attempts by workers to highlight or work on anti-discriminatory needs, if they have come for help with other needs.

Interculturalism/multiculturalism

This perspective emphasizes the importance of practitioners becoming 'culturally competent' but also emphasizes the *process* of interaction between different cultural groups. The ideal of multiculturalism 'embraces notions of tolerance between individuals and social groups' (Soydan and Williams, 1998: 10). But whether this ideal can realistically be achieved has been questioned. And it has been suggested that as a liberal principle it just disguises major inequalities and intolerance (Soydan and Williams, 1998). Tolerance, as a concept in itself, implies that there is something intrinsically objectionable to tolerate and can lead to a paternalism with which multiculturalism has become associated (Soydan and Williams, 1998). More recent definitions of multiculturalism go beyond ethnic/racial difference to include gender, socio-economic status, sexual orientation, age, religious affiliations, and physical and mental disabilities. Originating in North America, the multicultural model focused primarily on educating workers in the human services to become more culturally aware and culturally sensitive in a social context where there are large groups of recent immigrants and an indigenous native American population. The concepts and procedures in this approach are 'derived from the assumption that knowledge, understanding, acceptance, and sensitivity to cultural and human diversity are prerequisites for effective work with clients of diverse social and cultural backgrounds' (Chau, 1990: 126). Chau draws on the concept of 'sociocultural dissonance' to refer to 'the stress and strain of cultural incongruence and to the internal conflict caused by the social and cultural ramifications of being different', which is seen to occur when 'ethnic minorities seek to cope with their life situations while under the pressure to conform to the dual, often conflicting or incongruent requirements of both minority and dominant cultural systems' (p. 126).

Traditional multiculturalism has been criticized for focusing too much on attitudes without sufficient regard to the wider context – the institutional and socio-structural factors that perpetuate intolerance and prejudice (Harlow and Hearn, 1996) and the values of the dominant culture (Fontes, 2008). The concept of cultural competence has also been criticized:

knowledge about cultural difference is not enough to ensure good practice; on the contrary, it might even be harmful, by leading practitioners to make stereotypical assumptions based on their (inevitably limited) knowledge ... [which] will tend to deny the differences within categories and reduce individual choice and agency.

(Cree and Myers, 2008: 46).

Cree and Myers refer to Husain's (2006) model that encompasses three different dimensions – cultural competence, cultural awareness, and cultural sensitivity – as providing a more robust framework for practice. The development of 'interculturalism', which emphasizes the process of communication between cultural groups as a two-way system, challenges the one-way linear dynamic of the early literature.

Human rights perspective

Many of the core elements of human rights were present and enforced in western and non-western cultures and societies from ancient times. The 'modern' development of human rights evolved through three distinct phases: (1) a concern for civil and political rights in the eighteenth century in Europe and America; (2) an increasing demand for economic, social, and cultural rights from the time of the industrial revolution, progressing more slowly and at varied rates in different parts of the world; and (3) a third generation of rights currently being promoted – to peace, development, and a clean environment protected from destruction (United Nations Centre for Human Rights, 1994). The Universal Declaration of Human Rights adopted by the UN General Assembly in 1948 asserts that: '(The) recognition of the inherent dignity and of the equal and inalienable rights of all members of the human family is the foundation of freedom, justice and peace in the world' (UNCHR, 1994: 4). The human rights advocate maintains that human rights are universal and should apply to all persons without discrimination. The rights of any particular individual or group in any particular circumstances can be restricted only if they threaten to curtail similar or comparable rights of others. There is a risk that we might presume that in the modern western world most human rights are already guaranteed to the majority of people. Yet many of the conditions that cause people to seek help from social services are related to consequences of oppression and injustice; the profession's 'concern for meeting basic human needs, its respect for differences, and its social change orientation position it at the forefront of human rights struggles' (Witkin, 1998: 198).

To conclude, the importance of the helping professions' adopting a broad anti-discriminatory approach as a core value in their work is now explicitly acknowledged through its insertion into curricula on professional courses and as an item in various professional codes of ethics. The concept of human rights is one that is broadly in line with the helping professions' core philosophical values, especially in relation to: value for life; freedom and liberty; equality and non-discrimination; justice, solidarity, and social responsibility; and most organizations do work on developing intercultural competence, awareness, and sensitivity in their practices as part of continuing training programmes. But is this enough to accommodate the changing patterns of migration and transnational mobility that now characterize our globalized world? What about the broad ethical questions that arise from contemporary migration patterns?

Ethical considerations when working across cultures

Globalization in itself throws up many macro ethical issues, in particular focusing on the interplay between developed (North) and developing (South) countries, traditionally configured with the North consisting of European, North America, and Australia/New Zealand and the South consisting of Asia, Africa, and Latin America. More recent conceptualizations of the dynamics between developed and developing nations refer to new emerging economic powers in the former Soviet bloc and the Persian Gulf.

The interaction between migration and development

The first question to examine is whether migration hinders or promotes development of the countries of origin? One argument in defence of the increased importation of skilled professional migrants from the South to the North has been that of the value of income remittances back home. While they undoubtedly improve the lives of the family members left behind, there is little evidence that the benefit extends beyond this. A series of studies cited by Castles and Miller (2009) suggest that: 'migration undermines the prospects for local economic development and yields a state of stagnation and dependency' (Massey et al., 1998: 272). A second problem relates to the intensive recruitment drives launched by countries such as Britain and Ireland in countries such as South Africa and the Philippines to employ nurses, doctors, social workers, and social care staff. Despite the existing fundamental human right of individuals (in democratic societies) to exercise choice, this practice can be viewed as ethically problematic for two reasons: first, because it deprives the country of origin of their expensively trained, skilled professionals in what is often termed a 'brain drain'; and second, because of the inferior conditions under which such migrant workers may be employed – in particular in relation to temporary work contracts, payments for accommodation or restrictions to particular forms of practice. Given the often temporary nature of such migrations, and developing debates around the concepts of 'brain circulation' (whereby those temporarily migrating South to North may return home with new skills, knowledge, and practices they have learnt), it is important for both governments and non-governmental organizations at macro and local levels to promote an ethical exchange whereby there are benefits built in for the countries of origin. These may consist, for example, of initiatives from host countries in capacity-building and more structured staff and expertise exchanges and ethical agreements on how overseas recruitment is handled (as issued by the British National Health Service in relation to nursing staff), as well as the development of specific strategies in source countries to retain educated and highly qualified professionals (Castles and Miller, 2009; Kasiram, 2009).

Domestic labour, care work, and migrants

A second ethical dilemma that falls somewhat between the realms of work and home, but which cannot be ignored in any discussion on the ethics of working across cultures, is the use of immigrants for domestic labour, and in particular the increase in women who now migrate from the South to the North to meet the demands for childcare, domestic labour, and care for our ageing populations. In Britain, the pattern of increasing care provision in the private and voluntary sectors has led to a less-unionized workforce, vulnerable to low pay and poor working conditions (Bawden, 2009). In both Britain and Ireland, a high proportion of nursing staff and social work staff consist of immigrants. In both countries also, many professional families employ female cleaners, childminders, and carers who may themselves be mothers with their own children being cared for by others at home. Parrenas (2005) and Lutz (2008) describe the impact of this feminization of migration on both children and fathers at home in the Philippines by the former, and the invisibility of the migrant domestic worker market in official policies and practices by the latter. How many workers in health and social care owe their ability to be able to access the paid workforce to the contribution made by migrants in their home life? In effect, many Western mothers and fathers are facilitated in their ability to balance work and home commitments through the delegation of some of their family and childcare responsibilities to migrants. What, then, is our ethical responsibility to them, both as colleagues and as employers ourselves? The beginning, or first principle, is to examine our own practices for any suggestion of exploitation: What are the rates of pay? What are the conditions of service? What supports are in place to enable the individual migrant to remain in contact with their families at home; to link with each other; to have meaningful social supports of their own? The second principle should be to ensure that as colleagues and as employers, we accept that we have a collective responsibility not only to ensure that we don't engage in exploitative or oppressive practices ourselves, but that we also share a moral responsibility to promote decent conditions and respect for migrant workers.

Asylum-seekers and social policies

A third ethical dilemma relates to the treatment of asylum-seekers, both adults and children, and the extent to which many nations, including Britain and Ireland, have adopted policies on direct service provision, housing, and entitlement to benefits for this group that are harsh and designed to serve as deterrents. This is again one situation where our own personal attitudes play a major role in determining our professional response. The issue is whether our professional roles involve us in perpetuating (or even tacitly accepting) unfair and oppressive practices, and if so, what our response should be. The old dichotomy between the deserving and non-deserving poor is often replicated in the discourse surrounding asylum-seekers, with the result that the majority are often treated as suspect. Research confirms the levels of marginalization and social exclusion that current policies create (Vekic, 2003). Skills of advocacy are one response; more strategic initiatives by trade unions and professional organizations is another; and a third is at the individual level where the UNCHR (1994) recommends that in analysing the problems that refugees and asylum-seekers face, workers consider the causes for the flight of individuals, families or large segments of the population from their country of origin. This is an important step both in allowing individuals to tell their own stories, but also in providing a context for the individual's experience. Showing an understanding of, and some willingness to learn about, the conditions in countries of origin also demonstrates interest and commitment on the part of the worker, and ensures that workers' perceptions are based not only on impressionistic and politicized accounts from the media, but also on information from more credible sources. The situation becomes more complex, however, when the asylum-seeker's narrative has to fit into a particular mould to satisfy conditions for refugee status.

At a practice level, many ethical dilemmas will be encountered relating not only to endeavours to achieve legitimate status (or citizenship rights) but also to linguistic and cultural misunderstandings, and allegiance to different cultural values and practices and dynamics of cultural dissonance referred to by Chau (1990). Ethical practice across cultures requires workers to remain aware of their own values and beliefs and appreciate that theories and models of intervention framed for one culture may not be entirely translatable to others. In addition, given the negative media portrayal of many migrant communities, ethical practice may require an active effort to resist seeding negative images and prejudice against minority clients and patients.

Box 4.6 Practical example: ethical dilemma

You are working with a Bangladeshi family that moved to this country five years ago. The mother died one year ago, leaving the father to care for and financially support three children aged 15, 9, and 7 years.

The eldest boy, Ahmed Ali, aged 15, has done very well at school and is obviously very bright. Recently, he started missing a lot of school and the form teacher spoke to him about this. Ahmed informed his teacher that he would be leaving school at the end of the year as his father needed him to work, and had work lined up for him in a relative's restaurant.

You are assigned as a female social worker to Joyrun, aged 9, who has a mild learning disability. You are the only social worker involved with the family and it has taken a long time for you to establish a good relationship with the father. He still finds it uncomfortable talking to you.

The form teacher has contacted you. He wants you to involve yourself in this situation – to persuade the father to allow Ahmed to stay in school – or even to take action under child care legislation to force him, given that he is very bright intellectually and the teacher believes that his development will be impaired if he has to leave school prematurely.

Questions:
1   What should you do?
2   How would you go about working with this referral?
3   What components of solution-focused helping can you use?

Commentary:
This case example illustrates some of the value conflicts that can arise in cross-cultural work. Consider the needs of this family on a holistic level. Then consider how you would map this piece of work. Do you need to see Ahmed by himself first? Do you need to establish whether there is a problem that Ahmed would like help with? Then do you need to see the father by himself – or do you need to involve a cultural interpreter, possibly male?

Consider what Ahmed himself wants – if continuing in school means going against his father's wishes, what would be the outcome? For Ahmed, does obedience to his father and service to his family come first? What options might there be to allow Ahmed to continue with his education at a later stage, or can he combine paid work with part-time study? Consider what practical resources (information, referral, advocacy) you can mobilize or produce to help this family.

Consider how you might develop a solution-focused discussion with Ahmed and his father, both together and separately. Identify the difficult times that the family have already coped with. Brainstorm the strengths, past successes, and resources that are evident so far. Think about what questions you can use to develop your view of them as resourceful people who know how to map out what is best for them as a family, and for Ahmed as an individual.

The bridge between existing frameworks and solution-focused helping

While there are useful generic models devised specifically to address issues of racism, inequality, and discrimination in society in social care and health care services, many run the risk of becoming formulaic or tokenistic if applied uncritically to our work. The case for a broad social constructionist approach to our work across cultures is compelling given the myriad of experiences and processes that now embody migrants' experiences and sense of identity. But allied to this is the need also to consider the broader structural and societal forces that impact on migration patterns globally. For the solution-focused helper, this means going beyond the remit of the traditional model to encompass interventions at organizational and structural levels and to expand the understanding of solution-focused helping beyond individual treatment and interventions. Let us look at how they might merge:

1   Adopting the principle that for migrants (regardless of the pathway they have come on) the best route to good mental health and settlement in a foreign land is: first, to enable access to language classes and employment; second, to concentrate on securing basic living needs; and third, to allow for the fact that migration itself is a stressful and confusing time that does not necessarily denote pathology or dysfunction. Story telling and story listening is a powerful tool for validation of experience.

2   Current good practice guidelines, such as those drafted by the British Refugee Council (www.refugeecouncil.org.uk), advise 'therapeutic casework': a combination of individual therapeutic work and advocacy to address the needs of clients with mental well-being and psychosocial needs; hence combining a focus on structural and practical needs and emotional distress.

3   Another useful and effective strategy to facilitate communication between new immigrants and health/social services is the employment of cultural facilitators or health advocacy workers who act as a bridge between the migrant and service providers. Two organizations in Dublin, Cairde (www.cairde.ie) and Access Ireland (www.accessireland.ie), provide such services. Access Ireland has developed a Roma Cultural Mediation Project that currently makes available to health/social services trained Roma mediators who assist health/social services in both developing intercultural competence and in ensuring that Roma have greater equality of access to services.

Box 4.7   Practical example – using cultural mediators

Mirela Radu is a 16-year-old Roma girl from north-western Romania, resident in Ireland. She was married two years ago in her own country, according to Roma custom. She lives with her husband and his extended family here.

She has been arrested and accused of shoplifting. When she appears in court, the magistrate expresses concern that she may have been trafficked into the country or that she may have been forced into marriage. She does not speak English and the Roma/Sinti interpreter in court is unable to say whether this is the case. The judge asks the probation officer in court to assess whether this is the case, as he would then have to consider referring to Social Services under child welfare legislation. He remands the case for one week.

A female cultural mediator, Sabrina, is made available by a local voluntary agency. She speaks Sinto, the language the family use, and works with the proba-tion officer to make contact with the family; interviews Mirela by herself twice; speaks with her husband and his parents directly; and also speaks with Mirela's family back in Romania by telephone. She establishes that there is no indication of a forced marriage or trafficking. In addition, she establishes that Mirela is five months pregnant but has not yet accessed prenatal services or general practice services. Through Sabrina's involvement, Mirela is both registered with a local primary health care centre and given an appointment for prenatal services at her local hospital. She is also connected with a Roma/Sinti speaking health advocacy worker.

Questions:
1   What other services should Mirela be linked in with?
2   What work could or should be done with Mirela and her husband together?

Commentary:
Extending the concept of solution-focused helping to encompass advocacy, link-ing clients to services and practical assistance is necessary for ethical helping in public services when working across cultures and with migrant clients.

Solution-focused helping across cultures

The solution-focused model, developed in a private family therapy clinic in Wisconsin in the 1980s, has been successfully adapted for diverse populations both in North America and further afield. To a certain extent, this is unsur-prising given: its minimalist formula for effective therapy; the correlations between a broader literature focusing on the need to empower ethnic/migrant communities and solution-focused principles; the strong emphasis placed in SFT on the client's construction of the problem (and solution) and on the conceptualization of the client as a person of wisdom and resources. In the English-language literature, solution-focused helping is referenced in relation to its value with immigrants (Aambo, 1997; Azary, 2006), with Asian and Middle-Eastern families and clients (Berg and Miller, 1992; Song, 1999; Yeung, 1999; Ho et al., 2003; Lee, 2003; Lee and Mjelde-Massey, 2004; Lambert, 2008), for cross-cultural work (Lee, 2003; Fong, 2004), for work with bi-racial women (Edwards and Pedrotti, 2004), as a framework for work across religious and spiritual issues (Guterman and Leite, 2006), as well as specific applications to what might be termed culturally specific syndromes such as *Hikikomori* (Japanese social withdrawal; Narabayashi, 2003), and problems specific to refugees and asylum-seekers such as histories of torture (Berliner et al., 2004) and political trauma (Klingman, 2002).

Insoo Kim Berg's experience of being an immigrant in the USA led her to reflect upon the way to work across cultures. In an interview with Yalom, she airs her views on working across cultures:

> **Yalom:** what have you learned about applying these [BSFT] techniques in different cultures? How do you have to modify them?
> **Berg:** I think there are some modifications. Small ones. Again, I have a lot of gripes about the way that cultural differences are talked about in this country. My main gripe has to do with emphasizing the differences between cultures – what is different between you and me, instead of talking about what is similar between you and me. That we are all human beings with the same aspirations, same needs, same goals . . . Everyone wants to be accepted, validated, supported, loved, and to belong to a community. That's not different at all, no matter where you go. It's a different way of belonging to the group, but that's a small difference . . . So I think too many people talk about culture/ ethnicity as being a bigger difference than is necessary. I feel very comfortable no matter what culture I go. I just look at you as another human being rather than I am this group and you are that group. I think it's very divisive. So that's my main gripe.
> (Berg, 2003: www.psychotherapy.net/interview/Insoo_Kim_Berg)

Berg had already written on this theme of cross-cultural therapy (Berg and Miller, 1992), where she refers to the emotional and cognitive dilemmas faced by majority-class therapists who work with ethnically and culturally different clients and the risk of becoming over-attentive to difference. Of note is her support for a focus on the macro vision of difference – 'understanding the history, tradition, motivation for migration, the cultural orientation, manner of conflict resolution and orientation to problem-solving of an ethnic group often heightens sensitivity to difference and helps therapists respect human variation' (p. 357) – at the same time as emphasizing the need to avoid stereotypical labelling and appreciating the individual as a person with unique life experiences.

Aambo (1997) describes an innovative approach to capacity building within an immigrant population in Norway using solution-focused helping. Through a training programme, 'natural helpers' from a migrant Indian population were skilled to help others in their community with the aim of developing and educating women from different cultures to provide health information to other people from their cultures. In this pilot project, the use of a solution-focused philosophy in providing health information was seen to empower the women involved:

> Their independence and self-esteem are enhanced in ways which creates support from their families. Fitting the information to their pre-existing knowledge seems to facilitate behavioral change . . . [In addition] The program has been a mutual learning opportunity between the immigrant women and the health workers, and in this process different cultural backgrounds have been a source for inspiration rather than a source of conflict.
>
> (Aambo, 1997: 77–78)

Some minor modifications to the solution-focused model that might be necessary when working across cultures have been enunciated by several authors. Yeung (1999) identifies the specific appeal of a time-limited model such as SFT to a particular society: 'In a task-oriented, highly pressured and essentially pragmatic society such as Hong Kong, short-term, clearly understandable and focused therapies are generally more compatible with the culture' (p. 478). Citing de Shazer's construction of solution-focused therapy as a 'language game', he concludes that 'language must be considered seriously when any therapeutic approach developed in one linguistic setting is applied in another culture' (p. 479), and notes differences between the English and Chinese language in relation to lexical usage (key words and phrases central to the client's narrative; problems with translating presuppositional questions), syntactic usage (grammatical relationship of words, especially tenses and sentence structure), and intonation and rhythm. Yeung's analysis suggests that close attention needs to be paid, first, to the key interventions in solution-focused helping, and then, second, to barriers that may arise when translating these interventions into other languages. To this can be added the need to pay close attention to terminology within the same language but which has different meanings across the world. Research into the use of solution-focused interventions by Irish social workers indicates that the use of the Miracle Question is not universally acceptable due to the Catholic connotations of miracle in the Irish context; similarly, amplification of positive exceptions are toned down from exuberant American versions (Walsh, 2002).

Lee and Mjelde-Massey (2004) describe how a solution-focused approach helps East Asian migrants and their American-born children deal with the cultural dissonance caused by tensions between traditional and new cultures, whereby family members are helped to reframe their strengths to adapt to multiple world-views and values within the same family. They identify traditional values relating to filial piety, family centrality, and collective orientation to life; specific issues relating to shame and the need to incorporate face-saving strategies to retain dignity. They recommend the need for the helper to:

- enable different world-views and values of individual family members to be recognized and negotiated while at the same time respecting the unique intergenerational hierarchy in the family;
- adopt an empowerment-based approach that allows for each family member's unique experiences to be understood within their specific social and cultural context; which gives full participation to all family members in the process of change by defining their goals, constructing their solutions, and controlling the pace of change; and which conveys the message that family members are themselves the causal agents in achieving solutions to their presenting problems;
- utilize cultural strengths and resources by showing an active curiosity about the cultural strengths and resources that you need to be taught by the family;
- address possible cultural stigmas for Asian families to seeking help by adopting face-saving strategies such as an emphasis not on elements of 'blame' but on identifying how family members can contribute to desired solutions;
- note the cultural value of pragmatism, which can lead to the adoption of practical and useful assistance as well as talking therapies; remaining goal-oriented, focused on the present and future, and emphasizing small achievable changes;
- respect culturally embedded modes of communication – particularly the value of restraint, deference to elders and perceived superiors, and the restriction on openly discussing with strangers issues with a high emotional content; together with a traditional lack of direct eye contact in many Asian groups.

Lee and Mjelde-Massey (2004) conclude that: 'A solution-focused approach, by emphasising multiple worldviews, contextual knowledge, and clients' strengths and empowerment, offers a culturally respectful and responsive therapy process with East Asian families' (p. 510).

Berg and Miller (1992) specify that exception-finding, relationship-focused questions, future-focused questions, and scaling and coping questions are especially suited to Asian clients. Song (1999) also refers to cultural values, along with the relevance of face-saving and attention to traditional hierarchical family structures, when working with Korean families.

Ho et al. (2003) describe how solution-focused employee assistance counselling is better than many other western models imported for use with Chinese in Hong Kong because of its non-normative, culturally sensitive features. Narabayashi (2003) illustrates how solution-focused interventions can help meet the three goals associated with successful treatment for *Hikikomori* (Japanese social withdrawal) to find new meanings for the social withdrawal, to solve problems caused by it, and to assist family members to be healthy despite it. Lambert (2008) outlines how a solution-focused counselling model is particularly suited to work in the United Arab Emirates because it can accommodate cultural, religious, gender, and social hierarchy differences better than more traditional counselling models. Azary (2006) examines the extent to which solution-focused principles complemented Iranian culture, history, and religion with reference to American-based Iranian immigrant clients with mental health difficulties. She concludes that the emphasis on empowerment, problem-solving, face-saving techniques and encouragement for clients to identity their own resources and strengths complements many of the natural elements of Iranian clients' native culture and contemporary lives. Edwards and Pedrotti (2004) suggest that American bi-racial women fall between a rock and a hard place with conflicting demands on them, and that therapeutic approaches combining solution-focused interventions with narrative work can enable them to find their own solutions in a non-prescriptive manner. Georgiades (2008) gives an account of using a combination of solution-focused strategies with an empowerment philosophy in a four-year-long therapeutic intervention with a thirteen-year-old Greek-Cypriot teenager in a domestic violence situation. This intervention combined in-person contact with e-mail communications (the teenager in Cyprus and the therapist in the USA for much of the time), and within a worsening situation the e-mail connection between the therapist and the teenager appeared to be a real source of support and strength. Georgiades, however, also warns that the solution-focused intervention in itself might have failed if it had not been underpinned by a trustworthy therapeutic relationship including unlimited access to the therapist.

De Chesnay (2007) also looks at the use of solution-focused helping across cultures with survivors of sexual violence in an American context. She notes how cultural differences can also include cultures of violence in that attitudes towards violence against women (and children) vary across cultures. She also identifies the importance of recognizing the impact of 'cultures of poverty' on our clients' lives. Of importance in her interventions were the concepts of small stepping-stones of change, framing the problems as being solvable and emphasizing safety-seeking behaviours.

Guterman and Leite (2006) suggest that solution-focused helping is effective in helping clients with spiritual or religious concerns. Helmeke and Sori (2006) note that coping questions in particular can often elicit notions about clients' faith or religious beliefs.

Klingman (2002) evaluates an action-research project in Israel that aimed to 'help the helpers', school counsellors working with distressed children during the Intifada in 2000–2001. Group sessions initially meant to act as 'process debriefing' were run with sixty-four female junior high school counsellors; the main components of the final version of the programme combined process debriefing, cognitive adaptation to a threatening situation with an emphasis on coping, and a solution-oriented approach. Coping strategies and 'a future-oriented practical approach which emphasised the specific strengths and coping skills that the participants had already brought to bear in the present and similar stressful situations' were central elements, with the result that 'participants were helped to adopt more optimistic and self-confident expectations about both the situation and their professional role in it' (Klingman, 2002: 256). Berliner et al. (2004) are referenced (in an English-language abstract of an article in Danish) as using solution-focused methods with survivors of torture at a specialist centre in Denmark, in which the therapist helps the client find solutions and new possibilities in his or her current life in the community. Their interventions combine elements of both cognitive and narrative work with a focus on resources rather than symptoms.

Corcoran (2000) has described how she uses solution-focused interventions with both African-American and Mexican-American families referred with child behaviour problems, emphasizing the importance of context for understanding behaviours, the presumption of the inevitability of cooperation, and an emphasis on client-formulated, concrete, behavioural goals achievable in the short term, combined with the focus on the future and on behaviour and perception rather than feelings. In her case study, 'Isolated in Ireland', Shine (1997) describes how she used the approach with a single-parent, black African woman, separated from her white Irish husband. She expands on her difficulties in remaining culturally sensitive and eliciting details of differences between African and Irish child care practices while at the same time carrying out a child protection investigative role, but she concludes that the emphasis on the client as expert on their own life is an important validation of clients from diverse backgrounds. Souza (2005) completed a thesis on the interplay between culturally diverse childrearing practices and effective child protection practices, and concluded that a solution-focused based approach had particular strengths in this field of practice.

Box 4.8   Practical example

You work as a liaison nurse in a local maternity hospital. One of your patients is an Eastern European Roma asylum-seeker, Adina Pescu, who has a newborn baby girl (Sabina), just diagnosed with Down's syndrome. This is the fifth child for Mrs Pescu and her husband, Silviu. Their other children are aged 4–11 years. They are living in a local hostel for asylum-seekers with Mrs Pescu's widowed mother who is in poor health.

Mrs Pescu is very distressed at the news of her baby's diagnosis (conveyed with the help of an interpreter) and will not agree to feed or care for the baby. Her husband has not visited since the diagnosis was made. Both mother and baby are medically cleared for discharge.

Questions:
1   How would you approach this case?
2   What services/agencies/people might you involve?
3   How could you incorporate a solution-focused approach in your direct work with Adina?

Commentary:
It is important to remember that all new parents when faced with such news will be shocked. Do you know how disability is viewed within the Roma community? If not, is there someone you can consult to find out? What are the practical implications of this diagnosis for the baby and family? What supports will they need and how can they be put in place? Then, how does the family view the birth of Sabina? How are they going to cope? How have they coped in the past with difficult situations? What have they learnt from these past experiences that can help them now?

Conclusions

In this formulation of solution-focused helping across cultures in public services, I first propose that we broaden the scope for solution-focused helping to extend beyond individual or family therapy to encompass practical elements of helping, advocacy, and capacity-building at a local community level. Given the earlier analysis of migration patterns and economic needs, the risk of pathologizing immigrants or assuming dysfunction is great if interventions remain solely at the individual therapeutic level. Immigrants are, by definition, on the margins of two cultures, and increasingly through transnational activity remain linked to both home and away. The children of immigrants will have different experiences from their parents – for them adaptation is about developing an identity that combines aspects of both culture of origin and new society (Suarez-Orozco and Suarez-Orozco, 2001; cited in Fong, 2004).

Second, solution-focused helpers need to straddle two worlds when working across cultures. To do this effectively, we need to remain conscious of our own world-view and value system and how they might be different from those of the clients/patients we work with. As our workforces become more ethnically diverse, the opportunity to enrich our work through a growing familiarity with the general tenets of other cultures becomes greater but always with the caveat so well expressed by Berg (2003), Angelou (1990), and others: we are more alike than we are different.

Third, if as helpers we represent the dominant culture, then we have an additional responsibility to remain conscious of the values and world-view of the western world:

> Without at least an awareness of Western psychology's moral vision, counsellors [and other helpers] may believe that they can interact professionally with clients in a neutral manner, when many of our Western values operate implicitly . . . Our Western worldview . . . rests on assumptions of self-promotion, freedom from social restraint, self-development, and extolling our uniqueness as indicators of mental health. Yet, these are regarded as signs of immaturity and selfishness in collectivist cultures.
>
> (Lambert, 2008: 102)

Finally, the concept of resources and resilience with which solution-focused helpers will already be familiar is also extended to encompass family, culture, and possibly religion as important social supports and motivators for change. Lambert (2008) terms this 'culture-infused counselling' when culture is directly acknowledged and used as a resource. Fong (2004) similarly proposes the use of cultural values as strengths and protective factors.

Even more so than when we work with people from similar backgrounds and experiences to ourselves, we truly cannot know (or presume to know) when working cross-culturally the individual subjective experience. In cross-cultural work, a partnership approach is indicated – one which is led by the client/patient as expert on his or her own life (experts by experience as described by Cree and Myers, 2008) and which actively co-constructs solutions that are acceptable and achievable for both worker and client/patient. By actively eliciting and validating the service-user's experience according to solution-focused principles, one can avoid the danger of making assumptions according to simplistic stereotypes.

Box 4.9 Practice principles – developing your cross-cultural practice

---

1 Challenging mono-cultural, mono-ethnic, mono-religious views of society as presented in the local context
2 Appreciating the effects of dislocation, discrimination, racism and the experience of being a minority
3 Understanding our own biases and values
4 Using our ignorance of other cultural groups' values and views constructively – getting clients to tell us how it is for them
5 Treating any 'knowledge' we have of other cultures as provisional and not assuming clients from this culture will fit our expected picture
6 Understanding the differences within the difference
7 Knowing our own limitations and accepting that clients are the experts on their own lives

---

> Solution-focused therapy . . . provides a clinical practice orientation – a way of thinking – that is conducive to a perspective of multiple worlds and to strengths-based and an empowerment-based . . . practice that enables clinicians to participate in a culturally respectful and responsive therapy process with clients from different ethnoracial backgrounds.
>
> (Lee, 2003: 393)

5 The solution-focused helper working across the lifespan in learning disability services

I wouldn't say I was any different from other people but what I would say is that you know (my life) taught me one thing, that you shouldn't kind of keep silent like I did in the past. You have to talk about it. You have to speak out.
(excerpt from Bob's story, from 'A story to tell' project; reproduced from www.tcd.ie/nild/life-stories/stories/bob, accessed April 2010)

Introduction

The importance of language in shaping the construction of groups-in-need in society is powerfully demonstrated in this field of practice. Historically, the language used emphasized need, deficit, and handicap; only recently have these been replaced by terms that attempt to more accurately define the nature of the impairment. Whereas once the phrase 'mental handicap' was most prevalent, it is now seen as dated and inappropriate, although it endures among more conservative or traditional services and populations. It is still frequently used in Ireland and the phrase 'mental retardation' persists as a descriptor in the USA, sometimes now supplemented by the words 'mentally challenged' (Pollack, 2005).

In Britain, the term 'learning disability' is defined as including the presence of 'a significantly reduced ability to understand new or complex information, to learn new skills (impaired intelligence), with a reduced ability to cope independently (impaired social functioning) . . . which started before adulthood, with a lasting effect on development' (Department of Health, 2001: 14). In the USA, 'people with mental retardation or developmental disabilities are defined by legislation to include those with disabling conditions acquired before age 22 that cause lifelong and substantial impairment' (Keigher, 2000: 163). In Ireland, the term now favoured by advocacy groups is 'intellectual disability', which 'involves a greater than average difficulty in learning. A person is considered to have an intellectual disability when the following factors are present: general intellectual functioning is significantly below average; significant deficits exist in adaptive skills and the condition is present from childhood (eighteen years or less)' (www.Inclusionireland.ie). For the purpose of this chapter, the term 'learning disability' will be used throughout, although that of 'intellectual disability' is recognized to be equally appropriate. Appreciating that a range of terms still persist (some that might strike you as outdated, patronizing, and stigmatizing) is important because it alerts us both to the ways in which parents, carers, and institutions or organizations from particular contexts or cultures have historically understood this group-in-need and also how terminology changes over time. As a solution-focused helper, sensitivity both to subjective meaning and to the diversity of meanings that can exist in a family or group of workers or carers is an important element to convey. That language continues to develop and evolve is important also to consider as a tool in itself – although as solution-focused helpers we need to respect the cognitive frames with which our clients arrive, we also need to acknowledge the power of language and actively use the skill of 'reframing' to uncouple negative or unhelpful descriptors and to release the potential of alternative frames of meaning. For ourselves as helpers, we need to appreciate why it may be that certain terms continue to be used or continue to be challenged; for example, we need to appreciate why in the wider disability movement, distinctions are made (particularly in the field of physical disability) between 'impairment' and 'disability', with the latter used to describe how society constructs disability through social oppression and discrimination (Wilson et al., 2009). We also need to consider why some parents' groups continue to use handicapped as a descriptor; at least in part it may be because they fear that resources and services will be withdrawn or reduced if too much minimization of difficulty occurs. In the politics of resource allocation, they may well have a point. Hence an understanding of the perspective of those who use certain terms is important: language is not neutral and certain terms may be preferred for valid reasons.

Both British and Irish definitions of learning/intellectual disability cover three components: that of an impairment commencing in childhood, with lifelong implications, consisting of a combination of restricted intellectual and social functioning. A wide range of categories is included: from specifically genetic conditions such as Down's syndrome to those of the autistic syndrome; from mild forms of impairment where an individual may be integrated into mainstream educational and employment facilities, to severe or profound levels of impairment, to complex syndromes (possibly a combination of physical, sensory, communication, and intellectual impairments) where the possibilities of independent living may be severely compromised.

People with acquired brain injuries are not included because the definitions stress that the reduced ability is present from childhood. Learning or neurological difficulties such as dyslexia and dyspraxia are also omitted from

---

Box 5.1   Reflective exercise: the importance of language – Mind the gap!

- List the terms that you are most *familiar* with used to describe people with a learning disability.
- Connect these to the people whom you have most frequently heard use these terms – colleagues, friends, family, service-users, parents/carers, etc.
- List the terms that you are most *comfortable* with used to describe people with a learning disability.
- Is there a dissonance between your favoured terms and those used by others?
- If so, can you think of bridging statements or constructive remarks that you can use in your daily conversations with others that open up alternative descriptors but which at the same time respect the generational or cultural gaps that may exist?

---

these definitions as most people with these conditions are managed within the mainstream school and health services without the need for recourse to specialist services for learning disability. Levels of impairment for those with learning disabilities are most frequently described with reference to a continuum from mild/moderate through to severe/profound. Establishing the level of impairment is important if you are considering a solution-focused approach to your work, since some of the techniques and concepts will need to be adapted to suit ability.

In England in 2004, it was estimated that of a population of approximately 50 million, there were 985,000 people with learning disabilities, including 190,000 aged under twenty, 127,000 aged sixty-five or over, and 795,000 adults in total (defined as over twenty and under sixty-five) (Emerson and Hatton, 2004, quoted in Department of Health, 2009: 26). In Ireland in 2008, of a population of 4.2 million, there were

> just under 27,000 people with intellectual disability registered on the National Intellectual Disability Database in Ireland . . . 41% are registered as having a mild intellectual disability, 36% as having a moderate intellectual disability, 15% as having a severe disability and 4% as having a profound disability. There are another 4% whose level of disability is not verified.
>
> (Inclusion Ireland, 2009)

The tremendous difference in estimated prevalence rates (from one in fifty in the English figures to one in two hundred approximately in the Irish figures) suggests that such figures need to be interpreted with caution, as undoubtedly different definitions are being exercised. Keigher (2000) suggests that in the USA, of those diagnosed with 'mental retardation' only 5 percent have a severe or profound form that requires state services.

Ethical considerations

On a societal level, philosophers and bioethicists have over time grappled with issues relating to the needs and rights of people with disabilities. As modern medical technologies advanced, debates were sparked about prenatal diagnostic testing, abortion, the futures and outcomes for very premature babies, and the rights of those with disabilities. From Darwinian concepts of survival of the fittest through to the inversion of this concept in the eugenics ideology of the first half of the twentieth century and its adoption by the Nazi movement as a form of justification for beliefs of racial supremacy and purity, it has long been the experience of activists in this field that protection of, as well as advocacy for, those with learning disabilities has to be a central focus for helpers. The issue of reproductive rights versus protection remains a tension and an issue of ethical concern even if the practice of sterilizing girls and women with learning disabilities ceased in most European countries by the 1970s. How we treat the vulnerable such as those with learning disabilities raises questions not only about the type of society we live in, but also about the type of society we want to be part of. As societal norms and expectations in the developed world focus more intensely on notions and images of perfection and flawless lives, based on the ever optimistic dogma that universally 'Yes, we can', maybe we struggle more with how to incorporate real disadvantage and impairment into our world-view and contemporary lives. Are we instead, when faced with life-long impairment, inclined to lapse into a more fatalistic 'No, they can't'? (and hence insist on high levels of protection and care?). Or are we at risk of minimizing the impairment, of following a dogma of independence and choice at all costs, in a way that ignores a need for protection?

It can be argued that the extent and type of provision for those with learning disability is a fair measure of a society's moral compass and values. The sudden death in England in February 2009 of Ivan Cameron, the profoundly disabled young son of Conservative party leader David Cameron, received wide media coverage and tributes were paid to his family by many across the political spectrum, culminating in the closure of Parliament for a day as a mark of respect. Despite the seeming contradictions with espoused Conservative policy on reducing the scale of the public service, Cameron consistently paid tribute to the National Health Service and social services for the levels and quality of support and care Ivan received during his short life. Yet, the workforce that provides most of the hands-on nursing, respite, residential, and educational services to those with learning disability are in low-status and often low-paid positions.

Societies over time and indeed still in the twenty-first century vary both in their perception of, and provision of services for, those with learning disability. In some societies and cultures, the birth of a child with disability is viewed as stigmatizing, a mark of inferiority. In many societies, historically the traditional form of service provision was that of lifetime incarceration in large institutions. Although we may consider that the 'discovery' of large-scale, poorly equipped and abusive institutions in remote areas in Romania and Greece in the 1990s was an anachronism, it is a sobering fact that in many parts of the developed world, long-term incarceration in poor-standard institutions persists as a policy or has only recently been discarded. While the use of institutional care in the USA for people with learning disability halved between 1970 and 1990, rates still remain high in some states. Texas has one of the highest institutionalization rates (Braddock et al., 2008) and in March 2009 employees in one state institution there were charged with criminal offences following allegations of a 'fight club': coerced staged fights between adults with learning disabilities. In 2006, in the UK an official report confirmed numerous acts of institutional abuse against adults with learning disabilities living in both hospital and community-based facilities in Cornwall (Commission for Social Care Inspection and Healthcare Commission, 2006). Not only does it appear that abuse is a risk in institution-type facilities, but also so in community-based supported living arrangements, in a modern European country that is generally seen to have high standards of care for those in need. Why should this be so? Fyson and Kitson suggest that it is a failure on a policy level:

> the failure of policy makers at all levels to make the necessary connections between two parallel agendas: on the one hand the desire to promote choice and independence for people with learning disabilities, and on the other the need to protect them from abuse.
>
> (Fyson and Kitson, 2007: 429)

In England, the impact of two significant policy documents entitled *Valuing People* (Department of Health, 2001, 2009) cannot be over-estimated in their emphasis on the perspective of service-users and their families. The central principles of inclusion, control, independent living, and rights are enunciated and addressed directly to service-users themselves, as outlined in Box 5.2.

Yet, as new policies and community care practices are developed based on such principles, a central tension that has emerged relates to the evolving role of professionals. Kay (2003), among others, has suggested that the real issue underlying this tension is: where do power and control lie, with professionals and service providers or with service-users and their carers? This leads to another more fundamental question: how do we conceptualize power?

Box 5.2   Valuing People: A New Three Year Strategy for People with Learning Disabilities

---

Principles underlying official British policy:

Rights:
- People with learning disabilities and their families have the same human rights as everyone else.

Independent living:
- This does not mean living on your own or having to do everything yourself. All disabled people should have greater choice and control over the support they need to go about their daily lives; greater access to housing, education, employment, leisure and transport opportunities and to participation in family and community life.

Control:
- This is about being involved in and in control of decisions made about your life. This is not usually doing exactly what you want, but is about having information and support to understand the different options and their implications and consequences, so people can make informed decisions about their own lives.

Inclusion:
- This means being able to participate in all the aspects of community – to work, learn, get about and meet people, be part of social networks and access goods and services – and to have the support to do so. (DH, 2009: 30)

Department of Health (2009) *Valuing People: A New Three Year Strategy for People with Learning Disabilities* (www.dh.gov.uk/en/policyandguidance/socialcare/deliveringadultsocialcare/learningdisabilities/index.htm)

Rather than viewing power as a commodity possessed by either professional/service-provider or service-user/carer, a Foucauldian analysis of power allows us to view it as a generative quality: as 'something that people use and create, rather than simply possess' so that 'Every person, despite his or her social status and location, exercises and has the potential to create some form of power' (Fook, 2002: 52–53). This descriptor enables us to move beyond the rigidity of an either/or position, and into forms of practice as helpers that promote the voice of the service-user, which accepts the potential for those with 'expert knowledge' power to oppress but which at the same time believes in a multiplicity of voices, both service-providers and service-users, uniting to work out solutions to the daily issues of life. This conceptualization of power is worked into the fabric of a solution-focused approach: first, by acknowledging that the service-user or client is the expert on his or her own life; second, by acknowledging that the helper and client may have different goals and that negotiation may be needed; and third, by conveying powerfully that helping needs to be client-led and person-centred. This fits nicely with the policies of inclusion and person-centred planning that are the latest reforms in this field of practice.

Understanding that power is generative is one useful tool from social constructionist philosophy; another useful tool is that of explicitly acknowledging that client and agency agendas and goals may differ, which brings us back to a central concern for many helpers: balancing care and control. Workers in learning disability services describe how policy changes, welcome in their new emphasis on self-determination and choice for the client, involve risks if the individual's need for guidance, support, and at times protection is not also factored into service provision.

> There should be nothing wrong with acknowledging that, like most of us, people with learning disabilities can hope only to be interdependent rather than independent, that they need the support of others to make choices and to maintain an optimum level of independence. The danger is that, where organizations insist that people with learning disabilities are wholly responsible for their own, independent, choices they ignore the control exerted over them by others. In most cases control (or 'support') is proffered by caring family or staff members and is in the best interests of the person with a learning disability. But the pretence that such support does not also include an element of control leaves a dangerous gap in which abusers may find an all too comfortable niche.
>
> (Fyson and Kitson, 2007: 434)

As more people with learning disability live in supported housing in the community, participate in supported employment schemes, and exercise more choice over their lifestyle and habits, day-to-day ethical dilemmas arise for helpers, carers, and families regarding the balance between the right to exercise choice and the right to protection of individuals who may lack the ability to consent (or refuse) to engage in specific behaviours or practices. An ethical framework that 'seeks to promote the human rights of disabled people, their entitlements to equal opportunities, and to self-determination' (Sheldon and McDonald, 2009: 322), coupled with an appreciation of how, on occasions, this might need to be tempered with elements of protection, support, and/or guidance, might help to offset the dangers of an overly ideological approach to service delivery.

Shifting paradigms: how philosophies of care and service provision have changed over time

Kay (2003) describes four different philosophies of care that have emerged over time: medical, behavioural, educational, and social models. He notes that despite the inadequacies of each, developmentally they denote important shifts from a philosophy based on duty and ethics to a broader rights-based philosophy. Given that there are a range of state and voluntary/charitable organizations involved in service provision in most developed economies, it is probably more accurate to describe the current range of philosophies as diverse, with some emphasizing a rights-based approach, whereas others are derived from specific spiritual motivations such as the L'Arche communities developed by Jean Vanier and the Camphill Movement founded by Karl Konig. Both L'Arche and Camphill are based on a philosophy of mutual benefit for those with disabilities and their carers living in village communities, premised on a belief in the unique contribution each individual can make towards the mutual enhancement of all members of the community: the emphasis is on a communal way of life. At the other end of the continuum, a rights-based philosophy emphasizes freedom, individual fulfilment, and minimum restriction; taken to extremes it risks ignoring real needs for protection, thus creating situations where vulnerable people may be preyed upon, exploited, and abused. What, then, are the more accessible philosophies that can inform us?

Williams suggests that the social model is that which fits best with current thinking, concerned as it is

> with the place and the experiences of a person in their family and in society ... at risk of social oppression, social devaluation ... The model seeks to reverse the processes of vulnerability by supporting people in valued social roles, for example as family member, citizen, worker, tenant or home-owner.
>
> (Williams, 2006: 13)

The social model draws on the disability rights movement to emphasize the importance of society in shaping the extent and type of disability a person experiences. Attention shifts from concepts of individual problem or limitation to the environmental context that can either enable or restrict that individual's life choices. In addition, this perspective is built on the belief that service users are entitled to be active participants in service developments and views people with disabilities as experts on their particular disability (Galambos, 2004), a principle echoed in solution-focused theory (SFT) where the client is considered expert on his or her own life (de Shazer et al., 1986;

Walsh, 1997). The social model and disability rights movement gained an added impetus in the 1970s and 1980s not only from wider rights movements such as Civil Rights in the USA, but also from the development of specific movements within learning disability itself, most notably those of normalization and social role valorization.

Normalization had its origins in Scandinavia (Nirje, 1969), although its main proponent is a German-born psychologist working in North America (Wolfensberger, 1972). The central premise of normalization is that individuals with disabilities should experience the normal regular routines and experiences and conditions of daily life as much as possible. The emphasis is on the environment being normalized as opposed to the individual – in other words, schools need to adapt to take individuals of differing ability; health services need to ensure that people of all abilities are catered for in their services; residential care services need to be as close as possible to normal living conditions. In itself the development of this movement since the 1970s validated moves to de-institutionalize people with learning disability and shifted the focus towards community-based life and integration into mainstream services but may in itself be too normative or prescriptive if it results in decreasing choice. In addition, concepts such as 'the least restrictive environment' and 'mainstreaming' also influenced public policy (Bradley, 2000).

The Independent Living Movement in the USA also incorporates a belief that environments create disabling conditions, not individual impairments *per se*, and that personal autonomy and empowerment are core goals (Keigher, 2000). Styring (2003) suggests that an additional driver for change from the 1970s was the growing sociological critique by authors such as Goffman (1968) of institutional care. The developing awareness of the risks and actual occurrences of abuse in institutional services further focused changing policies towards community-based care.

Social role valorization – 'the application of what science can tell us about the enablement, establishment, enhancement, maintenance, and/or defence of valued social roles for people' (Thomas and Wolfensberger, 1999: 125) – is a theory from social psychology adapted for application in learning disability. An important concept is that of societal devaluation – the ways in which some groups or individuals are considered less worthy or acceptable than others. Social role valorization can be used to map out ways in which individuals with disabilities can be supported to take up socially valued roles in society. In addition, it pays attention to the psychological damage and 'wounds' that individuals can suffer when devalued in this way:

> The two main strands are achieving conditions that maximize opportunities for the development of competence in people to participate equally in society, and structures, settings and practices that promote

positive and helpful images and messages about people and their human and social worth and status.

(Williams, 2006: 31)

Tangible initiatives have been in the area of supported employment, events such as the Special Olympics, and publications that highlight some of the positive aspects of particular forms of impairment. Fitzgerald (2005) links creativity and autism spectrum disorders, writing about a number of famous artists, musicians, and philosophers across the centuries with clearly identifiable features of Asperger's syndrome. Both normalization and social role valorization can be considered as philosophies of care with a moral base that promotes a societal response to the needs of those with learning disabilities premised on respect, advocacy, and integration. Person-centred planning (O'Brien, 1987) is one particular expression of this change in emphasis, where inclusion and self-determination are core values to how services should be delivered (see pp. 124–125 below).

Mapping your own value base

How we approach people with learning disability is largely dependent upon how we see them, how we understand the nature of their needs and the context within which we frame our responses.

(Kay, 2003: 179)

Before deciding whether you can and, if so, how you can bring solution-focused concepts and interventions into your work, it is worth spending a bit of time thinking about your views, beliefs, and values as they relate to clients with learning disability. These will be affected by the amount and type of contact you have with such clients and their families and your own personal belief system, and thus the exercise in Box 5.3 is important.

The nature of the work in learning disability

Although many individuals with mild learning disabilities function well with minimal contact with specialist services, those with moderate, severe or profound learning disabilities and their families are likely to be long-term service-users in need of support and help either continuously or intermittently over their lifetime. That is a lot of contact with professional helpers! This is a particularly distinctive feature of working in learning disability services.

Another distinctive feature is that of the different phases of helping and contact that evolve over time: from initial diagnosis and early intervention

---

Box 5.3 Reflective exercise: mapping your own experience and value base

Example: My own lived experience is that of having a much-loved fifteen-year-old nephew with Down's syndrome; and of having had contact as a young child with a teenage neighbour with Down's syndrome. In addition, I worked as a community-based social worker in London with families where a member had a learning disability and also as a child protection social worker where parents have had mild learning disabilities.

My own mix of experiences have led to my current beliefs, which are that people with learning disabilities still face tremendous discrimination in the wider society; that peer-groups of children and teenagers can be particularly cruel to those with learning disabilities; and that normalization and inclusion policies only work if choice is accompanied by adequate resources for guidance and support. I think that more needs to be done both to recognize the unique qualities and interests that individuals have and that wider society can learn a lot from those with learning disabilities; it is to our own detriment as a society that we ignore or minimize the contribution they can make to us all. My maxim is: 'Listen, value, and advocate'.

Trish Walsh

Now it's your turn! Use the following headings to map out your own experience and value base; then devise your own maxim for how you approach your work:

(a) My experience of contact with people with learning disabilities includes the following:
  - as a relative or family member
  - as a neighbour or friend
  - as a childhood memory or experience
  - as a student in the helping professions
  - as a worker involved in direct care-giving, in the community or residential setting
  - as an educator teaching in a specialist or mainstream facility
  - as a professional – social worker, psychologist, doctor or therapist
(b) From these experiences I have learnt that what people with learning disabilities need most is:

_____

(c) In my work, I can make a difference to how my clients with learning disabilities experience their life through (three key qualities I bring to my work):
  1
  2
  3

services, through to developmental phases of childhood, education and ado-lescence into the transition to adult services. For parents, the natural pro-gression of milestones signalling increased independence and autonomy for their offspring is upended. Instead, their lives become woven in with the professional network of therapists, carers, psychologists, and doctors who monitor, treat, assess, and advise on unfolding needs. For those with profound or complex needs, life may consist more of hospital or residential care than supported home care.

For helpers themselves in this field, how contact and support is framed and offered becomes an important consideration. While this will be influ-enced both by the ethos of the service and established patterns of contact with families, the primary factor will be that of role definition and function. What is your job? How is it defined, and what does it authorize, enable or empower you to do? The advent of person-centred planning and establishment of key-worker systems has brought many positive changes to the roles of direct support staff and care workers in adult services, but working with the same service-users and families day after day is challenging for us all. How, then, as helpers in this field do you maintain a positive perspective and remain energized and innovative in your work?

How helpers in learning disability frame their work suggests that it is in finding a sense of personal meaning in the work that helpers can remain effect-ive and responsive (O'Brien and O'Brien, 2004). As one respondent put it: 'If you look at your job as the chance to make a positive relationship with people who can offer a lot if they have the right support, then you find your reason to work right there with the people themselves' (O'Brien and O'Brien, 2004: 3). A solution-focused outlook with the emphasis on making a difference, how-ever small, in the life of your client or service-user fits with this philosophy. Signposts for the journey are suggested by O'Brien and O'Brien (2004):

- expand your mindset;
- make time for renewal;
- build an organization that can support you;
- commit yourself;
- build good relationships
- be creative as the responsible person.

The role of the family both in providing direct care for those with learning disabilities and as advocates over time who have played a central role in devel-oping services at local, regional, national, and international levels is another feature of work in this area. Many service-users who need support and care services do remain in the care of their own families for most of their childhood and teenage years. Many people with learning disabilities, even of a profound or complex nature, are now living longer, in line with improved life expectancy for the general population. This then means that for much of the time there can be a triad of contact: service-user, family, and carer/helper. How, then, do you as the professional helper manage this dynamic? What skills do you need to learn and how can you honour your relationship with both service-user and family? Professionals working with children and their parents in child welfare scenarios describe how they learn to wear 'both hats' (Walsh, 1997), remaining mindful of their primary responsibility to the client but acknowledging that it is only in forming helpful alliances with carers and parents that the primary client's welfare is best ensured. Is this the same dynamic for you?

People with learning disabilities and their families are the one group for whom life-long contact with services is often a feature. Others include those with chronic, life-long illnesses. As such, they have particular needs but also offer additional rewards for those working in dedicated services. In other fields of work there is rarely the potential for such long-lasting relationships and contacts.

Parallel knowledge bases

The family life cycle will be a concept familiar to helpers and carers whose training included systemic concepts. Originally developed as a tool for the assessment of families in family therapy, Carter and McGoldrick's (2005) classic text, now in its third edition, has much to offer us in understanding the impact a child with learning disability has on the family. Although their conceptualization of the family life cycle can be challenged as too normative and simplistic for the complex family forms we now encounter, it nonetheless points out that families in general do go through a range of developmental processes and stages (such as the birth of children; caring for younger children; adolescence; launching young adults into independent living; 'the empty nest' syndrome; integrating the next generation of family form; preparing for death). We have developed across cultures a range of rituals and practices to mark these transition points. Although not all experience feelings of stress or loss at these transition points, as parents most of us take for granted that there is a natural progression to how our children will develop and change. With the birth of a child with learning disability, these certainties may be shaken or completely annulled. The hopes and dreams of a parent for a child with learning disability are not only qualitatively different but very likely to only take shape as the child gets older and the extent of his or her particular impairment becomes more apparent. Understanding the level of loss and adjustment that families need to contend with is essential for those not only in early intervention services but all along the service spectrum through to adulthood. Carter and McGoldrick map out the general stages of the family life cycle according to the emotional processes allied to each transition to a new phase, but also to the changes in the family structure and status that are required for the family to adjust accordingly. In acknowledging the immensely diverse paths and forms that family life now takes and the resultant minefields for helpers who will not now have the same backgrounds or life stories to compare with all their clients, Carter and McGoldrick (2005) encourage instead 'to go beyond the client's presenting problems to discuss their values and dreams. Encourage them to reflect about their real lives as they are actually leading them' (p. 17). Combining a knowledge of the family life cycle, the usual expectations of parents, and the particular pain that this can engender in families where a child or adult has a learning disability, with solution-focused questions evoking hopes, dreams, and plans for the future is one strategy for validating the pain of parents with a focus on mapping out realistic plans for the future.

The resiliency model of adjustment and adaptation (McCubbin et al., 1996) starts with the truism that families can be the one powerful constant in the lives of people with disability. Lustig (1999) applies this model to family caregivers of adults with learning disabilities, outlining how an understanding of how stressors combine with family strengths and taking into account the family's 'appraisal' can lead to more effective work by service providers around critical issues such as permanency planning, social support, and multicultural considerations. The family's ability to cope with emerging stressors informs the direction and content of professional interventions and services. Theoretically linked to family systems theory and family life cycle theory outlined above, it is noted that the 'stressor' load on a family will be increased when individual and family transition co-occur with prior family strains, situation and contextual difficulties, the family's own coping efforts, and any ambiguity that may develop between family members regarding the 'right' course of action. In Lustig's work, he relates the family's interactions and relationships with service providers as a potential co-stressor:

> Family resources are characteristics, traits, or competencies of individuals, the family, or community that can be used to meet the demands faced when confronted with a stressor. Family social support can be thought of as an important resource emanating from persons outside the family including support from relatives, friends, and community institutions.
>
> (McCubbin et al., 1996)

An emphasis is also placed on the family's appraisal, which broadly translates as their assumptions and perceptions about the world and their place in it:

> For example, the rehabilitation counselor may see a need for planning for residential options, while the family may have more immediate concerns related to supervision during day hours when the consumer

is not in supported employment. While it is essential that the counselor understand the potential issues confronting these families, the relative gravity of these issues for the family will vary at different times in the family life cycle and from family to family.

(Lustig, 1999: 29)

The linkage between solution-focused assumptions and the systemic concepts developed in this theory are strong: in particular, the use of solution-focused questions that explore the family's perception of the situation, their hopes for the future, their priorities and worries, fits tightly with the emphasis on the family's appraisal.

Person-centred planning (PCP) is an approach to life-planning for people with a disability, based on principles of inclusion and the social model of disability. In the UK context, it is seen to be at the heart of current policy as outlined in *Valuing People* (Department of Health, 2001, 2009) and is described thus:

A 'person-centred approach to care' by definition means having the individual at the heart of the process: taking on board a person's needs but also acknowledging their hopes, dreams and aspirations. Though ideal, this philosophy is difficult to uphold when the person concerned has a learning disability, not just because of their intellectual impairment but also because of the associated communication difficulties, which often compound the situation.

(Styring, 2003: 111)

In the USA, it is perceived more as an approach that emphasizes partnership between parents and professionals (Lustig, 1999). In both cases, similar steps are taken to first build a positive profile of the client, followed by network and support mapping, identifying significant people in their life, creating a vision for the future, and identifying goals and action plans. 'Circles of support' are another element of this approach. The introduction of this approach as a required element of government policy has been evaluated (Robertson et al., 2005) and the outcomes are promising with benefits in the areas of community involvement, contact with friends, contact with family, and the exercise of choice. However, in other areas such as more inclusive social networks, employment, physical activity, and medication, it had no apparent impact, leading these researchers to conclude that person-centred planning might be best considered an extension of good practice in increasing the individualization of supports and services but not a radical departure with strong outcomes. Variations in the levels of access to PCP plans also led the researchers to conclude that it was the availability of care managers and the commitment of facilitators to person-centred planning that was the most powerful predictor of whether people got a plan and the areas of benefit. In considering the PCP philosophy and contrasting it to that of solution-focused therapy, the link between the core philosophy of empowerment and personalization in person-centred planning and the emphasis on eliciting the client's priorities, strengths, goals, and vision for the future in solution-focused therapy is strong. Again, the use of solution-focused questions and techniques can be actively incorporated into the exercises involved in person-centred planning.

The Protection of Vulnerable Adults is another knowledge base that needs to be incorporated when working in the field of intellectual disability because the literature is so strong on the risk of abuse for this group (Westcott, 1991; McCarthy and Thompson, 1992; NSPCC, 2003; Fyson and Kitson, 2007; Pritchard, 2008). Although an awareness of the particular vulnerability of this client group is required, especially where clients have profound or complex needs and communication impairment, it is important not to allow the fear of possible abuse become a factor in restricting choice and independence unnecessarily. Fyson and Kitson make the point that it is equally important not to over-emphasize choice and independence to the diminishment of risk-awareness:

> Promotion of independence and choice for people with learning disabilities is an admirable aim ... [but] now run the risk of being fetishized to the point where they become the sine qua non of learning disability services: concepts beyond questioning. We believe that, in order to better protect vulnerable adults from abuse, these beliefs can and should be challenged ... [this is] a plea for a recognition of the obvious (if unspoken) reality that if these people were able to be fully independent and to make important life choices without support then they would not be receiving state-funded services in the first place.
>
> (Fyson and Kitson, 2007: 433–434)

Solution-focused helping and the learning disabled: why so little, so far?

While the application of solution-focused concepts and practices has advanced with speed in other areas of health and social care, it has had a slower start in intellectual disability as measured by the output of publications. One can speculate about the possible reasons for this time lag. My earlier research into its diffusion as an innovative approach in Irish social work (Walsh, 2002) would suggest that one possibility is that it simply did not filter into these helping systems so quickly, and so diffused more slowly. This in itself is an interesting detail, as it may also suggest that services for those with learning disability are somewhat at a step removed from other social services and perhaps out of the loop when it comes to new developments. Would the same be true in the UK?

Another possibility may be that the tag of 'therapy' onto the solution-focused model throughout the 1980s was a deterrent to workers who were just managing to uncouple the needs of people with learning disabilities from the field of mental health. For too long, from Victorian times through the earlier decades of the twentieth century, there had been a tendency to provide institutional care to both groups simultaneously (Beacock, 2003).

Solution-focused therapy has already proven itself to be effective and popular as an approach to direct work with young people and teachers in school settings. A small-scale study involving direct solution-focused work with young people with learning disabilities in a school setting (Franklin et al., 2001) suggests that they made positive changes on a range of behavioural problems following the intervention. As there are many publications covering the use of solution-focused concepts and practices in school settings focused primarily on those with special education needs (Thompson and Littrell, 1998; Mall and Stringer, 2001), in this chapter I concentrate on its potential at different stages across the life span within learning disability services.

From the year 2000, a number of articles began to appear describing (and in some cases evaluating) solution-focused work across a range of issues in learning disability. Lloyd and Dallos (2006, 2008) analysed solution-focused first sessions with mothers of children diagnosed with severe intellectual disabilities; Stoddart et al. (2001) developed a modified approach in a Canadian multidisciplinary clinic offering therapy to individuals with developmental disabilities across the life span; Smith (2005) describes its use with a man with mild learning disabilities referred for 'anger management'; and Murphy and Davis (2005) combined solution-focused techniques with video work to offer a creative and effective intervention to a nine-year-old boy with significant developmental disabilities to improve his communication abilities. A chapter in a book on solution-focused nursing (Musker, 2007) outlined its potential for general disability nursing and another text by a speech and language therapist outlined many examples of its use with clients with communication and/or swallowing difficulties, including those with intellectual disabilities (Burns, 2005).

There is consensus across these publications that adaptations need to be made when using solution-focused concepts and techniques in learning disability. First, in work with parents, the Miracle Question was found to be actively unhelpful; second, in working with adults with learning disabilities, techniques had to be adjusted to allow for simpler formulations of scaling, supplemented by graphic aids; and third, that account needs to be taken of the unique needs and stresses of this client group, in particular in relation to social isolation and the absence of naturally occurring supports and networks of friends.

Initial diagnosis

There is no doubt that the initial diagnosis of a disability in a child can be a traumatic crisis. Sometimes a disability is diagnosed soon after birth; sometimes parents can have an anxious wait for weeks or even months before a definite diagnosis is made. Children born with Down's syndrome and other particular syndromes often have pronounced physical features. Early intervention services are designed to work actively with the family in the early years to both provide what support services are needed as well as direct therapy assessment and inputs for speech and language, psychology, and management of medical or nursing needs.

Trute et al. (2007) found that while a persistent negative perspective regarding disability persists in the childhood disability literature, many parents respond positively and with resilience to the challenges of rearing a disabled child with many examples of parents reporting subsequent enriched lives and enhancement of personal qualities of mastery and self-esteem.

Abery (2006) suggests that although negativity may be the generally expected reaction to the birth of a child with disability, 'many families take it [rearing a child with a developmental disability] in their stride, adjusting over time, adapting to higher demands, and growing as individuals and families along the way' (p. 1). Many parents may prefer to highlight the positive aspects of the situation; they may be more interested in getting your help to mobilize necessary resources and less inclined to dwell on a 'tragic' situation. The focus of intervention needs to be wide-ranging and take into account the many practical needs that may emerge.

Sheldon and McDonald (2009) highlight research that establishes the lower incomes that families with disabled children tend to have as well as the additional expenditure they can incur. Abery (2006) suggests that attention needs to be paid to three different aspects of the family's life: the 'meanings' the family and individual members attribute to the situation; the 'resources' they have available or are able to acquire; and their general 'coping' behaviours and styles. Trute et al. (2007) highlight a potential focus on 'cognitive coping': thinking about a particular situation in ways that enhance a sense of well-being. They also highlight the fact that, over time, and even at any one point in time, there can exist a paradoxical mix of sadness and joy, of positives and negatives.

Culturally specific beliefs and values also need to be explored. Lustig (1999) describes how a qualitative study of older American caregivers from African, Chinese, Haitian, Hispanic, Korean, and Native American communities (McCallion et al., 1997) identified elements that distinguished particular cultural groups: (a) how the disability is perceived; (b) who is considered part of the family; (c) who provides care; (d) how the family makes decisions;

(e) what family members expect of each other; (f) what level of support is received from friends and community; (g) whether and how closely the family adhere to traditional values; (h) how willing the family is to accept help.

The teenage years

Despite evidence that policy changes and the increasing emphasis on normalization, inclusion, and choice is increasing the number of children with disabilities now cared for primarily at home and attending local community schools or education units, adolescence remains a time of change both in service provision and in demands on families and carers. The early years

---

Box 5.4   Practice example: working with parents of children with a learning disability – starting off

---

Suzanne Subira is the mother of 7-year-old Sushani. They are Egyptian and Muslim and have lived in the London area for eighteen months since Suzanne and her husband divorced in Egypt. Sushani has a moderate learning disability but has never been engaged with services because her mother has chosen instead to send her to private educational facilities. Her GP is now worried about both mother and daughter following Sushani's expulsion from a private facility and her mother's distress at the situation. The GP is worried about the mother's mental health as she is inconsolable and drinking whisky. He has insisted on a referral to social services and she has agreed to this. He is asking you to do a home visit.

Questions:
1   What solution-focused principles will you draw on in your initial visit to the family home?
2   What messages will you hope to convey both to Suzanne and her daughter, Sushani?
3   What specific solution-focused questions and topics is it appropriate to include?
4   What specific solution-focused questions and topics would it be wise to leave out?

Commentary:
The following interventions could be useful: coping questions; eliciting meaning, both cultural and personal; identifying past successes and achievements in overcoming adversity; developing a sense of personal qualities; offering as much choice and control as possible.

of adolescence see a transition from a primary school setting into either a secondary school or special school unit. Increasingly, the expectation will be both from service providers and the young people themselves that they will have an increased say in life and day-to-day choices. How might you draw on solution-focused techniques and concepts in this situation? What changes might you need to make? In direct work with young people with learning disability, Murphy and Davis (2005) suggest a general approach that discovers and amplifies what a client does well, that can incorporate video feedback (or self-modelling) to demonstrate and reinforce preferred behaviours, and that also identifies strengths and unique positive characteristics: 'Competency-oriented interventions are particularly refreshing for young clients who are unaccustomed to being viewed as capable or being asked about their strengths and resources' (p. 70). Graphic depictions of improvements in desired behaviours can also reinforce in a way that language may not. Exception finding is also highlighted by Smith (2005) as an especially effective technique, and that the natural focus on the present and preferred future also fits well with young people with learning disabilities. Let us continue with Sushani and her mother Suzanne as an example (see Box 5.5).

Planning for adult life

Increasingly, the focus now shifts towards permanency planning for young adults with learning disabilities before their parents become frail, elderly or unable to cope. This can lead to situations of tension and frustration both for the parents themselves but also for care managers or key workers who will be trying to introduce change. As part of the philosophy of normalization and inclusion, it is no longer seen as appropriate for adults with learning disabilities to remain in their parents' care, often with limited social and educational outlets, when facilities of group living and active social lives are possible. This is not always easy for parents to understand or accept, especially if they have devoted many years of their lives to the primary task of caring for their child. Clashes with service providers can often occur at this transitional point. Lustig (1999) notes that professionals sometimes give messages to parents that they are either doing too much or too little. He also notes that older parents, in particular, are more likely to be sceptical of service systems because they cared for their child at a time when institutional care was the only other option and contact with professionals was thought to lead to institutionalization.

This is a time where active planning for both parents and offspring can be complemented by a solution-focused focus on preferred realities. What hopes do the parents have for their son's or daughter's adult life? What sort of life in five or ten years time? How is it best to prepare for that? What sacrifice does the

---

Box 5.5   Practice example: the teenage years – dilemmas of freedom and protection

---

Sushani is now fifteen and well settled in a local special education centre. Her communication skills are good; she remains extremely close to her mother and she now enjoys going shopping with her for clothes and make-up. Her mother Suzanne is very proud of how attractive her only child as a teenager is and she enjoys buying her clothes and make-up. At the same time, she is concerned that Sushani is now beginning to flirt with some of the young men at her special school and is pushing her mother to let her attend a teenage disco at the centre scheduled for the school holiday break in two weeks' time. She has asked you as Sushani's key worker to come and visit the home to address this issue.

Questions:
1   How will you approach this meeting?
2   Will you want to meet with both Sushani and Suzanne together?
3   What is your view on whether Sushani should be allowed to go to the disco?
4   How can you reassure her mother?
5   What solution-focused techniques and concepts will help you?

Commentary:
The right to sexual expression and the ethical dilemmas that can arise around the related right to reproduce are probably core concerns for this mother. It will be important to locate these in the context of cultural, societal, and class values and to spend time with this family while they work out what is best for Sushani.

---

parent need to make in the short term, in the letting-go to enable the longer term future to develop?

Sensitivity to the parent's acute awareness that cultural norms have changed and less parental involvement is now expected can be shown by normalizing some of these changes. References to the ways in which all parents become redundant in the end as adult children require them less can be coupled with an acknowledgement that this is a particularly bitter-sweet transition for parents of children with learning disability because the combination of care and protection needs have been so great. For some families where closeness has become the only constant in their lives, for example in the case of Suzanne and Sushani cited above, much effort would be needed to develop new support networks and activities for Suzanne before there would be a chance of success in moving Sushani to a new group home. It is also not unusual for a family crisis of some kind to precipitate a decision to explore new options, although it is obviously better if a planned move can be implemented rather than the sudden need for an emergency placement.

The young adult may also experience feelings of loss and displacement. Lustig (1999) also points out that unanticipated changes in placement can also disrupt other valued components of life such as supported employment or leisure activities.

Box 5.6   Practice example: loosening the bonds and creating a preferred future

Sushani is now twenty-two and is in supported employment in a local centre. She has good friends there but she still lives with her mother and tends to spend every evening and weekend in her care. She would like to go out with her friends sometimes but is also insistent that she does not want to upset or displease her mother.

Suzanne meanwhile has been unwell for some time and as key worker you are worried about her declining health. She has now told you that she has an inoperable but slow-growing cancer and may only have a couple of years to live.

Questions:

1   How can you work with Suzanne on increasing Sushani's independence and ability to cope by herself while still respecting their very close tie?
2   Should any work be done with Sushani to prepare her for her mother's death? Do you need to get Suzanne's consent for this and if so how do you go about it?
3   What other services might you involve and how?

Commentary:

Work hard with Suzanne to ensure that her solutions are heard and her wishes worked out so that she experiences being valued and respected. Use recent and past history to track how well she has managed to put her daughter's interests first, and how over time she has being letting her go and preparing her for independence. Make explicit use of the cultural elements of both disability and death in eliciting from Suzanne her personal perspective as a Muslim both on death and on her responsibilities to Sushani. How about her distant family's responsibilities?

Conclusions

The professional literature on helping in the field of learning disability suggests that helpers themselves can become too focused on the impairment and lose sight of the essence of the individual him or herself. Referring specifically to social workers, Galambos (2004) asserts that:

> Data from studies infer that social work interactions with this population and their families tend to focus less on abilities and more on the disability and presenting problem . . . social workers appear unable to move beyond this approach to concentrate on client strengths.
>
> (Galambos, 2004: 163)

To resist this tendency and instead to build services based on empowerment, humanistic principles, and respect requires of the helper the capacity to remain focused on maximizing the individual's potential through creative and optimistic planning and interventions. Solution-focused concepts and interventions have a role to play here.

6 The solution-focused helper working in primary, acute, and specialist health care settings

> Illness is the night-side of life, a more onerous citizenship. Everyone who is born holds dual citizenship, in the kingdom of the well and in the kingdom of the sick. Although we all prefer to use only the good passport, sooner or later each of us is obliged, at least for a spell, to identify ourselves as citizens of that other place.
>
> (Sontag, 1983: Preface)

Introduction

All of us are humbled by the experience of personal illness or of bearing witness to the illness of those close to us. Workers in health care settings deal with a broad spectrum of distress and often anguish as both patients and their families and friends deal with illness and its effects, be they recovery, disability, prolonged incapacity, and/or death. From the emergency service worker to the mortuary worker, from the home help to the community nurse to the specialist surgeon, all have to find a way both of making sense of their experiences with those in distress, and of coping with feelings that are engendered in us all by close contact with those in pain, distress, and experiencing trauma and loss.

There are different ways of 'making sense' of work in health care settings but most helpers share a common core purpose: that of wanting to alleviate people's suffering and to help them in their journey through illness and pain. In addition, to make work in this area a career and a satisfying form of work, you have to feel that you are making a difference, and that you *can* make a difference.

What, then, has solution-focused therapy (SFT) to offer you in the way of making sense of your work, as well as giving you ideas, tools, and strategies to weave into your personal framework for practice? This will depend, as in all other settings, on three different elements to your work at present: first, the contexts in which you work and the type of contacts with patients that your work entails; second, the roles that you need to take on to carry out your day-to-day work; and third, the knowledge bases – the theories, ideals, and beliefs – that comprise your current personal framework for practice. But first, let us tune in to the particular pressures and challenges of contemporary health care, for it is replete with ethical challenges and dilemmas that powerfully shape the patient–helper encounter.

Ethical dimensions

Most health care professional groups adhere to codes of ethics, designed to help ensure that appropriate ethical values guide practitioners. The values that commonly apply across the health care professions centre round issues of autonomy (the rights of individuals to self-determination), the rights to dignity and honesty (in providing patients with sufficient information for them to exercise informed consent), beneficence (the requirement to act in the patient's interests), non-maleficence (the requirement not to do harm), and the value of justice (in allocating scarce health care resources). Values such as these do not provide simple answers on how to handle a particular set of circumstances but they can help guide practitioners through complex situations, especially where conflicts arise. Different values can be held and conflicts can arise in these situations between health care providers and families, or indeed among different members of a family; conflicts may also arise between different values. In extreme cases, recourse may be needed to higher authorities: hospital or health service ethics boards, the courts or professional bodies. But on a day-to-day basis, workers in health care services grapple with moral and ethical dilemmas that develop in their work. What, then, are the most significant ones?

Illness and stigma

Sontag (1983) describes how two diseases – tuberculosis in the nineteenth century and cancer in the twentieth century – became in turn 'the disease that doesn't knock before it enters' and an illness 'experienced as a ruthless, secret invasion' (p. 9), regarded as a mystery and acutely feared. Her polemical essay on *Illness as a Metaphor*, first published thirty years ago, is illustrative of how disease terminology changes over time both in its impact on individual sufferers and its perception within societies as a whole. Cancer is no longer the death sentence that it was; neither is tuberculosis, nor HIV infection, nor an array of other ailments. However, Sontag's work reminds us that illnesses can be extremely stigmatizing and lead to prejudicial attitudes and behaviours. Infectious diseases are a particular category that can evoke negative reactions in health care workers. Taking the example of the moral panic that HIV infection triggered across many societies in the 1980s and 1990s, lessons can be learnt about how to minimize the risks of discriminatory attitudes and practices permeating the health care setting.

First is the importance of education and knowledge, both at the public level and for professionals in the field, about the true risks of infection and the practical steps that can be taken to manage this risk. Second is the importance of collaborative partnerships with patient advocacy groups both to humanize the illness for professionals and to normalize the illness for the patient. Third is the importance of clear protocols for the management of information, especially in relation to legal requirements regarding the notification of infectious diseases and the ethical requirement to inform individuals who may have been infected of their need for testing. The latter is one area where the solution-focused emphasis on the individual's right to identify their own goals has to be limited, as is the absolute right to a confidential service, given the predominant claim of a 'third party' possibly infected with a life-threatening virus to be informed, offered testing and, if necessary, treatment. In this situation, the requirement to work for the common good outweighs certain individual rights. Does this mean, however, that a solution-focused approach is completely ruled out in such situations? Not necessarily. Examples do exist of a solution-focused approach tailored for work with people with HIV and AIDS (Pomeroy et al., 2002; Orsulic-Jeras et al., 2003).

Health care rationing

Research and medical advances have provided interventions and treatments that can now cure many serious illnesses and defer death. People now live longer, albeit often with chronic conditions that still require intensive management. Medical advances in the last thirty years have been truly incredible to the extent that one of the greatest challenges for societies now is to decide how to ration health care. However, no society can afford to treat all its members for medical problems to the extent that advances in health care can now allow. This is one of the most significant social policy problems of our times and it permeates the health service sector. In the USA, health care provision is largely rationed on an ability to pay basis; in the UK, in the context of a health care system available to all, efforts have been made to allocate resources in line with an evidence-based strategy, with the National Institute for Health and Clinical Excellence (NICE) and its social counterpart, Social Care Institute for Excellence (SCIE), evaluating interventions and publishing guidelines for practitioners based on research evidence. In other European countries such as Ireland, a mixed economy of public and private provision underpinned by a system of health care insurance determines the extent and level of care individuals receive. In Canada and Scandinavia, a comprehensive system of public insurance means there is only one health care system with no private component.

How, then, does this issue – the need to ration health care resources – impact on practice at the level of the individual patient? Taking the particular context of acute hospital care, decisions have to be made on a daily basis regarding the continuance of an existing treatment, the instigation of new or experimental interventions or the withdrawal of treatment altogether. While equality of access to treatment is a component not only of the ethical codes of several health care professions (McAllister, 2007; International Federation of Social Workers, 2008) but also of various international and national legislative frames such as human rights and equality legislation, in both the UK and Ireland a two-tier health care system persists, allocating some resources on the basis of ability to pay rather than clinical need. This aspect of the health care environment presents serious challenges to a solution-focused helper who wishes to integrate respect, hope, and a future-focused vision in his or her work, challenges for which there are no easy answers. For some, activity outside the clinical workplace helps alleviate the unease engendered: advocating for change on a structural level; lobbying politically; joining pressure groups and helping to advise and inform those who are committed to seeking change. For others, practical measures such as enlisting additional resources for individual patients through advocacy and social brokering can help to restore an element of social justice to their work. Finally, some organizational structures allow for a commitment to work only in the public sector and a rejection of the additional rewards of private practice that can, for those who opt to make such a commitment, prove satisfying. Health care colleagues remind me of how, in the early days when HIV medications were just coming on stream and were scarce resources, some medical staff baulked at prescribing these expensive triple-therapy treatments to HIV sufferers who also had heroin addiction problems, reasoning that their drug problems made them less likely candidates for long-term maintenance of health through medications. In such situations, discussions are needed about the judgements being made and advocacy provided for the rights of less-educated and more socially disadvantaged patients who would otherwise lose out on access to necessary treatments.

Managing expectations

Health care provision has consequently become one of the most publicized and politicized issues in modern societies. In Ireland in 2008, the media was dominated by a range of stories highlighting the 'dysfunctional' health service, the scandals of 'missed' cancer diagnoses, and political lobbying for the retention of local cancer treatment services in rural communities. In the UK, media coverage likewise focuses on issues such as the role of local health authorities in approving (or not) expensive treatments for particular conditions. Such media coverage is revealing because it highlights some underlying assumptions and expectations regarding health care service provision. On one level, the language used in media reporting reveals the increased expectations of people that not only should doctors and health care workers be infallible but that they (or their organizations) should also be able to meet an ever-increasing demand for new and expensive treatments. Patients and their families/carers now come with a mass of information obtained through the Internet or on-line chat-rooms and support groups. This creates a great deal of pressure for individual health care workers, and doctors often take a deep breath when a patient turns up with a pad and pen and a list of treatment options outlined in red! On the one hand, it can be argued that for patients to be so much better informed about their illness is to alleviate the pressure on health care workers to be educators. In solution-focused thinking, it means that patients are more likely to be collaborators and co-creators in dealing with and managing their medical problems. This has the benefit that a more traditional expert–patient relationship does not have to be dismantled first. Yet, on the other hand, the combination of vast knowledge about a range of interventions coupled with a hazy knowledge about the specifics of their own unique case can mean that patients and their families/carers may be more likely to challenge treatment decisions made and need more time with specialists on their case to understand fully the implications of different treatment regimes and options in their own case.

Managing expectations and negotiating agreed treatment options is thus another feature of health care in the twenty-first century that can throw up many ethical dilemmas for workers. Solution-focused questions can play a part here, coupled with honesty about the clinical reality, treatment options and side-effects, and a commitment to empowering individuals to make their own choices. Of particular help can be the reminder from the solution-focused literature that the role of the helper is to facilitate, not to persuade or cajole; the belief that people generally are experts on their own lives and will know what is best for them; and the importance of the ability to convey this to the individual – that you believe that she will make the right choice for herself (see Chapter 4). Honest and timely information, delivered with respect, coupled with sufficient time for the information to be absorbed and questions answered, can go a long way towards motivating patients and their families/ carers to work with you. Related to this is the need to avoid giving false hope or false reassurance. Some health care workers, particularly in their early years of work in the field, describe how devastating it is to them personally to be the bearer of bad news and how easy it can be to fall into the trap of giving false reassurances especially when pressed by desperate patients or parents/ carers. Conversely, it can be devastating to paint too bleak a picture in the hours immediately after an accident or health crisis, as the retention of hope is an important aspect of how people cope with stressors and crises in their lives.

Autonomy and self-determination

Recognizing the right to refuse treatment can be a particularly difficult 'call' for the health care professional. In a highly publicized case in the UK in 2008, a teenage girl with a chronic, life-threatening heart condition refused the option of a heart transplant asserting her right to have her wishes respected. This decision supported by her parents led to a child protection referral from the hospital anxious to ensure that they were not seen to be complicit with a 'right-to-die' request from a young person. No further action was taken by the authorities once they were satisfied that the teenage girl was fully aware of the choices facing her and was making a well-informed decision that she did not wish to undergo any more invasive and painful medical interventions for her condition, having undergone a series of hospitalizations and treatment regimes all her life. This individual case can lead us to consider the capacity of young people and children to make their own decisions and the issue of what constitutes 'informed consent'. Of particular note for health care workers reflecting on this story was the importance stressed on the young person's experience of illness and intervention as constituting a powerful form of knowledge not available to those professionals who were treating her. In other words, no one of us can be better informed than the patient with a chronic illness of the choices facing them, and the advantages and disadvantages of each option. This has, of course, to be coupled with a developmental level of cognitive understanding, such that the patient appreciates the implications of refusing treatment if it will lead to further illness, disability or death. With younger children, or those sick from birth, the situation may be much more complicated. In paediatric settings, workers struggle sometimes to find an agreed course for action with families, for a child with a chronic terminal condition. The need of parents to do everything possible to save the life of their child is powerfully captured in the 1992 award-winning American film based on a true story, *Lorenzo's Oil*, which details a couple's fight to identify and make available medication for their child's rare condition. In real life, this couple did manage to defy medical expectations and kept their child alive until he was aged thirty, but a miracle cure it was not. Day after day, in paediatric settings, parents fight for continued treatment 'at all costs' even if told it will be unsuccessful. They may not consent to treatment being withdrawn; they may insist on their right to bring the child to other specialists for second, third or even fourth opinions. This poses a real ethical dilemma for hospital and medical staff when a child is suffering and in pain as a result of these efforts to find a cure or a treatment. When a child is young and/or unable to articulate their needs and wishes, hospital staff may be compelled to advocate on their behalf, sometimes forcefully, against the parents' wishes. How, then, can the hospital staff simultaneously help the parents to accept that life is at an end? Is there a need in such situations for a more formalized system of advocacy, either for the child or for the parents? Is there a need to involve ethical committees in hospitals, so that a higher-level authority can adjudicate and take the heat out of the direct interaction around the child? These are complex, emotion-laden questions but ones that need constructive solutions all the same.

Issues regarding personal agency and the need for advocacy for those unable to advocate for themselves, also arise in the context of the increasing emphasis in the current health care discourse on individual responsibility and the importance of disease prevention and primary care interventions. In the UK, one of the dominant health-related themes in the popular media throughout 2008 was that of obesity, which is arguably the current 'health scourge' of our time. In the USA, obesity is if anything an even greater pre-occupation. Parents can now be accused of 'killing their children with kindness' for refusing to deny them unhealthy foods. Clinicians have to consider whether to ration scarce and expensive treatment resources such as liver or lung transplants on the basis of whether continuing (and self-inflicted) risk factors diminish the possibility of successful outcomes. Sometimes such debates seem to parallel the Victorian distinction between the deserving and the undeserving in the allocation of charity, or as one Irish colleague describes it, the depiction of the 'good' versus the 'bad' patient. The former footballer George Best was, prior to his death in 2007, excoriated in the British media for his continued abuse of alcohol following a successful liver transplant operation. This, then, is another ethical challenge of health care work – how do you remain respectful towards individuals who self-destructively undo your fine work, reject your advice and treatment regimes, and 'waste' scarce resources? Many social work, psychology, and social care workers in medical settings find themselves having to advocate for socially disadvantaged patients and groups, many of whom have compromised physical and mental health, and may present as 'less-deserving' than the 'good' patient.

The solution-focused principle of separating the person from the problem is a start and ensuring that clinical decisions take into account the patient as he or she presents and their unique situation at that time, not just the stereotype that is the first image or impression. A reminder of the principle of 'not-knowing' about the unique contours of an individual's life at this precise time challenges the tendency to assume judgemental attitudes and formulaic solutions. This coupled with efforts to link with the person as being an expert on their own life can go some way towards preventing a judgemental blaming or cold attitude creeping into the encounter; one which provides no motivation or hope to the individual in difficulty but which can create an unhelpful attitude of isolation and anger.

Culturally specific practices and beliefs

The cultural specificity of health care systems and practices in developed countries needs to be acknowledged, as do the complexities of working cross-culturally, particularly where there are language difficulties. Some cultures attribute diseases and illness to spiritual and magical elements. Working with language interpreters is a skill in itself; access to cultural interpreters can help to deepen knowledge and raise awareness about specific cultural beliefs and practices. In Dublin, Ireland, an innovative refugee social integration project Access Ireland (www.accessireland.ie) has created a team of trained cultural mediators to work with health and social care services and families from minority groups on understanding each other's beliefs and practices. For Irish health care workers used to practising in a seemingly homogenous culture, shaped primarily by Catholic, and to a lesser extent Protestant, religious beliefs and practices, the transition in recent years to a more culturally diverse population has been a challenge. With over 10 percent of the population now from diverse ethnic and religious groups (Commission for Social Care Inspection and Healthcare Commission, 2006), workers have had to learn new strategies for communicating understanding and working effectively with patients from different backgrounds without resorting to simplistic and often crass cultural stereotypes. In the UK and North America, ethnic diversity and mix similarly challenge all helpers to be less certain that their own solutions will fit the lives of their clients; in such circumstances, the notion of being expert on the client's life has to be abandoned. Solution-focused strategies can be useful in this context; in particular, the emphasis placed on a respectful curiosity, a positioning of the helper as someone who is interested in how this patient thinks and how this family works. The emphasis on 'not-knowing' is a genuine and honest acknowledgement of the level of ignorance many of us feel when working cross-culturally; and the importance of linking and establishing a bond with the person before turning to the problem together creates a humanistic link to transcend difference. In addition, health care workers may sometimes have to take the role of advocate for a family who wishes to use healers from their own community alongside a more orthodox medical regime.

Two ethical issues that have proved particularly challenging in health care have been those of patients presenting with female genital mutilation (FGM) and Jehovah's Witnesses refusing blood transfusions: 'Female Genital Mutilation includes procedures that intentionally alter or injure female genital organs for non-medical reasons' (WHO, 2008). While international agencies including the World Health Organization and UNICEF unite in a campaign to eradicate the practice as a violation of the human rights of girls and young women, it is estimated that between 100 and 140 million girls and women worldwide currently live with the consequences of female genital mutilation (www.who.int/mediacentre/factsheets). The most common presentation of female genital mutilation has been in maternity hospitals when complications arise during childbirth and in general practice surgeries where women present with medical problems arising from the procedure. For many workers educated and socialized into societies where women are considered equal, the practice is shocking and engenders feelings of revulsion and anger. Concern can also be felt that the practice will be perpetuated on younger girls and dilemmas arise about whether child protection procedures should be invoked. While female genital mutilation is now viewed in many European countries as an illegal act consisting of an assault, uncertainty remains about the extent to which it may still be practised. What, then, are useful strategies for health care workers when working with women presenting with FGM-related issues? For many, the use of information and education can go some way towards highlighting both the illegality of the act in developed countries as well as the immediate and long-term health consequences involved. The roles of educator and advocate can be invoked but in working with women for whom female genital mutilation is a reality, a non-judgemental acceptance of their situation is called for and the best practical, medical, and supportive facilities offered. Yet when it comes to the issue of whether the practice is perpetuated on younger females in this family or community, issues of human and legal rights and responsibilities to protect vulnerable children prevail.

This is also true when parents refuse to allow blood transfusions either for children or during childbirth. Health care providers in the UK and Ireland have in these situations applied to courts for permission to impose the treatment of blood transfusion where the life of a baby or child is threatened, despite the practice being contrary to the Jehovah's Witness religious movement. Here again the ethical responsibility and social mandate to be mindful of the human and legal rights of the vulnerable, especially the young, overrides the individual parent's right.

New ethnic communities, comprising migrant workers, refugees, asylum-seekers, and students, can be resented when they present with specific health care problems, such as sickle-cell anaemia, which previously did not warrant a dedicated service. Racial prejudice may trigger protestations that these communities are 'taking' scarce resources; health care workers and agencies need to have in place well-conceived anti-racist policies to ensure that they maintain their mandate to be open and accessible to all comers.

In conclusion, ethical challenges and dilemmas permeate the contemporary health care field: some illnesses continue to stigmatize; individuals can be blamed for not following healthy lifestyles or abandoning life-threatening habits and practices; advances in medical technologies have created higher expectations and new inequalities in how health care resources are rationed; the individual's right to autonomy can be threatened by the medical institution's aim to save life where possible; the ethical requirement to do no harm can be compromised when patients and their families wish to prolong treatment where no positive outcome is possible; the requirement to 'do good' can be challenged by religious or cultural practices. The health care professional may be in conflict with patients and families in particularly extreme situations. While consensus can be aimed for, it may not always be possible. Working for the common good and the need for protection of, and advocacy for, the vulnerable may be two particular ethical values that can mean limiting a right to choose and the concept of the patient as expert on his or her own life.

Context and contact

The context of your work is important in several different ways. First, it will influence the patient base with which you work. In an economically and socially deprived inner city health centre or hospital, for example, 'solutions' may come in the form of a mixture of practical assistance, advocacy for services or rights, as well as one-to-one or family work on how the patient and their family and carers are coping with their illness or health problems. As a social worker, nurse, therapist or hospital counsellor in a particular specialist unit, for example a paediatric oncology unit, solutions may also need to include practical assistance, but particular skills and knowledge in dealing with loss and bereavement will be central to your work. Second, in addition to the *type* of environment – both external in the socio-economic profile of the community serviced, and internal to the specific health care setting in which you are based – the unique *culture* of your workplace will have an impact. For example, how are patients perceived? What hierarchies of care or professional status exist? What style of leadership is in place? How integrated is your workplace in, or isolated from, the communities served? It is worth bearing in mind the context in which you work, for we all become acculturated or socialized into these contexts, and this affects how we view our role.

Many health care settings can be characterized as busy, with a high turnover of patients coming for clinics, for check-ups, for diagnostic or developmental tests. The turnover and the nature of the work may be such that you may only ever have one-off contacts with patients and their families. In some other settings, you may have the opportunity to have contact with people over a longer, sustained period (for example, in a longer-stay hospital ward or convalescent and rehabilitation settings). In primary care settings such as GP surgeries and health centres, you may have a mix of contact types: short, intensive contacts with families with new babies as midwives and public health or district nurses, or others recently discharged from hospital; longer, less frequent contacts with families with young children through developmental clinics and with young and older people with chronic illnesses. There is scope for the solution-focused helper across these different contact types,

---

Box 6.1   Reflective exercise: the impact of context

Review the following account of how a specific health care setting can impact on the worker.

As a young social work student in the 1970s, I spent one summer working in a local 'hospital'. It was only ten minutes walk from my home, yet I had remained completely unaware of its presence. Why? This hospital had several features that created a distance between it and the local suburban Dublin community. First, it was a British Army hospital, established and funded by the British Home Office as a hospital and long-term care facility for Army veterans; second, it was isolated physically, hidden behind stone walls, the buildings nestling in a low single-storey formation at the end of a long avenue.

As a nursing auxiliary, I found that the context had an enormous impact not only on how I was expected to perform my function but also on how the entire range of staff–patient relations were worked out. The structure and hierarchy of the Army system was embedded in how the hospital wards were run: on the long, twenty-bedded open wards were the former privates and corporals and technical officers; in the private single rooms closest to the nurses' station and first to receive their meals and medications were the former officers. Yet, as a nursing auxiliary, I had a good deal of intimate contact with patients, from feeding to washing to emptying bedpans to giving medications to making beds. I had more time on the open wards and because of this and the extent to which I was able to observe other staff in their interactions with the patients, I became more aware of the needs of those men, their likes and dislikes, and the ways in which 'small acts of kindness' could humanize what was an oppressive institutional setting. In contrast, the privacy awarded the officers in single rooms also created a form of isolation: as a nursing auxiliary I had to remain mindful of their presence and make more of an effort to remain as sensitive to their needs as I did to the larger numbers on the open wards.

Consider your own setting. Identify two features of your workplace that are related to the structure, hierarchy or culture, one negative and one positive. Consider how the positive feature impacts on your work and how you can make the most of it.

---

whether you have only one opportunity to make an impact or whether you know that you will be working with a patient or family over a longer time-frame but you may need to tailor your use of the approach depending on the types of contacts that you have with patients and their families/carers.

As I have explained in earlier chapters, the solution-focused helper does not impose therapy or assume it is needed in distressful circumstances. Rather, he or she connects with the broader concept of instilling hope and presuming

---

Box 6.2 Practice example: the potential for solution-focused talk across different types of contact

---

One young mother, who in a time of great distress attempted suicide through a drug overdose, told of how in the midst of her distress the words of an ambulance worker 'pulled her short' and helped to lift her out of her despair. He simply said to her: 'Look, what about your four children – they need you. You can't do this to them. You are too important to them'. He used a powerful future-focused comment to link with the best hopes of this young mother for her children. She described how he 'drew her out of herself' so that she could look beyond her present state of mind. This helped her to engage with the health care workers who took over her care, with the focus of getting better so that she could resume parenting her children.

An Irish colleague, describing how she approached her counselling work with the dying and bereaved, talked of how she saw her job as being there for 'the long haul' in a role of 'bearing witness' to the other's pain; of sharing a journey and by being a sympathetic companion, helping to carry that burden of grief for the time that the bereaved needed that support. By remaining available, but not imposing contact, she is able to both convey the message that this is a natural process of grieving, at the same time as acknowledging that as an experienced worker in a health care setting, she is available to a bereaved person over time, simply to listen and acknowledge the pain and suffering of the bereaved person.

Questions:

1   Can you identify one client or service-user who appears despairing and hopeless?
2   What, if anything, do you know about what really matters in their life?
3   How might you construct some solution-focused questions that would allow you to have similar conversations with your client?

Commentary:

People who become depressed often feel isolated and alone with their troubles. Just to be reassured that they matter and that they are not alone can be a great comfort and motivator to keep going.

---

resilience while remaining congruent with the emotional context and essence of their encounter with a client. The solution-focused helper's aim is to have the client leave the encounter enriched by the contact. For the ambulance worker in the first example given above, and for the social worker counselling the bereaved in the second example, simple actions and words can turn the encounter into an enriching experience.

Box 6.3   Reflective exercise: seizing the moment

Think of a recent patient you dealt with, or saw others deal with, who was in a moment of crisis, of distress or strong emotion.
  Think of how you felt at that time.
  Were you able to interact effectively and sympathetically?
  If not, what could you or someone else have said or done that might have been meaningful for that person at that time?

Roles

In most settings, both health and social care professionals need to perform a range of roles in a day's work in addition to their hands-on clinical specialisms. McAllister alerts us to an important aspect of health care work – that of the transient nature of the contact and the transitional process the patient is experiencing:

> Being a transition worker means working during times of transition for people and helping them to cross a bridge between one state (perhaps illness) into another (perhaps wellness or adaptation). So nursing is about being able to be with clients and their families so that they transform what may be a life crisis into a turning point, something manageable. It is about giving people self-belief, resources, hope and facilitating change.
>
> (McAllister, 2007: 33)

Workers in health care settings have found Compton and Galaway's (1999) template of five different intervention roles useful (Bachman and Lind, 1997; Sun, 2004; Guthiel and Souza, 2006). As *social broker*, helpers connect patients to the resources and additional supports they need. As *advocate*, the helper either helps patients and their families/carers to be heard in their own right or speaks up for them, which may be particularly important in the multidisciplinary context where matching the patient's wishes and needs with clinical plans is an ongoing process. As *mediator*, it may be necessary to help resolve disputes between the patient and others – perhaps even between the patient and family or carers; or between different members of a family system, especially if it comes to plans around discharge or treatments. As *enabler* – or clinician/therapist as Sun (2004) reframes this role – helpers move into a more direct change-agent position, using one or several of a range of interventions to help mobilize the person's own resources to deal with or overcome specific problems. And finally, as *educator*, the helper may be directly involved in teaching the patient and family/carers about medical conditions themselves, about treatment regimes, about dietary or physiotherapy elements, about tests and procedures. Compton and Galaway's (1999) list is not exhaustive but it gives us a useful starting point to this element of our work: the diversity of responses we need to develop.

This is a skill you already have – the abilities to be flexible and responsive to diverse need in the specific context in which you work and to be aware of the boundaries of that context and your professional position in it. Let us just take time to develop this aspect of our work.

Many health care workers are genuinely surprised to discover the range of roles they need to occupy in carrying out their day-to-day work in addition to their particular clinical specialism. Furthermore, the skills that these roles require – skills of eliciting, clarifying, communicating, reframing, teaching, and supporting – are all skills that are integral to helping in a therapeutic manner. In other words, many health care workers are already well versed in the core skills necessary to be a solution-focused helper.

The next element to weave into developing your own personal framework for being a solution-focused helper is to identify the parallel knowledge bases that you are already using: the theories, beliefs, and practices that you have

---

Box 6.4 Reflective exercise: mapping your current work roles

Taking Compton and Galaway's (1999) five main role types, identify which combination of roles you undertake in your job. Leaving aside your direct clinical/treatment work, map out which activities take up what percentage of the total.

Social broker   %
The skills I use include:

Advocate   %
The skills I use include:

Mediator   %
The skills I use include:

Enabler   %
The skills I use include:

Educator   %
The skills I use include:

developed over time. These may need to be considered in a different light, tweaked or discarded if you wish to develop a deep solution-focused aspect to your practice.

Parallel knowledge bases

Apart from the technical and specialist knowledge bases associated with different roles in health care, solution-focused helpers also draw on other theories to understand and support clients with health care problems. These include the following, although it is not an exclusive list. These are merely the ones that have been most frequently mentioned by workers that I have surveyed.

Ecological and systemic theories

As a helper in a health care setting, the individual referred is invariably the focus of your attention. Yet, understanding the individual-in-context is almost always an integral part of effective helping. Similarly, understanding your position as part of a network of helpers in a health care setting is also vital, so that as well as 'living with the overlap' of effective interdisciplinary relations you can work out with colleagues when you should undertake certain tasks and when it is time to involve others. Bennun (1999) uses systemic concepts to analyse the functioning of a hospital intensive care unit, noting that it was a useful framework 'to identify some of the systems or stakeholders and consider where they interact and . . . some of the issues they raise' (p. 99). Although the original solution-focused model (de Shazer et al., 1986) was limited in its focus on the wider system, subsequent developments of the model have placed a wider systemic emphasis at the heart of the approach (Walsh, 1997).

Theories of attachment and loss

In addition to the applied work on the importance of attachment for the development of children, the original work of Bowlby and Ainsworth (Ainsworth and Bowlby, 1967; Bowlby, 1999) has been developed and applied to assess adult attachment styles and their impact on the individual's ability to cope with stressors and develop resilience in their networks (Parkes et al., 1991; Simpson and Rholes, 1998). Health care workers find these concepts useful both in working with mothers and their children when hospitalized and also in understanding individual reactions to illness in adults. Some hospitals are developing assessment tools based on attachment theory to assess how families will cope with a challenging diagnosis of childhood illness. One source of such materials is the Circle of Security Project, originally American but now with centres in the UK and Australia. Generally, how people cope with loss is a central element of the work in health care settings.

Theories of trauma and loss

Since the 1970s, increased attention has been paid to the concept of psychological trauma, both in terms of its impact on a person's well-being and the risk of the development of more extreme anxiety disorders, often referred to as 'post-traumatic stress disorders' (PSTD) (Van der Kolk et al., 1996; Harvey, 2000). Health care workers are often involved in the community aftermath of war or major disasters such as that following the events of 9/11 in New York; they themselves can be traumatized by this work. Individual patients and their families/carers who have come through traumatic experiences such as physical or sexual assault, violent deaths, suicides, road traffic accidents or localized gang violence may need special attention. Harvey (2000) suggests that narrative work (telling the story, or writing about the event) can be an effective and supportive intervention in post-traumatic work. Coupling this with a solution-focused frame in which the person is viewed as innately resourceful but temporarily knocked off-course allows for the worker to convey the message that this too shall pass; that this is not a permanent state of stress but one that will come to an end.

Theories of crisis intervention

Crisis intervention theory suggests that with crisis comes opportunity and the potential for change (assuming that change needs to take place). With the questioning of old, established patterns of being and behaving comes the potential for new patterns and practices to be developed. In therapeutic terminology, crises represent opportunities. A crisis can be 'any transitory situation in which a person's usual coping mechanisms are no longer adequate to deal with the experiences involved' (Wilson et al., 2008: 692). In the case of health care, a crisis could be a diagnosis, an injury, an accident, an unexpected 'turn for the worst', a death. Not all of these will necessarily be crises. Indeed, after long painful periods of illness, death may come as a relief and a resolution, rather than a crisis. It is not so much the event but the meaning of the event for a person that determines whether it is a crisis or not. Workers in acute health care and emergency settings will invariably see more people in crisis: following accidents, traumatic illnesses, even disasters with multiple casualties. With the exception of chronic conditions where the patient may already be as familiar with life in hospital as that at home, a hospital admission or the need for treatment in a casualty department may well trigger a crisis for the patient or people close to them. Partners, parents, friends, siblings, and colleagues can all be greatly affected by a hospitalization, particularly if it could have been avoided.

Lifestyle issues and choices may need to be re-examined; the unintended consequences of actions accepted and change planned. With experience, many health care workers learn how to instinctively recognize 'magic moments' in crisis situations, those unique combinations of time and place, which, as a worker, you need to seize as a golden opportunity to make a difference. Solution-focused questions and strategies can be used at these times.

Theories of motivational interviewing

Motivational interviewing (Rollnick and Miller, 1997; Rollnick et al., 2007) shares many features with solution-focused therapy and these links have been recognized over time (Lewis and Osborn, 2004). What they have in common are: the importance of understanding the person's frame of reference; the active expression of acceptance and affirmation; the active elicitation of the client's own perspectives, goals, and strategies; building in reviews of progress and acknowledgement that helpers have the responsibility to find strategies that are acceptable to this client. Together with SFT, motivational interviewing highlights: clients' intrinsic values and goals; the importance of the client's motivation to change; the concept of 'resistance' not as a fixed value on the part of the client but as useful feedback on the behaviour of the helper; and the quality of the working relationship as being more of a partnership than the traditional expert/client roles. Motivational interviewing is a popular approach in addiction work and also has its uses in health care work with patients facing rigorous and tough treatment regimes. Advocates of motivational interviewing, like those of SFT, emphasize the danger of using techniques without adopting the spirit of the therapy. In essence, if you already have an affinity for motivational interviewing, you should not find it difficult to combine elements of it with some of the solution-focused ideas and concepts outlined here:

> Solution-Focused Counseling and Motivational Interviewing combined can encourage clients through a collaborative and respectful counseling relationship, honoring client stories, and recognizing client strengths, intentions and preferences as important components in the client's own healing.
>
> (Lewis and Osborn, 2004: 48)

Spirituality and the role of religion

One cannot consider work in health care settings – with the dying and bereaved, with sick children, premature illnesses, and loss of ability or function – without also considering the meaning of it all, mankind's ultimate nature and purpose, matters of religious faith and belief and ritual.

> The spiritual issues that clients raise are as diverse as the clients them-
> selves. For some, grief over the loss of a loved one, a job or career, a
> marriage or a child, is spiritual. For some, decisions over pregnancy,
> marriage, separation and divorce, disease, terminal illness, or debili-
> tating illness are spiritual . . . Spiritual questions deserve thoughtful,
> deliberate and authentic responses.
>
> (Bullis, 1996: 9)

With the emphasis in solution-focused theory on understanding the client's
own personal belief system and way of making sense of their situation, the
inclusion of spiritual aspects of illness is not inconsistent. Indeed, a person's
religious beliefs can be used as a powerful voice for change and belief in that
possibility.

Theories of resilience and coping

The concept of resilience has received a lot of attention in recent decades,
particularly as it applies to vulnerable children and youth in adverse environments. Resilience can be broadly understood as 'relative resistance to psychosocial risk experiences . . . [it] means that there has been a relatively good
outcome for someone' (Rutter, 1999: 119). Cross-culturally, the concept can be
understood as the capacity to bounce back from adverse experiences. Resilience
theory has also been extended to the notion of family resilience (Walsh, 2006)
and environmental or community resilience. Coping theories are most often
related to overcoming stress (Lazarus and Folkman, 1984), with coping strategies tied to an individual's appraisal of a situation. Cognitive processing is
also identified by Rutter (1999) as a factor in the promotion of resilience: 'there
is a need to pay attention to the suggestion that the psychopathological effects
of risk experiences are strongly moderated by how individuals cognitively and
affectively process their experiences' (p. 139). Solution-focused strategies and
sequences of questioning are heavily but not exclusively focused on cognitive
aspects of problems and the possibility of replacing problematic beliefs or attitudes with more hopeful or helpful understandings. The skill of reframing is
central to this. Meaning-making has been identified as one strategy for helping
patients and their families cope with chronic and acute illnesses. Lee et al.
(2006) describe how a structured intervention with adult cancer sufferers that
focused on meaning-making improved self-esteem, optimism, and self-
efficacy. Paediatric social workers in one Irish setting place a great emphasis on
helping parents focus on what they can do when dealing with a sick child;
helping them to retrieve an image of themselves as copers, helping them
regain control and adapt to the situation.

In conclusion, many health care workers already have useful theories and
ways of thinking about their work that guide their practice. These may include

---

Box 6.5   Reflective exercise: mapping out your current tool-kit of theories

Make a list of the theories or practice frameworks that you already use and how.

On a scale of 0–10, rate each theory against its similarity to the solution-focused model presented in Chapter 3. Note the similarities and the differences.

Taking one situation type (e.g. working with a young person who is not following their treatment regime) for which your current strategies are not working, consider how you might introduce some useful solution-focused questions or comments in your next contact with them.

---

the theories outlined above but should not be seen as a barrier to the adoption of solution-focused practices. In outlining how a philosophical model of solution-focused nursing (SFN) can be implemented alongside existing nursing models, McAllister (2007) notes that it is possible for differences to exist alongside shared understanding: 'It is possible, as SFN is, to be both for humanism in the sense that it values each person's uniqueness and for science and what it can offer in the treatment of disease and the amelioration of suffering' (p. 4). Research studies of how practitioners move between different roles and activities in social work show that they can juggle interventions from seemingly conflicting paradigms without difficulty (Harrison, 1991; Walsh, 2002).

Examples of solution-focused health care

As people can now live longer with medical conditions as opposed to dying from them, more health care workers will have contact with patients with chronic illnesses. While the management of the illness itself may require constant monitoring of medication and treatment regimes, frequent short hospital stays, and regular contact with primary care workers, the psychological impact of chronic illness is another aspect of care both for patient and carers. Demoralization, depression, and social isolation can all occur. Patients often need to exercise courage every day to avoid being overwhelmed by their condition. How, then. can you act as a solution-focused helper in such situations?

Structured interventions, using the solution-focused therapy model in a formal programme, such as the example in Box 6.6 are one idea. Another is to look at how you can use 'stories of success' from other patients to give 'clues' and indirect guidance to patients on how they too might cope with the adversity of illness.

Box 6.6 Practice example: long-term illness and returning to work

---

Cockburn et al. describe how an orthopaedic rehabilitation programme in an American hospital effectively utilized a solution-focused group therapy intervention to help patients and their families adjust and re-enter employment. While this was a small-scale study involving less than fifty participants in a type of randomized controlled trial, the results were promising if not generalizable, and suggest that solution-focused interventions can play a part in motivating those recovering from a long period of illness to feel more able to return to work: 'Both work hardening and solution-focused therapy ostensibly share a mutual interest in promoting and affirming patients' sense of control and strengths, and the setting of negotiated goals that are health oriented' (Cockburn et al., 1997: 103).

Questions:
1   Can you identify clients or service-users who have similar problems adjusting to illness and/or returning to work?
2   How do your current interventions match with this example of solution-focused work?

Commentary:
The key points from this intervention are as follows:

- Interventions built on the individuals' frame of reference when identifying goals that are important, meaningful or useful were most pertinent.
- De Shazer's advice on the features of well-formed goals – that they be small, realistic, involve hard work; the creation of new behaviours rather than just the cessation of negative ones; and excluding previous failed solutions – was also central to their programme.
- The formulation for goal-setting was centred on it being behaviourist and involving a: ' "who, what, where, when and how" set of descriptions' (1997: 98).
- Reframing of difficulties was a central intervention – of particular use was helping participants to overcome feelings of isolation, hostility, and discouragement by inviting alternative solution-focused conversations on changing how relationships might be viewed or acted upon.

Dietary and treatment regimes

Apart from the lifestyle or behaviour changes often advocated in the wake of acute conditions or early-warning signals of ill-health such as high blood pressure and heart disease, people with chronic or life-long conditions may need to follow rigorous dietary or treatment regimes for life. Children suffering from

---

Box 6.7 Practice example: coping with chronic pain

Irish author Bill Long described how a combination of health care problems, including a heart transplant, an aneurism repair, two hernia operations, a gallstones operation, and the removal of cataracts, had 'put a stop to his gallop' while in his early sixties. Now fourteen years later, he is crippled with osteoporosis and chronic arthritis and lives in a wheelchair, dependent on a mixture of twenty-eight different medications a day to keep going. He is in constant pain and describes himself as sometimes feeling like 'a poor, flickering flame that, at any instant, may be snuffed out', yet describes how he has come to terms with this in words that are powerfully resilient:

> I am, as we all are, alone with my pain. In the land of pain, comparisons are not valid. Your pain and mine are very different. We must handle them in our different ways. We must come to terms with our pain and let it enhance rather than ruin our lives.
>
> For myself, I have found that you can never beat pain. It will always be the winner. So, I decided that some compromise was necessary. I decided to establish a good relationship with my pain. Pain had come into my house as an uninvited and unwanted guest. I had a choice to make. Fight it, or befriend it! So, I talked to my pain. I said, 'I will not, cannot fight you. You are too strong and I am too old and too weak. So, I will just let you wash over me. Let you teach me something. Something beautiful and worthwhile. How about humility? Teach me humility'.
>
> And that, for me, has worked . . .

(Bill Long: Race against remaining time, *Irish Times Health Supplement*, p. 8, Tuesday 27 November 2008: healthsupplement@irish-times.ie; permission to reproduce granted by *Irish Times*)

Questions:

1 What can you take from this account into your work with patients with chronic pain?
2 How could you introduce this 'idea', this suggestion to them?
3 How could you lead the conversation to a magic moment when sharing Bill's story?

Commentary:

This is a powerful example both of how individually we each need to make sense of our illnesses and pain. In addition, it is a good example of how 'externalizing the problem' and talking to it as an external phenomenon can help give us a sense of mastery and control.

blood disorders or metabolic conditions and those with cystic fibrosis are just two examples. One particular practice issue that can arise is how to motivate children and adult patients to 'stick with' the regimes required? Lightfoot (2003) describes how she finds that solution-focused concepts blend well with the concept of the 'expert patient' in her work as a dietician. She highlights the unhelpful nature of the term 'compliance' as carrying an expectation of obedience and the yielding to an expert with power. The active use of the solution-focused concept of the client being expert on their own life blends well with the notion of the expert patient and thus reframes the role of the helper to be a facilitator to the patient working on how best to implement treatment regimes. Lightfoot's three strategies are: (1) give people choices; (2) recognize that every behaviour makes sense and explore its meaning; (3) don't ever do what the patient can do nor decide for them.

Let us look now at how these principles might be applied in practice. One useful concept here is that of 'creating a yes-set' (Erickson and Rossi, 1979; de Shazer, 1982), of linking with a client in such a way that their experience is one of being heard, being validated, and being complimented.

The aftermath of accidents, excess, and overdoses

Workers in accident and emergency departments speak of increasing frustration and demoralization with the increases in teenage gang violence in cities and of young people admitted with alcohol- and drug-related accidents and injuries across the UK and Ireland. The increasing volume of such cases has stretched services and often the first priority has to be medical. Yet the social contexts and circumstances leading to these admissions may also need to be addressed. Should parents and carers be engaged with, and if so, how? What about those troublesome cases where the injuries are minor, where drunkenness or drug overdose is treated successfully?

What responsibilities do health care workers have to intervene where lax parenting controls may be putting young lives at risk? Is there an important role for the hospital to play in a public safety capacity? Can an intervention be structured to highlight the 'lucky escape', empower parents and young people to call a halt to encouragement to engage in risky behaviours, and strengthen a caring network around a vulnerable youngster? What is realistic and how far should interventions go? How can it be informed by solution-focused ideas and philosophies?

The importance of hope

In Chapter 3, I outlined the centrality of hope as a guiding concept in my understanding of solution-focused work. Hope as a motivator; hope as a

---

Box 6.8   Practice example: creating a 'yes-set'

Kelly is a nine-year-old child with a metabolic condition that requires strict adherence to a particular diet, which restricts normal childhood treats such as sweets, crisps, and fizzy drinks. While she was younger, her mother, Paula, did not have too many difficulties in getting her to stick with the diet, but she has struggled with it over the past year. This has meant that Kelly has had two hospital admissions for her condition to be stabilized – admissions that in the eyes of the hospital staff were unnecessary if Paula had only 'done her job' as mother.

The hospital social worker, Clive, knows that the family have had difficult times recently. Kelly's father was killed eighteen months ago in a fight outside a bar; Paula's drug-use has increased in recent times; Kelly's older brother, Lee, has just been given a jail sentence for drug-dealing.

Questions:
1   How might Clive work with Paula and Kelly to create a 'yes-set'?
2   What compliments can he genuinely give – which involve Kelly and Paula's own hard work?
3   How might he frame their difficulties so that they experience a sense of their own coping, their own strengths and potential resources?
4   How might he help them identify how much better life could be and how can he map out a plan with them towards those goals? What are Kelly's dreams and goals? What are Paula's?
5   How might Clive work with the multidisciplinary team to advocate for a less-blaming attitude towards the family?
6   How can he reframe the issues so that the team develop a more positive picture of the family?

Commentary:
Such cases as this can be extremely difficult for hospital staff, evoking as it does concepts of 'good' and 'bad' parents, and staff can revert to blaming attitudes if not helped to acknowledge the difficult feelings such distress evokes in them.

---

transformative energy that helps create new possibilities; hope as the catalyst that all helpers need to offset the dangers of routinized, dehumanized responses to human distress. In health care in particular, the concept of hope has an added significance.

Box 6.9 Practice example: slowing down in emergency care

Naomi is a fourteen-year-old who was admitted to hospital late on a Friday night over the Hallowe'en half-term holidays. She had passed out in a local park after drinking half a bottle of vodka and five cans of cider. Her friends called an ambulance but 'legged' it once the ambulance arrived. Dressed only in a mini-skirt and skimpy T-shirt, Naomi was suffering from hypothermia when she was found. A fake adult I.D. card was found in her handbag and her mobile was used to call her father to the accident and emergency department where Naomi had regained consciousness after treatment. It is now 3 a.m.

Questions:
How to prepare for meeting the father using solution-focused concepts.

1 Can you imagine yourself in the father's shoes – how must he be feeling? What do you think the father's priorities will be?
2 Can you put aside your feelings of frustration that your workplace is now littered every weekend and half-term with drunken, injured teenagers?
3 Can you find a way of slowing yourself down before you meet the father so that you engage him with a calm acceptance and a readiness to hear what he has to say?
4 Can you identify what needs to happen after your meeting with the father to strengthen the caring network for Naomi without pathologizing or blaming either Naomi or her family?

Commentary:
In one paediatric hospital setting, workers have told me of the tendency that can exist for medical staff to reprimand parents about their wayward teenagers, the abuse of hospital resources, and the frustration of medical staff with having to clean up the mess, without first finding out if there are important issues that need to be addressed. In one case, it transpired that the teenage overdoser's father had been recently diagnosed with terminal cancer; in another case, the teenager had been sexually assaulted by an older man.

Conclusions

Health care workers have many opportunities to use a solution-focused philosophy and strategies in their work. Being solution-focused does not mean being unrealistically optimistic about unlikely outcomes, however.

Box 6.10   Practice example: recreating hope

Claire Booth (1992) describes how she recreated hope in her counselling work with HIV sufferers in the days before effective therapies had been produced:

> the language of disease can be reframed, to recreate the person that was eclipsed by the military metaphor. The client can be enlisted to fight back against the virus, using the weapons of nutrition, gentle exercise and a positive focus. The therapist can talk about the 'side effects' of negative thoughts or behaviours, and look for less damaging ones. 'What happens when you do that?', 'How does your partner react?', 'Do you think that is still useful for you?', 'What is different about those times when things were going better?', 'What are you doing differently?', 'How do you manage at some times and not others?' Such questions challenge the view of self as powerless and help recreate the sense of personal agency so often lost during chronic illness. The use of these kinds of questions, simple though they appear, helps build a context of success and control rather than one of defeat and despair.
>
> (Booth, 1992: 39)

Questions:

1 How can you balance encouragement to be hopeful along with a recognition of the pain and fear that serious illness engenders?

2 Is it necessary to go slowly – and to start by naming the fear?

Commentary:

Booth describes how she finds the concept of 'one thing at a time' helpful at the diagnosis stage when shock and despair are often prevailing emotions, 'trying to maintain the delicate balance between reality and hope, despair and struggle, faith and disillusionment' (p. 40).

> Client and therapist together work to make certain important features of ordinary life seem extraordinary. The therapist marvels at how the client has, in face of such daunting obstacles, still managed to have good days. How does he do this? The focus is on how living day to day is a feat in itself and to be wondered at. Sickness is reduced from being a life-style, to being a side effect of having a life.
>
> (Booth, 1992: 39)

Interventions need to be framed within the confines of the medical situation and the patient's own life.

- *As a newcomer* to solution-focused helping, you can review and reframe your own perspective – if it is a problem-saturated view of a patient or family, then practising a more solution-focused frame can bring a new hopefulness to your work. Retaining your hopefulness in the client's ability to bring positive change to their life is central to this approach. You must believe in them.
- *As an experimenter*, wanting to develop your practice further, you can start with generating sequences of questions, tailored to your own work and setting. Use goal-setting, exception-finding, coping and overcoming questions to generate enough to take you through a session. This is an important precursor to using it directly with clients.
- *As an innovator*, committed to establishing a solution-focused practice, you need to think more systemically and strategically. Sometimes work will also be needed at team and unit level to regain a positive approach to work. Feeling that you can make a difference is an important buffer against burnout. Constructing new protocols and interventions with colleagues is one way of regaining some momentum and energy at team or unit level. Helping colleagues to view troublesome or troubled patients with a more helpful and hopeful lens is another effective strategy.

7 The solution-focused helper working with older people and in end-of-life care

> It is hard to have patience with people who say 'There is no death' or 'Death doesn't matter'. There is death. And whatever is matters. And whatever happens has consequences, and it and they are irrevocable and irreversible.
>
> (C.S. Lewis, 1961: 15)

Introduction

Death is part of the human condition. All of us at some stage of our lives need to face not only our own mortality but that of loved ones, relatives, and friends. Death can come suddenly, life can linger slowly, death can come as a relief or it can be seen as a terrible tragedy. Similarly, the experience of bereavement can have many shades of meaning, running the gamut of emotional states and experiences. Given the strength of feeling that loss evokes, as so well articulated by C.S. Lewis, what can solution-focused helping offer the dying and bereaved? While a death is indeed irrevocable and irreversible, are the consequences automatically also so? Or is there scope for sensitive, hope-kindling interventions?

There is a growing recognition in the helping professions of the importance of the quality of care offered to the dying and bereaved people. The hospice and palliative care movements are probably the most significant drivers for improved end-of-life and bereavement care in Western Europe, North America, and the Antipodes. In addition, the organ retention scandals of the 1990s, which publicized undeveloped practices in many hospitals in the UK and Ireland, have led to improved policies and procedures and increased sensitivities to ethical and care issues. Yet, despite great efforts to increase both specialist palliative and hospice services, more people continue to die in hospital or institutional settings than at home or in hospice care (Van Doorslaer and Keegan, 2001). It is reckoned that across the developed world around 80 percent of deaths are predictable and expected, yet the majority of people continue to die in hospital or institutional care. The 2007 mortality statistics gathered for the UK indicate that of over 500,000 people who died that year, roughly a fifth died at home; and less than one-twentieth died in hospice care (www.statistics.gov.uk); most of the remainder were either in hospital or institutional settings.

Location of death is important because it will have a significant influence on the type and quality of care available. Cause of death is also important, as there is some evidence that it alone affects location of death. Mitchell et al. (2005) found that those suffering from dementia were more likely to die in nursing homes, whereas those with cancer either in their own homes or hospitals. However, Canadian researchers claim that a 'paradigm shift' in end-of-life care is occurring across developed countries, as research shows a significant drop in Canadian hospital deaths between 1994 and 2004, down from 77.7 percent to 60.6 percent. This shift in location of death indicates the need for 'increased support of EOL [end-of-life] care in homes and nursing homes . . . as these two sites have increasingly become a default or perhaps chosen place for death and dying' (Wilson et al., 2009: 1757).

The terminology used in this field of care and practice illustrates some of the influential strands in operation. Palliative care is a rather medical term, yet in its fullest description describes very well the range of values and active multidisciplinary work that encapsulates the best of end-of-life and bereavement care.

Box 7.1 Policies and definitions

Palliative care is an approach that improves the quality of life of patients and their families facing the problems associated with life-threatening illness, through the prevention and relief of suffering by means of the early identification and impeccable assessment and treatment of pain and other problems – physical, psychosocial, and spiritual. Palliative care:

- provides relief from pain and other distressing symptoms;
- affirms life and regards dying as a normal process;
- intends neither to hasten or postpone death;
- integrates the psychological and spiritual aspects of patient care;
- offers a support system to help patients live as actively as possible until death;
- offers a support system to help the family cope during the patient's illness and in their own bereavement;
- uses a team approach to address the needs of patients and their families, including bereavement counselling, if indicated;
- will enhance quality of life, and may also positively influence the course of illness;

- is applicable early in the course of illness, in conjunction with other therapies that are intended to prolong life, such as chemotherapy or radiation therapy, and includes those investigations needed to better understand and manage distressing clinical complications (WHO, 2008).

This World Health Organization definition illustrates the medical origin of the term 'palliative care' as a concept in cancer treatment. The more generic term 'end-of-life' care is now increasingly adopted to give an essentially broader, more inclusive frame for work with the dying and bereaved.

The English National Health Service now run a National End of Life Care Programme with a designated website. However, their mission statement suggests that it has a narrow patient-focus: 'To improve the quality of care at the end of life for all patients and enable more patients to live and die in the place of their choice' (www.endoflifecare.nhs.uk/eolc).

In Ireland, an End-of-Life Forum was set up in March 2009 to: 'develop a vision of how modern Ireland can address the challenges of dying, death and bereavement . . . The proceedings and outcomes of the Forum are governed by the principles and values of hospice and palliative care. Life is affirmed and dying is regarded as a normal process. Death is neither hastened nor postponed. Pain and other distressing symptoms are relieved' (www.hospice-foundation.ie).

The interweaving of the hospice movement, palliative care as a medical specialism (and also as a value-based approach to the dying and bereaved), and the emergence of the new term 'end-of-life care' all point to an increased focus and new emphasis on improving this area of health and social care. Why should that be necessary?

Now let us address this question by examining further the diverse needs of those who die.

> Over 500,000 people die each year in England of whom two-thirds will be over 75. Death occurs in a wide variety of settings from hospitals, care homes and hospices to the home. Many people will be transferred many times between these different settings in their last years, months, days and hours. So being responsive to their individual needs and preferences is an enormous challenge.
>
> (www.endoflifecareforadults.nhs.uk/)

Thus, for health and social care workers in the community, in care homes, in hospitals, and in hospices, the older person (defined here purely in age terms as being over seventy-five years) facing death will be part of daily working life. Older people are, of course, not a homogeneous group, although often they are referred to as such. The demographics in most developed societies have changed significantly in recent years. Increased life expectancy, improvements in medical care and treatments for chronic illnesses mean that more people are living longer but now with two distinct phases to 'older age': the third (active and independent) and fourth (frail and dependent) ages. Some of the ethical dimensions of caring for those in the fourth age will be considered later in this chapter. For now it is important to bear in mind that of the two-thirds of people who die each year over the age of seventy-five, many may have been active and independent and for them (and their partners and contemporaries), illness and death may be unexpected and sudden.

The reference in the English quote above to the high proportion of older people who will be moved between different settings prior to death is replicated in Irish figures. Almost 30,000 people die annually in Ireland (Health Services Executive, 2005) and up to 66 percent of all Irish deaths take place in some form of hospital or institution (www.cso.ie), with 40 percent of deaths occurring in acute hospitals (Irish Hospice Foundation, 2006). In a recent Irish study, it was found that of nearly 1000 deaths in a large acute hospital, 63.6 percent of people had spent fifteen days or less in the hospital and 234 (25.1%) were recorded as dying within one day of admission (Walsh et al., 2007). This raises an important practice issue for solution-focused helpers: given the brief and often time-limited nature of contact, what is it ethical to set out to do?

While two-thirds of those who die each year may be over the age of seventy-five years, substantial numbers of younger people also die: children, teenagers, young adults, and those in middle-age. Most of these will be what are termed unexpected or traumatic deaths, many of which will occur in acute hospitals and emergency clinics. Helpers in acute hospitals (from ambulance crew to A&E nurses, attendants and doctors, to hospital porters, mortuary and administrative staff) will all face challenges in relation to the large number of sudden and unexpected deaths that they encounter. Acute hospitals with specialist centres such as oncology, paediatric and neonatal, and neurosurgery services will have increased numbers of patients who will die in tragic and traumatic circumstances following sudden fatal illnesses, workplace accidents, car accidents, assaults, and suicides. What do we know about what helps?

Parallel knowledge bases

The international theoretical and research base around death and bereavement is extensive. One of the reasons for this is that the experience of loss (in many different forms) is seen as central to the human experience and is intrinsically linked with meta-theories such as those on the importance of attachment for healthy psychological development. Significant contributions to the literature have been made by iconic figures such as Kubler-Ross and Murray-Parkes as well as Saunders, founder of the modern British hospice movement. Kubler-Ross (1973) produced one of the first modern theoretical frameworks for understanding the process of coming to terms with terminal illness: a five-stage framework of denial, anger, bargaining, depression, and acceptance. While the notion that there are set stages in the grieving process is no longer accepted by most theorists in the field, Kubler-Ross's pioneering work highlighted the lack of recognition of the subjective experiences of the dying and bereaved at that time. Murray-Parkes set up the first hospice-based bereavement service at St. Christopher's Hospice in London in addition to researching and publishing extensively on bereavement and hospice care (e.g. Murray-Parkes, 1972; Murray-Parkes et al., 1996). Saunders pioneered a modern hospice and palliative care approach to care of the dying, focused on expert pain and symptom relief accompanied by a holistic approach to the care of the dying patient.

Drawing on existing research and a review of the literature (Walsh et al., 2007, 2008), the following points can be made. Although much research in the 1970s to 1990s focused on issues of pathology and risk assessment, it is now generally accepted that most people will recover over time from normal bereavement experiences without any professional interventions or with low-level interventions only (Stroebe and Stroebe, 1987; Bonanno et al., 2004; Prigerson, 2005). Contemporary holistic theorists call for a move to 'normalize' grief and for more community education to improve existing social support systems (Klass et al., 1996; Stroebe and Schut, 1999; Neimeyer, 2001, 2005; Field and Friedrichs, 2004). Evidence does not support the provision of routine specialized therapeutic interventions to all. Different grieving styles and experiences require a choice of intervention approaches responsive to individual need. Interventions should be flexible and customized to suit different genders, cultures, ages, coping styles, and perceived individual need (Jordan and Neimeyer, 2003). The argument is made by some for a public health approach with a view to developing a seamless health care response towards the human experiences of death, dying, and loss, including bereavement care (International Work Group on Death, Dying and Bereavement, 2005). Greater community awareness of grief and bereavement is seen not only to increase people's preparation for death and the community's capacity to support individuals (Nucleus Group, 2004), but to essentially normalize death as an everyday part of life, emphasizing social and collective dimensions of loss (Conway, 2007). Strategies such as self-help/support groups may be particularly relevant where cultural barriers prevent particular groups from accessing traditional service models (e.g. indigenous or immigrant minority groups) (Nucleus Group, 2004).

The indications are that bereavement services located within acute hospitals help the grieving process, provide a positive image of the hospital, and are beneficial to staff. Aspects of care that are particularly valued include sensitive facilitation of viewing the body, privacy, belongings returned considerately, written information on bereavement and available support services, correspondence concerning hospital records and procedures, sympathy cards from staff, phone calls, and referrals to community services where needed (Fauri et al., 2000; Browne et al., 2005). A range of professionals has a role to play in effective palliative and bereavement care. A 'whole-hospital' (or 'whole-institution') approach that encompasses all staff from ambulance crew to mortuary staff, telephony to specialist nurses to clinical managers has been found to be effective in improving the quality of care experienced by the bereaved (Walsh et al., 2007). Relationships and communication with staff are of key importance to the bereaved (Cuthbertson et al., 2000).

Tiered models of outreach care for the bereaved are seen to be the ideal model of care given the variability of individual responses to loss, the importance of building communal and self-help services that normalize the grieving process, and saving specialist interventions only for those who need them (Walsh et al., 2008; Stephen et al., 2009). Outreach services may be needed to reach the bereaved who are not likely to improve with time and informal support but who are unable to access either self-help or professional support. Field et al. (2005) found that the bereaved access support from voluntary bereavement organizations, general medical practitioners, and churches. Those who decline bereavement support services either had enough support from other sources or preferred to cope on their own. The specific needs of caregivers for the dying or bereaved, both formal and informal, are increasingly emphasized (Harding and Leam, 2005; Papadatou, 2006).

Since the early 1990s, many support groups have existed online for those bereaved through suicide, murder, sudden infant death syndrome, for widows and widowers, or for those who have lost a child (Nucleus Group, 2004; Wagner, 2006). For those living in rural areas, or further afield, the Internet can allow access to social support from afar. Today's adolescents turn to cyberspace for information and support in the hunt for immediate results (Oltjenbruns and James, 2006). Bebo.com and Myspace.com are both frequently used to mourn the death of friends, especially those who died tragically through accidents, murder or suicide (Oltjenbruns and James, 2006; Roberts, 2006). In the context of studies that emphasize how marginalized bereaved youth can be (McCarthy, 2007), modern technologies that are particularly accessible to young people have potential. One caution in relation to the use of websites or chatrooms for the bereaved is the potential for copycat actions, particularly relevant for suicides or tragic adolescent deaths. A second is the difficulties of evaluating the benefits of Internet sites (Clark et al., 2004) and there has been little systematic evaluation of their effectiveness (Nucleus Group, 2004).

Memorial services are one communal response to the need for ritual, allowing mourners to experience the support of others and lessen their isolation (O'Reilly, 1990). Feedback from those who attend is generally positive (Ormandy, 1998; O'Connor et al., 2004); they provide an opportunity for both bereaved relatives and nursing home/hospital staff to acknowledge the loss of the deceased.

Schut and colleagues' (2002) review of the effectiveness of general preventative interventions for the bereaved found no evidence that counselling or therapy helped those who did not seek professional help. Specialized interventions are most effective for those suffering from complicated grief who identify themselves as being in need of professional help (Stroebe et al., 2005). The importance of the self-identification of difficulty is therefore established, suggesting that higher awareness of complicated grief reactions among the general public may lead to more individuals self-referring if offered outreach services. One model of 'family focused grief therapy' (Kissane et al., 1998; Kissane and Bloch, 2002) promoting healthy family functioning during palliative care and bereavement has resulted in positive outcomes for families.

Group support may benefit those experiencing traumatic or complicated grief (Neimeyer, 2000; Sikkema et al., 2004). Some research has shown that group intervention for people coping with AIDS-related loss had a positive impact on their general health and quality of life (Goodkin et al., 1998; Sikkema et al., 2004). Farberow (1992) found that participants in a suicide survivor group showed deterioration of some emotional responses after participation. Interventions have also been shown to have negative effects in some cases, such as group interventions for fathers of murdered children (Schut et al., 2002).

British guidelines for best practice recommend that those assessed as being at risk should be engaged with proactively, either by telephone or letter, around eight weeks after their bereavement (NICE, 2004). In one Irish bereavement service for children, time between death to referral varies (O'Daly 2006). The fact that 18 percent of referrals are made over three years after death indicates complicated or ongoing grief reactions can still cause distress and concern years later.

Alongside the development of an extensive research and theoretical/conceptual base into the experiences of death and grief, there have been sociological critiques of the repositioning of loss as primarily an individual experience.

Walter (1994, 1999) examines how both culture and time impact on the phenomenon of bereavement and experiences of loss, grief, and mourning. In tracking the sociology of bereavement (as outlined in the typology in Box 7.2), he demonstrates how the process of bereavement is conceptualized, regulated, and integrated into societal norms and practices.

The social context of bereavement

In related works, Van Doorslaer and Keegan (2001) and O'Connor (2008) adapt this template to demonstrate the range of responses to death in contemporary Irish society, in particular capturing the co-existence of traditional

Box 7.2 A typology table

	Traditional	Modern	Late modern	Postmodern
Social context	Community	Public vs. private	Professional expertise defines private experience	Private experience becomes public
Authority	Religion	Medicine	Therapist	Self
Bereavement experience	Social mourning	Private grief, anomic grief	The grief process, counselling	Expressive/ narrative talk
Required language	Ritual	Stoical reserve	Expressive talk	Expressive/ narrative talk
The dead	Group ancestors	Privately experienced, publicly forgotten	Let go	Live on in conversation

Reprinted with permission from O'Connor (2008), adapted from Walter (1999: 187) and Van Doorslaer and Keegan (2001).

rural practices of 'waking' the dead at home; the community-based nature of rural grieving and the dominance of religious rituals; and more modern urban practices – more often involving secular services and funeral homes/professional funeral directors; expressive/narrative talk in the form of eulogies; and the increased use of both professional and mutual-help individual and group services. In many cases, these traditions or expressions of ritual co-exist together so that there may be a range of ways in which members of the same family or social circle grieve their loss. The tensions between individual and communal responses also have wider societal implications, fuelled in some part by various media giving widespread coverage to celebrity deaths such as Princess Diana and Jade Goody, leading to what has been termed 'a new art of dying' (Conway, 2007).

Walter (1994, 1999) highlights some of the contradictions that exist therein: that in contemporary times we are seen to have postmodern choices to create our own individually unique death rituals, yet all societies still seem to need to tightly regulate 'the intense fears and emotions of those who are dying and grieving' (Walters, 1994: 199). His concerns about the limitations of an individualizing/pathologizing approach to death are echoed by others who espouse a 'public health/community' perspective:

> While accepting that these [health care] services have important roles to play, they can be regarded as regulatory discourses limited by their individualising frameworks. The danger of this is that death and loss

will continue to become privatised and conceptualised as individual rather than societal issues. There is also the further danger of the exclusion of the 'disadvantaged dying'.

(Conway, 2007: 200)

An international charter for the normalization of dying, death, and loss has been produced (International Work Group on Death, Dying and Bereavement, 2005), as a response to the increased medicalization of grief. Essential elements of a public health approach towards end-of-life care include: recognition of the inevitability of death and universality of loss; cultural sensitivity and adaptability; and equal access for all. Greater community awareness of grief and bereavement is seen to increase people's preparation for death, the community's capacity to support individuals, and promotes a more integrated approach to health promotion (Nucleus Group, 2004). The case is also made that the expansion of community education on grief and bereavement could improve the social support networks of the bereaved. Strategies such as self-help/support groups might be particularly relevant where cultural barriers have been found to impact on particular groups accessing traditional service models (e.g. indigenous or immigrant minority groups). Walsh (2007) extends the notion of resilience to encompass 'relational networks' to help families and communities recover from traumatic loss and major disasters. Pointing out that the predominant therapeutic models for treating trauma and survivors of major disasters are individually focused and pathology based, she proposes a

> multisystemic, resilience-oriented practice approach [which] recognises the widespread impact of major trauma, situates the distress in the extreme experience, attends to ripple effects through relational networks, and aims to strengthen family and community resources for optimal recovery.
>
> (Walsh, 2007: 207)

In summary:

- Bereavement should be viewed as a process that occurs over time, where the integration of the experience of loss can be facilitated for most through informal support systems, rituals, and the general accommodation of death and loss in existing social and community networks. The essential process is seen to be one of individual meaning-making, whereby the individual learns to live with their loss in a dual process of letting go and retaining memory.
- The individual's response to loss is multifactorial, and influenced by age, gender, culture, personal, interpersonal, and social factors. A person's prior, current, and subsequent situation and experiences will

also shape the individual reaction. The meaning of the loss to the person, the combination of risk and protective factors, and the level of internal resilience and coping skills are important aspects.

- Bereavement can cause a wide range of practical, social, and emotional needs. Some people will need information about practical matters, finances, processes of grief. Some will benefit from peer support, especially those who are particularly isolated or lacking in social supports themselves. A small number will need more specialist therapeutic intervention.
- Clinical interventions offer most benefit when they are of a high quality, delivered by specially trained professionals and targeted at the 5–20 percent of specific groups who may experience complex or complicated grief, necessitating high-quality risk assessment.
- Service users want a 'human' touch, communication, partnership, and access to advice, information and support that is both accessible and flexible. Parkes (1986) said the bereaved need 'knowledge, normalisation and listening' and this is still what service users themselves are seeking.

The implications of this work for us as strengths-based, solution-focused helpers are important:

- first, because of the emphasis on the need for active, attentive listening when working with the dying and the grieving: 'For people to die and grieve their own way, they need carers who can truly listen . . . But if the revival [of choice] is to succeed, if communities are to be strengthened and a secure base for values laid, then the struggle to keep on listening cannot be abandoned (Walter, 1994: 199–200);
- second, the call for an approach that emphasizes the development of personal skills (which in a solution-focused frame links with the task of 'reminding' distressed or problem-saturated clients of the skills and resources that they do indeed have);
- third, the emphasis on ensuring that the 'disadvantaged dying' – those currently not receiving hospice or palliative care and also minority groups (such as immigrants, ethnic populations, and those with disabilities) – are not excluded from services;
- fourth, recent research work into meaning reconstruction and the experience of loss emphasizes the individual and subjective experience and meaning-making process as being of central importance in understanding how people grieve (Neimeyer, 2001); and finally,
- the reminder that group and communal experiences of loss and grieving can be actively mined to help both normalize the experience and create longer term social networks of support that foster resilience

and the potential for transformation and positive growth: 'Times of great tragedy can bring out the best in the human spirit: ordinary people show extraordinary courage, compassion and generosity in helping kin, neighbors, and strangers to recover and rebuild lives' (Walsh, 2007: 208).

Death, when it occurs, brings to an end for a range of medical, nursing, and clinical support and administrative staff, their role in that individual fight for life. With the urgency of need and the pressure on beds that exist in modern hospital settings, staff must move on quickly to the next patient, the next critical situation, the next emergency. For those in residential care outside of hospice settings, the pace may not be so pressurized but staff still need to grapple with complex issues around the wishes and needs of the dying and how these impact on other residents; and how best to support families and carers in the time before death as well as that following death. But what sense do workers make of these experiences? How do they (and their organizations) frame their role – or, indeed, do they see that they have a role at all in dealing with the dying patient? In the next two sections, we will first consider the personal dimension and then what the ideal organizational framework for improving care for end-of-life and bereavement care might look like and ask you to compare it with your own.

The personal dimension

One experience that is frequently identified by social work and social care students as one of the most challenging in their training is that of working with dying and bereaved clients. While this might partly be to do with the age profile of many students – most often in their twenties and many without any experience to date of the loss of a significant other – it also points to the centrality of loss experiences in our own personal biographies as being an important influence on how we work in this area. On many professional courses, special attention is paid to this area because it does have such an impact. An important start, therefore, is to examine our own experiences (and fears) around getting old, death, and loss.

The organizational dimension

In July 2008, the English NHS launched a government strategy for end-of-life care that 'aims to provide adults approaching the end of life with more choice about where they would like to be cared for and die. It encompasses all adults with advanced, progressive illness and care given in all settings'

Box 7.3 Reflective exercise: taking stock of death and loss

My first experience of death was at a distance – that of my grandmother's sudden death in Co. Cork and my parents' need to travel to her funeral. This coincided with my sixth birthday and eagerly awaited birthday party. My only fear was that my party would need to be cancelled. This concern superseded any sensitivity to my father's grief and loss.

My second experience was that of my aunt's eagerly awaited first child and her travel from a rural part of Ireland to stay with us in Dublin before the birth in the 1960s. Childbirth was not actively managed in those days and she was in labour for three days before an 'emergency' caesarian was performed. Her big baby boy, weighing over ten pounds, was born severely brain-damaged and died a few hours later. The house was full of sadness for weeks as all the baby clothes, Moses basket, and toiletries were put away. Quietness, sadness, and grief filled the house at this time.

My first experience of seeing a dead person was when I was eighteen years old and working as a nurse's aide in a convalescent hospital setting. One of the older patients died after a short illness. His death on a public ward, with the curtains drawn and family and priest present, was expected and peaceful. Following death it was my task, together with two male orderlies, to prepare him for removal to the mortuary. I was unprepared for the crude humour the orderlies used while we completed this task (after family and priest had departed). I was shocked by what I saw as disrespect for the dead.

My first experience of the death of someone close was when my father died unexpectedly of cancer of the pancreas, when in his sixties, in an acute hospital, when I was twenty-two. His death had a profound effect. Most of all a sense of distress and anger towards the hospital for their 'failure' to save him and for the pain and loss of dignity he suffered in his final days. My father had been moved from an intensive care bed to a side-room with no facilities in his last two days, as his distress was upsetting other patients. He died ten days after being admitted to hospital for exploratory surgery. The cause of death was peritonitis.

Reflection on the effects of these experiences on my work in this area now:

Young children have their own priorities; often rooted in the here and now of their own lives. I now understand why some helpers use dark humour as a defence mechanism against the psychic pain of working closely with the ill and dying through my exposure to psychoanalytic theory, especially work on defence mechanisms against anxiety. My aunt's experiences remind me of the significant losses through stillbirth and early childhood death that parents experience. My father's death in such pain makes me a committed advocate for developing better end-of-life services, not only in nursing and hospice centres but also in acute hospitals.

Exercise:

1 Describe your own experiences of loss and death as far back as you can remember.

2 Consider how these experiences impacted on you at the time: How did you feel? What helped and hindered?

3 Consider how these experiences impact on you now – in what ways do they influence the work you do and your orientation to the work you do?

(www.dh.gov.uk/en/Healthcare/IntegratedCare/Endoflifecare). While this provides a useful policy imperative for championing improved practices and innovative approaches, the exemplars outlined on their website demonstrate how this is a 'work-in-progress'; a driver for improved practices but with still a long way to go. Key components of improved services are seen to include, wherever possible, elements of a good death such as:

- being treated as an individual, with dignity and respect;
- being without pain and other symptoms;
- being in familiar surroundings; and
- being in the company of close family and/or friends.

(www.dh.gov.uk/en/Healthcare/IntegratedCare/Endoflifecare)

Important as these elements are to the construction of sensitive and appropriate services for the dying and grieving, their pursuit must be tempered with the recognition of the utter variability of death: 'The physical diversity of modes of death, from traffic accident to frail old age, indicates that no one idea of the "peaceful" death can characterise every death' (Walter, 1994: 199).

It has been suggested that the NICE guidelines should be adopted for hospital and community health settings in Britain. This guide suggests a three-tier model of bereavement support to ensure that the bereaved have access to support to facilitate grieving and to prevent any detrimental consequences: (i) provision of information; (ii) access to bereavement support; and (iii) specialized interventions. Bereavement support should be provided in such a way that encourages people to use their own resources and network (NICE, 2004). Health care professionals are likely to be most effective if they provide support to natural helpers, including family, neighbours, friends, and 'members of familiar religious, social or business groups' (Center for the Advancement of Healthcare, 2003: 69). While bereaved individuals are likely to display a wide range of grieving styles and experiences, the most fundamental need is for information, support, and acceptance.

Box 7.4   Reflective exercise

---

1   Taking the core components of a 'good death' as outlined by the NHS above, consider how your organization or agency might rate, on a scale of 0 to 10, in meeting these standards:

   (a)   Being treated as an individual, with
       dignity and respect   0 1 2 3 4 5 6 7 8 9 10
   (b)   Being without pain and other symptoms 0 1 2 3 4 5 6 7 8 9 10
   (c)   Being in familiar surroundings   0 1 2 3 4 5 6 7 8 9 10
   (d)   Being in the company of close family
       and/or friends   0 1 2 3 4 5 6 7 8 9 10

2   Can you list three actions that you can take in your current capacity to improve ratings?
3   Can you name three actions that need to take place at an organizational level that could improve ratings?

Ethical considerations

For both the dying patient and the bereaved, the concept of a 'good death' is important, one

> free from avoidable distress and suffering for patients, families and caregivers; in general accord with the patients' and families' wishes; and reasonably consistent with clinical, cultural and ethical standards. A bad death in turn, is one that is characterised by needless suffering, dishonouring of patient and family wishes or values, and a sense among participants or observers that norms of decency have been offended.
>
> (Trice and Prigerson, 2009: 96)

Yet, for the approximately 20 percent of deaths each year that result from accidents, suicide, violence, and traumatic conditions, circumstances at the time of death may not be ideal. What, then, are the principles that need to be adopted to ensure that whatever the circumstances, the best that is possible is done for the comfort of the dying person and those bereaved?

Ethical issues abound when working with a patient or resident who is terminally ill. Issues arise in terms of balancing the voice and needs of the patient and their loved ones, as well as in relation to balancing the medical

---

Box 7.5   Practice example: competing needs at the time of death

---

Millie is a woman in her mid-fifties, married with adult children. She has been hospitalized due to severe pain resulting from a terminal brain tumour. Although she is still lucid, she is asking for any relief possible from the pain. Her husband and adult sons want a planned operation to go ahead that might prolong her life but also is likely to result in increased pain and discomfort.

Questions:
1   How are Millie's needs and the wishes of the family to be balanced?
2   Who is going to help them make this decision in the hospital?
3   What potential use are solution-focused questions in this scenario?

Commentary:
Although there is a range of ethical frameworks of potential value in dealing with complex end-of-life issues, the most widely used and espoused is that called the Four Principles approach to health care ethics (Gillon, 1994; Beauchamp and Childress, 2001). The four principles are:

(i)   *Beneficence*: the obligation to provide benefits, to do some good – to improve health and well-being.
(ii)   *Non-maleficence*: the obligation to avoid harming the patient.
(iii)   *Respect for autonomy*: the obligation to respect the decision-making capacities of autonomous persons.
(iv)   *Justice*: obligations of fairness in the distribution of benefits and risks.

The four principles are all important but no one of them is superior or takes precedence over all the others. In any given situation, the circumstances and relative worth of each of the principles need to be weighed up in reaching a final decision. Confidentiality, truth-telling, and informed consent are three other commonly cited values in health care, which in the Four Principles approach are incorporated under non-maleficence and respect for autonomy.

---

care and interventions offered – Is too little being done? Is too much being done? Are some patients offered better interventions than others? How are these decisions made?

Although advocated by health care professionals, the Four Principles approach (or principlism) has been criticized by others for its rather prescriptive, formulaic approach to the resolution of ethical issues. McBeath and Webb (2002), among others, argue for a 'virtue ethics' (VE): 'Instead of focusing on moments of decision, on the dilemmas of action in our morally complex world, VE stresses the character of the moral agent' (Campbell, 2003: 292). Through self-examination, using a blend of 'intuition, reasoned choice and empathy's for one's fellow humans' (ibid.), a resolution to an ethical dilemma can be sought. Houston (2003) raises concerns about the central issue of how virtue is defined and established in the first instance, although he favours the approach above the more rule-bound, defensive approach taken in some social care fields of practice for its reflexive-interpretative process. Drawing on the German philosopher Habermas, he proposes that important elements of decision-making include inclusivity, open communication, impartiality, and empathy.

Because of the heightened emotions that accompany personal beliefs of 'the right' resolution of ethical dilemmas in end-of-life care, there is an increasing recognition of the need for a team approach to decision-making, which can incorporate medical, nursing, social work, and family perspectives in reaching the best decision in individual cases. Finally, it is worth remembering that:

> The increasing popularity of living wills, the interest throughout the modern world in euthanasia, the publicity given in the UK to the idea of the Natural Death Centre, the flexing of muscle by American patients, all indicate a vociferous minority of people who want to control their own dying and death. Minority though they be, they cannot but cause doctors [and other health care helpers] to stop and think before paternalistically assuming they know what dying patients want or need.
>
> (Walter, 1994: 198)

Let us now examine some of the most common issues that emerge when caring for the terminally ill and the bereaved.

Communication and truth-telling

Many of the complaints that hospitals receive relate to issues of information-giving and communication around terminal illnesses or conditions, and is an area of some complexity.

> Underlying the principles of achieving a good death, however, are the basic assumptions that patients want to know, are told, and accept that death is coming. Unfortunately, for oncologists [and other medics] alike there remains uncertainty regarding how to avoid distress, suffering, and the dishonouring of patient wishes while participating in communication of diagnosis, and prognosis and during the transition from active treatment to end-of-life care.
>
> (Trice and Prigerson, 2009: 96)

Trice and Prigerson's research suggests that there are still problems in communication between doctors and terminally ill patients, often exacerbated when there is a significant class and status imbalance between doctor and patient or where time is not given for patient and family to both absorb the prognosis and take time to consider its implications. 'Peacefully aware' patients who accept the prognosis and engage in proactive planning for their death through advance care directives were found to 'have the highest overall quality of death as reported by their caregivers . . . In turn, surviving caregivers of peacefully aware patients are more physically and mentally healthy six months post-loss than caregivers of patients who were "aware" but not peaceful' (Trice and Prigerson, 2009: 102). Palliative-care practitioners suggest the art of breaking bad news in the best possible way relates both to whether information is given gradually or in one blunt session and also to the timing of a confirmed terminal prognosis to avoid depression and loss of hope.

Assisted dying and euthanasia

These are issues that trigger strong emotional reactions not only in many health care professionals but among ordinary people. Most emotive are cases that involve progressive diseases that are painful, involve paralysis or relentless loss of function. High-profile right-to-die court cases in both the USA (Terri Shiavo) and UK (Diane Pretty) led to much public debate on the issues involved, as do current cases of individuals who travel to Dignitas in Switzerland for an assisted death. Many people voice opinions that left in intolerable situations themselves they might want to exercise the option. Yet for health and social care professionals, codes of ethics generally rule out any potential involvement. While doctors and nurses with the influence of the palliative care movement generally now accept death as a natural end to life and avoid inappropriate interventions, most oppose any moves to legalize euthanasia. Reasons include: the research base on the levels of depression in those with a terminal illness, which, if treated, can significantly improve general psychological well-being in the end stages of life; the complex emotions of guilt and despair that are part of the process of accepting a diagnosis of terminal illness; and the numbers of patients who may not be thinking clearly, who may lack the capacity to make a reasoned decision or may need to be protected against the risks of being encouraged to engage in euthanasia in the context of expanding need and diminishing resources for health care provision.

Specific ethical issues relating to dementia

Dementia is a loss of brain function that occurs with certain diseases. The two most common syndromes are Alzheimer's disease and vascular dementia, both of which are irreversible. Dementia with Lewy bodies (DLB) is another common form of dementia. Dementia usually occurs in older age and is rare below the age of sixty years. As the number of older people living for longer increases, so also has the subset with dementia. Once diagnosed, treatment is focused on reducing symptoms such as changed sleeping patterns, disorientation, decreases in communication and problem-solving skills, and maintaining independent living skills for as long as possible. Advanced care directives can be drawn up when a person is still able to make decisions, and these can be of use subsequently in deciding on the care plan. One problem that may arise, however, is that advances in medical science in the intervening period may make better treatments or interventions available that were not factored into the advanced care directive. In this case, health care professionals can face difficulties fulfilling their ethical commitments.

A second practice dilemma that can arise in dementia care is that of balancing the needs of clients and carers, especially when the State is heavily reliant on the services of unpaid family and relative carers against a backdrop of tight budgetary constraints for formal State nursing and hospital care. In such cases, Wilson et al. (2009) advocate an approach that assesses and weights up the needs of both client and carer in trying to work out the best outcome. Wilson et al. (2009) also provide an alternative perspective on the needs of those with dementia as advocated by Kitwood (1997), who highlights the need for a person-centred approach to dementia care, one that endeavours to maintain 'personhood' for as long as possible, rather than biomedical management of different symptoms. This is very much the approach that Mary Warnock (2009) calls for in work with all older people (see Box 7.7).

An ethical issue that may well arise relates to the sharing of information by family members with care staff; sometimes sensitive or confidential information that the person with dementia, were they not to be ill, would not wish to have divulged. In such cases, the practice principle that if it is in the client's best interests and will benefit them in enhanced care, then such information can be shared on a 'need to know' basis.

Ethical dilemmas in working with older people

When working with older people, Lloyd (2006) suggests that feminist ethics of care (although now relating both to men's and women's caring roles) has a lot to offer. She identifies the relationship or dynamic between rights, justice, and care as being of particular importance, and taking the example of English social policies such as the expansion of direct payments (for people to commission care and support services for themselves in their own homes) she highlights the assumptions of autonomy, independence, and rationality that underpin such policies, whereby 'The interpersonal and emotional dimensions

---

Box 7.6 Practice example: end-stage dementia and peg-feeding*

Mary is an eighty-two-year-old patient in a nursing home with vascular dementia. Her condition has deteriorated in recent months and she is now in end-stage dementia. One characteristic of this stage can be a lack of appetite/refusal to eat. Care and medical staff need to make a decision on whether to commence artificial peg-feeding, a procedure that causes discomfort and a certain amount of pain as well as a risk of infection and complications. Her family are distressed and adamant that she must not 'be starved'.

Question:
How can this ethical dilemma be resolved, using the Four Principles approach?

Commentary:
The first test is beneficence – that the intervention needs to be of benefit to the patient. The common-sense belief would be that it is of benefit because it will keep her alive. In many circumstances this is true. It is a validated intervention that has been shown to be of benefit. But what if research shows (Finucane et al., 1999; Rimon et al., 2005) that those who are peg-fed in end-stage dementia do not in fact live longer? Then, it is arguable whether the intervention brings a benefit.

The second test is non-maleficence – that the intervention avoids harming the patient. But peg-feeding can have many complications and unpleasant side-effects, so a guarantee cannot be given under this test.

The third test is that of autonomy – but for a person with dementia, communication problems and confusion can make it difficult if not impossible to know what they want, let alone determine competence to make a decision. If so, can the issue of what this patient would have wanted if she had been in a position to make a decision and communicate it be worked out with her family? There are some dangers in this but in general it is certainly better that a decision is reached with the family, after they have been fully informed of the issues involved. The provision of clear and unbiased information is important here; in addition, the family need to know that loss of appetite is an end-stage symptom in dementia just as it is with some cancers. The question can be posed to them: If she had cancer, did not feel like eating and was refusing food, would you want to peg-feed her?

The fourth test is that of justice – a final balancing up of the benefits and risks of this intervention. If Mary is terminally ill and is refusing food, and if her family still insist that she should be peg-fed even if it does not prolong her life and does cause discomfort and possible infection, should someone act as advocate for Mary to work out a decision?

* With acknowledgment to Dr Regina McQuillan, Palliative Care Consultant, St. Francis Hospice/ Beaumont Hospital, Dublin.

of human life have been overlooked through our preoccupation with individual rights' leading to 'a partial and impoverished view of the human condition' (p. 1175) and a less than adequate understanding of the human need for care. The human need for care, central to the development of the autonomous adult, needs to be recognized in debates about rights and justice. Like Houston (2003), Lloyd places a heavy emphasis on the relational and contingent dimensions to moral decision-making. She describes research conducted by Minichiello et al. (2000) that showed that, for older people, increased dependency was dreaded: 'These older people showed an acute awareness of the risks inherent in being seen to have become "decrepit" and they often went to great lengths to avoid giving the impression that they were "giving up" ' (Lloyd, 2006: 1180). Lloyd makes the point that the right of both articulate and vulnerable older people to be heard requires care on the part of professionals and helpers in powerful positions, in order for it to become a meaningful reality. Finally,

> Hearing older people's voices is therefore a complex matter at all levels . . . The moral orientation of those in contact with older people is crucial to establishing the conditions in which older people can articulate their needs and perceptions. However, this entails also recognition of older people's rights without making assumptions that older people must take responsibility for asserting these.
>
> (Lloyd, 2006: 1182)

Solution-focused helping with older people and their families/carers

For both fiscal/pragmatic and consumer expectation reasons, in official policy an increasing emphasis is now placed on maintaining older people in independent living situations for as long as possible; older people in this 'third age' of being active and independent are lauded and referred to as having 'grey power'. Those in the fourth age of increasing dependency and need for services are treated somewhat differently:

> Those in the third age (active and independent) are able to engage with the agenda of individual responsibility and self-care while those in the fourth age (frail and dependent) are not regarded as having rights but must rely on the discretion and benevolence of others to care for them.
>
> (Lloyd, 2006: 1173)

This change in status and independence is an important watershed in the journey through life but one beset by ageist assumptions and prejudices. Mary Warnock (2009) writes powerfully about her experiences of getting older.

Warnock's call is for us to treat each older person as an individual with their own particular likes and dislikes so that we can protect them 'against a life bereft of any of the pleasures they value'. Does solution-focused helping have a role in this?

Solution-focused concepts have been used successfully in work with older populations by Bonjean (1997, 2003), Dahl et al. (2000), and Seidel and Hedley (2008). None claim that they have provided an evidence base to demonstrate

---

Box 7.7 Case study: Baroness Mary Warnock – Don't call me vulnerable just because I am growing older

'What [do] we think is the role of the old in society, now that they are getting so very old and so very numerous? First, we have to ask who should count as old. Chronology is no longer enough to define a category of people who, as we are often told, are "vulnerable". I am often shocked when I realize that some people are counted among the old who are 20 years younger than I, simply on the grounds that they are retired or have grandchildren.

Of course we know that people age at different rates, according to their genes, their health or their environment; but many people in their 60s and 70s are no more vulnerable than the rest of the population, all of whom, after all, are pretty vulnerable: they may be robbed, mugged, run over by a bus, choked by a field of rape the local farmer has sown next to their house, fall victim of swine flu, whatever their age.

In fact, the very concept of vulnerability is suspect, if applied to the old as a class defined solely by date of birth, It should be reserved for those who are manifestly at risk, those whose bones, or grasp of reality, have become fragile, or who have become blind, or unable to walk . . . I believe that I am as capable as any other householder of detecting a bogus offer from a cowboy builder, or a fraudulent telephone call offering me the chance to win millions of pounds. That is a matter of education and common sense, not of age. Nor does the fact of living alone itself render me vulnerable, as people often suppose . . . I'm certain that I am not the only old person who does not want to be pitied or patronized, but left to get on with life on my own, until that becomes impossible . . .

Looking after the old ought essentially to be a matter of trying to understand what they like and hate, what they have always liked and hated, and of trying to protect them, not against their own supposed mental frailty and dependence, but against a life bereft of any of the pleasures they value.'

(*Observer*, 17 May 2009, p. 31, my emphasis; reprinted with permission)

that solution-focused helping is superior to other forms but the more nuanced findings give some rationale for its use with older people.

Bonjean (2003) suggests that solution-focused techniques are ideal for reminding older people who may be disheartened with life of the lessons that they have learnt and the strengths they have shown over a lifetime. In particular, solution-focused questions about how they have found solutions in the past can be powerfully drawn on to boost self-esteem and restore a sense of competency.

In Tucson, Arizona, Dahl and her colleagues (2000) carried out research to examine the clinical efficacy and cost-effectiveness of treating 'seniors' with solution-focused therapy through an outreach 'wellness-based' nursing programme. Data were collected from 46 patients who received two or more sessions of SFT for a range of problems, including depression, anxiety, marital, family and relationship problems, and stress related to chronic illness and loss of functioning. Most participants were aged between seventy and seventy-five years; there were more women than men and all lived in the community. A standardized scale – the Global Assessment of Functioning (GAF) – was used before and after the intervention; patient satisfaction questionnaires and self-scaling questions were also used. The findings pointed to modest increases in both self-scaling scores and GAF scores but high motivation and satisfaction scores. In all,

> 95% of the patients exhibited clinical improvement by moving at least one self-scaling point from the first to the last session . . . Both GAF and self-scaling scores increased in the same direction . . . preliminary results indicate that SFT is clinically effective with seniors. High patient satisfaction scores also show SFT was well accepted by elderly patients. Finally cost-effectiveness was demonstrated by significant rates of improvement achieved within very few sessions.
>
> (Dahl et al., 2000: 45–56)

Seidel and Hedley (2008) make the case for the suitability of SFT with older clients due to the extent to which age-related challenges may hinder more traditional and time-intensive therapeutic interventions. Their Mexican study recruited Spanish-speaking people, aged sixty or over, who had identified a problem in their lives and were motivated to attend therapy sessions. Recruits to the study were aged between sixty and eighty-six years and consisted of seventeen women and three men. Problems ranged from relationship difficulties to reduced psychological well-being due to sadness, depression, worry, health or loss. The twenty participants were allocated to either the treatment or control group. The treatment group received three sessions of solution-focused behavioural therapy (SFBT) consisting of seven solution-focused elements (scaling questions, outcome questions, exception-finding questions, the miracle question, relationship questions, solution questions, and compliments). Standardized measures were used for the pre- and post-test measurements, including a Spanish language Stress Appreciation Scale for Older Adults, the Lambert Therapy Outcome questionnaire, a Participant and Assessor Problem Severity rating scale, and a Participant Goal Achievement Rating scale. The treatment group showed significant differences and medium to large effect sizes between the pre- and post-test scores, although the effect sizes did not quite reach clinical significance, leading the authors to conclude that 'this study provides tentative support for the provisional inclusion of SFBT as a treatment model for the older age population in Mexico' (Seidel and Hedley, 2008: 251).

Solution-focused therapy and residential/nursing home care

Sidell (1997) and Ingersoll-Dayton et al. (1999) specifically promote solution-focused helping for helping families to adjust to nursing home care and for addressing 'problem behaviours' among nursing home residents, respectively. Bonjean (1989) emphasized the need for systemic family-focused interventions to address the developmental and relational context and provide flexible solutions that take into consideration the needs of all members of the family in which one individual has Alzheimer's.

Building on the work of Bonjean (1989, 1997) and Ingersoll-Dayton and Rader (1993), Ingersoll-Dayton et al. (1999) focused on problem behaviours among residents, most frequently encountered when patients have dementia. In a small research study in one nursing home, they devised a solution-focused intervention offered to both nursing staff and family members of residents with dementia who were either verbally or physically aggressive or wandering. The innovative programme – an individualized Suggested Approaches Plan – was built on both family members' and nursing aides' views of what worked in alleviating the problem behaviours and exceptions to the problem. The results were not significantly different between the experimental group and control group in terms of improved behaviours. However, some problems with research design were identified that may have contributed to this, in particular the small numbers of residents involved (just twenty-one), and the possibility of a 'generalization effect' in that both experimental and control groups came from the same areas of the nursing home and the same staff covered both groups. Nonetheless, some of the results were promising: for those who received the solution-focused intervention, both nursing staff and family members were more agreed about problem behaviours and

> nurse's aides and family members reported significant changes over time in wandering and aggression among residents. Specifically, they

indicated that both problem behaviors decreased in their frequency and severity. In addition they experienced more mastery over these problem behaviors over time.

(Ingersoll-Dayton et al., 1999: 59)

Ingersoll-Dayton et al. (1999) highlight the particular importance of nurses' aides (or care staff) in determining the quality of the care experienced by residents. As they provide most of the direct care to residents, they develop 'a special understanding of residents' needs and desires. They often observe what exacerbates residents' problem behaviors and then develop strategies for preventing and managing such problems' (p. 50). Family members can often be considered as more of a hindrance than a help by nursing home staff, yet they are an 'often overlooked resource'. The Suggested Approaches Plan combines the family members' ability to offer emotional support and helpful biographical information to nursing home staff with nurses' aides' intimate knowledge of the resident's current issues and their professional skill and experience in developing strategies for managing problem behaviours. The Plan establishes useful communication channels between the two and encourages collaborative, solution-building action. One example cited by the authors gives a good illustration of how carers' perceptions can be altered (and empathy and tolerance increased) when historical information is shared by family members:

> For example, nurse's aides were frustrated by one resident who hoarded food, clothing, and other items in her dresser drawer. When her daughter explained that her mother's preoccupation with possessions began when her farmhouse had burnt to the ground during the Depression, the nurse's aides had more understanding for the resident's insecurity. Together with the daughter, they sought alternative approaches for providing her with a sense of security.
>
> (Ingersoll-Dayton et al., 1999: 61)

Let us now look at how these practice tips can be applied to your work.

Sidell (1997) notes how little attention has been paid to the move to nursing care as a significant life event, both for the resident and their family, and the importance of managing this transition well for the benefit of both resident and family. The task for a solution-focused helper is 'to help those affected find a new way of living' (p. 25).

For the incoming resident, losses can be multiple and include 'adjustment to group living, loss of health, disruption of personal space, loss of self-esteem, a sense of separation from family, friends and the immediate community and decreased opportunities to retain a sense of meaning in life' (Sidell, 1997: 22). Against this, however, can be countered the advantages of a move to

---

Box 7.8   Practice principles: generating solutions to problem behaviours among nursing home residents with dementia (Ingersoll-Dayton et al., 1999)

At the organizational level

1   Ensure a consistency in resident care over time. The solution-focused approach was generally more effective when nursing assistants worked with the same residents over time – they developed a greater appreciation for the unique history of the resident and what worked in managing behaviours.

2   Intervene at multiple levels within the nursing home. Managers, nursing directors, and care/nursing staff all need to be included in psychosocial interventions. The support of supervisors is essential if direct care staff are to feel confident in this work. Also, a well functioning communication system is needed whereby staff can share strategies and solution behaviours with each other.

3   Careful planning for how to approach and involve family members. The emphasis should be on their involvement being a resource and the wish of the staff to collaborate with them, support each other, and work together to devise effective solutions.

A caveat to the assumption that involving family members is always a good thing (or indeed that it is unproblematic) can be provided by recalling the family inter-actions in the TV series The Sopranos *when Tony's mother, Lydia, was both in hospital and residential care; similarly when Uncle Junior entered a nursing home. Family politics continued to play and be played out!*

At the individual level

1   Involve direct care/nursing staff. Research has already established that when involved, they identify effective strategies for dealing with the problems.

2   Actively mine and share the resident's history to increase empathy and toler-ance among staff. Include positive qualities and pleasant interactions in the past as well as useful biographical information that helps contextualize current problem behaviours.

3   Include and welcome the resident's family not only in visiting but in frequent contacts with staff. Develop multiple care-giving strategies and try them out. No one approach is likely to be successful in the long term.

---

residential care for those still with independent living skills: for older people living alone for whom completing daily chores has become a struggle, there can also be a relief in relinquishing this responsibility and handing them-selves over to be cared for and, in the right setting, nursing home care can offer more stimulation, more opportunities to socialize and consequently less loneliness.

For families, a parent's move into residential/nursing care can engender complex emotions and ambivalent stressful feelings. Sidell (1997) lists these to include: 'stress surrounding the placement decision, distorted expectations of what the nursing home is like, uncertainty in knowing how to respond to perceived deficiencies in care, role ambiguity, discomfort in visiting, chronic grief and loss reactions, decision making dilemmas and the imminence of death' (p. 23). She suggests, first, that solution-focused principles can offset the 'extreme sense of helplessness' often experienced as long as the helper remains mindful of each family's uniqueness and looks 'for what is right and try to use it' (p. 26). Her emphasis on the need to establish (rather than assume) the impact of a move to nursing care for the resident and their family leads to an acceptance that interventions cannot be constructed according to a norm but need to be built on an individual basis tailored to that family's unique needs and coping skills. Hence the solution-focused technique of establishing past experiences, successes, strengths, and resilience comes into play. Second, to allow solution-building, close attention needs to be paid to the specific meaning of the transition for this person given their past and present resources and coping strategies. Third, for family members overwhelmed by the transition, discouraged or hopeless, the solution-focused emphasis on small specific concrete goals can be helpful:

> A family member feeling overwhelmed with the transition related to the nursing home might forget that coping is possible. This approach stresses small measures of success that the family member might not otherwise focus on. The emphasis is on what is possible and changeable.
>
> (Sidell, 1997: 28)

The technique of focusing on exceptions allows for the identification of the moments in the day, the diversions, the pleasurable activities still available that help adaptation to the changed situation.

Solution-focused therapy in end-of-life and bereavement care

> Counseling a terminally ill client means facing the dying process with that person and helping her or him make sense of the loss of life.
>
> (Itzhaky and Lipschitz-Elhawi, 2004: 51)

Butler and Powers (1996) point to the surprise often expressed by solution-

---

Box 7.9 Practice example: language use

Molly is an eighty-four-year-old widow who was admitted to your nursing home from hospital following a fall. She is French but has lived in England for over fifty years. She has no family but for over twenty years has shared her inner-city rented flat with a lodger, Bill. She has been diagnosed as suffering from dementia with Lewy bodies and needs high-support nursing care. She wanders and is often verbally abusive (in French) to staff, especially when they are dressing or bathing her.

Questions:
1   How might you work on both organizational and individual levels, using the principles listed earlier, to generate some care-giving strategies for Molly?
2   What other ideas do you have for how Molly's welfare might be advanced?
3   How might you use solution-focused questions with both Molly and staff?

Commentary:
Speaking in French to Molly may be a useful strategy. It is possible that she has reverted to speaking and thinking in French with the advent of dementia. She may still express her views, which should form the centre point of any interventions.

---

focused trainees that the approach could be used with terminally ill or grieving clients. Yet, Insoo Kim Berg provided an early powerful example of its use with a dying young woman in London in the training audiotape *Dying Well* (Berg, 1993). In this piece of work, Insoo helps the young woman to identify what it is she wants to achieve before she dies. For the young woman, a former sex worker dying of HIV/AIDS who had a somewhat troubled life, some contact with her estranged family is a key goal. Insoo works slowly, sensitively, and with compassion to help this young woman figure out what she can achieve in the short time she has left, while not offering any false reassurance or false hope.

Insoo, who died suddenly in 2007, when in her early seventies, had a few years previously described in an interview what life and death meant for her (see Box 7.10).

Gray et al. (2000) developed a model of solution-focused helping for use with bereavement groups in rural communities in the USA, emphasizing how the focus on coping and adapting draws on experiences of the group members. It adopts techniques of negotiating goals and possibilities, using future-oriented questions, scaling questions, and expectations about ability to cope. Morrison (2007) suggests that a solution-focus can be a process whereby others are helped 'to find *their* own answers, responses or ways of acknowledging the

---

Box 7.10   Case study: reflections on life and death

Berg: What am I living for? What is the purpose of living on? What do I want to do with the time I have left? That kind of stuff. I'd like to be able to . . . I don't know whether I'll have the opportunity or not . . . to say on my deathbed (this picture of one dying, surrounded by friends and family . . . who knows? It may never happen that way). I'd like to be able to say I had a good life. And what's the definition of a good life? I made some difference. That's it. If I could just say that. I've made some difference because I've been here in this world. Life is a little bit better and I contributed to that. I think that would be a good life.

(Interview with Insoo Kim Berg, 2003: www.psychotherapy.net; accessed June 2009)

---

realities of their lives.' (p.165, original emphasis) and that bereavement work needs to be person-centred, attending closely to the individual's experience, and allowing them to continue to live with the presence of the lost loved ones. Rituals can be important, as can narrative work (White and Epston, 1990), which allows the bereaved to 're-story' their lives to incorporate the loss.

Butler and Powers (1996) and de Castro and Guterman (2008) provide informed and technically detailed examples of how SFT can be used in grief work and with families coping with suicide, respectively. In framing solution-focused helping as having at its core a dual process of acknowledgement (or validation) and possibility (a hopeful future-focused frame), Butler and Powers describe the particular need to go at the client's pace and follow the client's lead in grief work:

> When the issue is grief, it is especially important to move at the client's pace. Obviously, the reinforcing behaviours often associated with solution-focused therapy – smiles, exclamations, and gestures – need to be toned down for the grieving client. Any tendency for the therapist to be ahead of the client, or to minimize pain, will shut down the process and possibly result in the client dropping out . . . prematurely.
>
> (Butler and Powers, 1996: 242)

In the work of de Castro and Guterman (2008) also, the emphasis is on staying with the client's current state of loss for as long as this takes, even into a second or third session. Language needs to be adapted to allow for the state of loss and sadness, so question sequences may be focused on how someone is 'coping', how they stop things from 'getting worse', or how they manage to get up and get on with life, day after day. The shift of attention from validation to possibilities needs to be managed with sensitivity. Butler and Powers suggest that future-focused questions are particularly useful in grief work, as they serve to elicit clients' own goals and enable them to construct their own solutions as opposed to being prescriptive. Although they suggest that the Miracle Question is useful, others have found that it needs to be amended. The Miracle Question was not considered to be appropriate in work with nursing home residents and their families (Sidell, 1997) or with cancer patients (Neilson-Clayton and Brownlees, 2002) in its original format; however, it can still be used in an adapted form when made more specific to address the current difficulties.

Pre-suppositional future-oriented questions are asked in a sequence to allow for as detailed a picture as possible to be constructed of how life might be – the future life to be aspired to. Exception-finding, coping, and scaling questions are also recommended, as are relational questions that link the individual client's experience with family, friends, relatives, and neighbours who form a natural support network in the community. As with much other solution-focused work, the emphasis is on positive behaviours, exceptions, and signs of hope in as much detail as possible. Goal-setting is also important if the work is not to drift. The essence of the work is maintaining a dual focus: 'continuing to acknowledge difficulty while pursing the possibilities' (Butler and Powers, 2006: 242).

Spirituality is another element of grief work highlighted and discussed by Butler and Powers (2006) and de Castro and Guterman (2008). Butler and Powers (2006) have found that often a resolution of grief appears to involve a belief in a God and that 'SFBT is inherently respectful of people's spiritual beliefs. Because the model is focused on clients and their natural resources, people feel free to discuss their spiritual values' (p. 238). de Castro and Guterman (2008) provide a detailed examination of how solution-focused helping works with families coping with suicide. They emphasize the need for clients to set goals in their own language and on their own terms. This is important because the experience of loss is so unique and in addition individuals' ways of coping and views on ideal outcomes are so diverse. Their emphasis is on going very slowly and processing feelings first before moving into 'change-work'. They emphasize the importance of establishing the client's 'world-view' very thoroughly because the experience of suicide in particular can be related to many different causes; in addition, suicide in some religions and cultures is a very serious transgression. In the three detailed examples provided, de Castro and Guterman demonstrate their work with a Pakistani-American Muslim family, a European-American white Catholic family, and a European-American Jewish family. They remind us that not all negative emotions can or should be 'talked away', and that sometimes it is best just 'to be with clients in their despair, grief or depression'. They conclude that solution-focused strategies have important advantages over existing cognitive-behavioural and psycho-educational approaches because 'solution-focused therapy highlights families' existing or potential resources and emphasises the resiliency of families coping with suicide' (de Castro and Guterman, 2008: 104).

Box 7.11   Case study: working with bereaved parents of a young child

Bobby, a three-year-old child, dies in hospital following an accident in his home, when he managed to pull a heavy wardrobe down on top of himself. His mother, Joanne, was in the adjoining room but could not prevent it. He was rushed to hospital where he was found to have catastrophic head injuries and is placed on life support. His parents, Joanne and Bill, were told that he would not survive. The social worker assigned to the family combined her knowledge of solution-focused helping with her experience base of working with bereaved parents of young children. She described the following points as being of importance in her work with Bobby's grieving parents:

- Give the parents time to get over the initial shock before planning for the life support machine to be turned off. Do not go into solution-focused mode at this time.
- Make yourself available to spend as much time with them as necessary in this intense time – listen to their stories about their child, Bobby; help them to remember him in as much detail and in as many forms as they want to share.
- Stay with them in the past and the present until they show signs that they are ready to move on. Do not rush them or the process. Give them full licence to feel the pain and loss.
- Make sure they have privacy and as much uninterrupted time as necessary with Bobby while he is still alive.
- Help them to claim the process of loss; do not let others dictate (professionals or family and friends). Build in as much choice as possible – let them guide the process as much as is feasible.
- Look at what good might come from their child's death. Consider how this tragic loss and death may have some meaning. Is organ donation possible? How might that be approached? Further down the road, might they want a role in public accident prevention programmes?
- Convey your belief in them as individuals; convey your unconditional positive regard for them. Convey your belief that they can and will get through this difficult time. Remind them gently, and at their own pace, that they are resourceful people with unique strengths.

The loss of a child is not an event; it's a process. Solution-focused ideas are not immediately applicable in the immediate crisis of traumatic death where the Miracle is just not possible; but the approach has been found to be of value in bereavement work in the medium to long-term phase of helping.

The importance of hope

A core element of solution-focused helping in working with the dying patient is that of hope. Specialists in this field describe how it is important to maintain hope for as long as possible, if that is how the patient is coping, when faced with a terminal illness; likewise for families. Hope also has a more important presence in shaping how professionals and carers interact with the dying, in particular the need for helpers to retain a sense of hope and purpose themselves in work with the terminally ill – no mean feat.

Itzhaky and Lipschitz-Elhawi (2004) describe how hope can be used as a strategy for staff supervision and support of social workers in palliative care. Their definition of hope is useful to us as it allows for what is possible, not a perfect future: 'Hope involves recognition of reality and the difficulties it involves and an effort to cope with and overcome them by offering a more effective behavioural alternative for coping than denial' (p. 47). They also describe hope as 'an active process of recruiting strength and finding solutions' (p. 50). The strategies they suggest for the maintenance of hope among helpers are useful for all solution-focused helpers. Cutcliffe (2004) describes a form of bereavement counselling that has at its heart the process of inspiring hope.

Box 7.12 Practice principles: strategies for maintaing hope (Itzhaky and Lipschitz-Elhawi, 2004)

- Acquiring knowledge and information on the characteristics of the terminal illness and the possible reactions of those suffering from it.
- Setting realistic goals for your work with individual clients/patients and their families – 'hope is possible only if it has some grounding in reality'.
- Active problem-focused coping (coping in which efforts are directed to defining the problem, creating solutions, considering alternatives in terms of pros and cons, and choosing possibilities for action) prevents workers 'from retreating to passivity and helplessness and encourages recognition that although it may be impossible to affect the physiological course of the disease . . . [you] can affect the client's psychological condition' (p. 50).
- A positive attitude can be fostered by identifying and highlighting the 'little rays of light' in the work, by the use of humour, and by being reminded (or reminding yourself) of the value of your work and small successes in it.
- Cultivating hope by finding meaning, such as reorganized priorities (such as family over work) due to illness; a reactivation or discovery of a faith and religious belief; a general re-evaluation of relationships and making sense of these as a helper/carer to accept that, in the ultimately negative experience of death, something good can also come.

Conclusions

It is important to emphasize that solution-focused helping with older people and in end-of-life/bereavement care is not aiming to deny the significance of the events taking place. As C.S. Lewis (1961) notes, 'There is death. And whatever is matters'. Similarly, there is loss and sadness and grief in growing older. None of this can be ignored. Yet, solution-focused concepts and a solution-focused attitude can perhaps help carers to balance the loss and sadness with a belief, a hope, that life does go on and that in the small routines and details of life, there can co-exist hopefulness, sense of purpose, and worth. While advances in technology and communication have led to globalized economic and banking systems frighteningly sensitive to economic and political policy shifts thousands of miles away, these have been accompanied by innovative assistive technologies as well as information and communication technologies that 'may improve quality of life, extend length of community residence, improve physical and mental health status, delay the onset of serious health problems and reduce family and care-giver burden' (Blaschke et al., 2009).

The following practice principles are worth bearing in mind.

When working with the bereaved, less important is the concept of moving people on – more important is the acknowledgement of present pain and distress, combined with a hopefulness that life can and will get better. Attention can be focused on the small steps towards change; the small differences that might be found. A self-directed pace of work and goals for the work is important in counteracting a sense of hopelessness and powerlessness.

Dying well – the concept that people at the end of life may have unfinished business and tasks that if completed will help them to die more peacefully can be a useful starting point in work with the terminally ill.

Finally, 'The key to SFBT is the understanding that the therapist and the client make up a therapeutic system that collaborates on the construction of solutions. This understanding is crucial in addressing bereavement' (Butler and Powers, 1996: 228).

8   The solution-focused helper working in community development and with groups

> We often look inward or to the family to explain and understand behaviour, but the immediate context – interpersonal, built, and physical – is a powerful influence on how we feel, think and act. So the environment – be it school, neighbourhood, or playground, and its people and structures – can be a major force in helping people to turn around their lives.
>
> (Saleebey, 2005: 243)

Introduction

In this chapter, I outline the extension of solution-focused principles and interventions beyond individual and family work to group and community work. The increasingly rich literature demonstrating the value of the approach in such initiatives in health and social care services is summarized. First, community work as a method of intervention is reviewed. Then, some of the parallel knowledge bases pertinent to solution-focused community development, and in particular capacity-building activities, will be outlined.

Historically, community work was viewed as one of the three main methods of intervention in British and American social/human services, alongside individual/family casework and groupwork. The debate about whether workers should focus on developing improved environments and communities or focus on individual and family change intensified in the 1980s in the UK. While the Barclay Report (National Institute of Social Work, 1983) proposed a structure for social services based on local community-building activities, a combination of political influences and policies (in particular the purchaser–provider split introduced by the Conservative government of the time) and the advent of several high-profile child deaths and subsequent inquiries in England in the late 1980s led to the reorganization of social services into specialist streams with child protection emerging as a particularly dominant form of practice. Work in social services departments became framed around managing risk, meeting individual needs, and working primarily on individual and family levels. Only in the voluntary sector and in service-user-led organizations did community development activities continue to flourish. Similarly in the USA, appreciation of community development and community organization as a valid form of helping diminished in the thirty-year period from the 1970s to early 2000s (Saleebey, 2005). Sullivan and Rapp (2005) infer that one barrier to community development initiatives between different organizations and/or individual therapists/helpers is the nature of the health insurance market in the USA and the reimbursement arrangements that are in place.

Community development as a method was gradually marginalized and then dropped from social work curricula in the USA and England, Scotland, and Wales. It now only survives within the British Isles as a core competence in Northern Ireland (Sheldon and McDonald, 2009) and in the Republic of Ireland (National Social Work Qualifications Board, 2003). Yet, in recent years, as the faults in existing systems of service delivery became more obvious and pronounced (particularly evident in service-users' feedback), and as political concerns move to a focus on the needs of socially excluded communities living in poverty and substandard environments across Britain and Ireland, there has been somewhat of a rediscovery of the value of community development approaches. Saleebey (2005) records the re-emergence of a community dimension in North America also. He puts the renewed interest in community work down to three factors: first, the discovery of community dimensions to a range of phenomena outside of social services contexts; second, the 'virtual explosion' of knowledge in the area of individual, family, and community resilience ('founded on the idea that each individual, family and community has capacities, knowledge, and means that enhance revitalization . . . and there is thought to be a complex and abiding calculus of resilience – that community and individual or family resilience are inextricably bound together' (p. 241–242)); and third, the notion of empowerment, of which more later.

Sure Start, the ambitious nationwide programme to tackle childhood disadvantage in the UK, is built along community development lines with integrated services provided through local community-based children's centres:

> Sure Start Children's Centres are building on existing successful initiatives like Sure Start local programmes, neighbourhood nurseries and early-excellence centres, and bringing high-quality integrated Early Years services to the heart of communities. By 2010, there will be 3500 children's centres, so that every family has easy access to high-quality integrated services in their community and the benefits of Sure Start can be felt nationwide.
>
> (www.dcsf.gov.uk/everychildmatters/earlyyears/surestart;
> accessed October 2009)

Similarly in the health care field, there is a renewed focus on public health approaches as it becomes increasingly evident that many chronic health problems are created and/or exacerbated by environmental and life-style factors. Rather than waiting for problems to develop to the point of needing expensive specialist interventions, whole-population approaches are now advocated for significant health risks such as obesity (Nestle and Jacobson, 2000). In Northern Ireland, a community development and health network (www.cdhn.org) has been established in one health trust area. Its mission is:

> to end health inequalities using a community development approach. By this we mean campaigning, influencing policy and developing best practice work which shows that communities, both geographical and of interest & identity, can define their own health needs and design and implement preventative and radical solutions.
>
> (www.cdhn.org; accessed October 2009)

Across a range of fields such as general adult health, child and adolescent mental health, education, family support, and migration integration, the orientation is increasingly broad and includes outreach, groupwork, and community capacity-building. Public health approaches are now advocated for therapeutic work for families in difficulty, in an attempt to reach the estimated 70–80 percent of children and parents in need who do not make it to specialist CAMHS services (Baruch et al., 2007; Jones, 2009). Family therapists, too, now emphasize the community dimensions of their work, noting that 'Community programs may have therapeutic effects in themselves, be a help to the therapy goals, or be an alternative to therapy' (Falicov, 2007: 166). Well-being and positive health promotion focus on group interventions in cardiac and cancer rehabilitation, and for those with chronic conditions such as diabetes and high blood pressure. The power of both self-help and treatment groups has long been recognized in the addiction field, ranging from Alcoholics Anonymous and other twelve-step programmes to motivational interviewing approaches. In addition, a body of literature has developed around the concept of strengthening community resilience following major disasters such as 9/11 and mass shootings in the USA and Europe. Walsh describes this development as a

> multisystemic, resilience-oriented practice approach [which] recognizes the widespread impact of major trauma, situates the distress in the extreme experience, attends to ripple effects through relational networks, and aims to strengthen family and community resources for optimal recovery.
>
> (Walsh, 2007: 207)

Landau (2007) describes a specific programme, the Linking Human Systems

(LINC) Community Resilience model, which is based on the aim of building community resilience following rapid and untimely transition and loss where the focus is on nurturing competence within the community itself.

Whether public health promotion, community education, self-help groups or user-led organizations, an additional dimension to the potential of community-based action lies in new technologies and the speed with which information and advice can now be broadcast and lobbying movements or campaigns launched through social networking sites such as Facebook, mass communication channels such as Twitter, email, and text messaging. Virtual communities therefore now represent another potent force for change and mobilization.

In summary, community development has re-emerged as a valuable form of practice across many social care and health fields. Before considering how good a match solution-focused concepts and practices are with community development theory and practice, let us define the field and outline the parallel knowledge bases.

Parallel knowledge bases

Community development over time

Most work that falls under the umbrella of community development is reflexive -therapeutic or reformist in nature, meaning that it 'seeks the development of relatively small groups within the present social order . . . or improvement in the present social order' (Payne, 2005: 208), rather than aiming for collective empowerment and liberation, or radical change on a structural or societal level. Historically, there has often been a radical agenda attached to collective action and collective organizing, particularly when associated with the Marxist concept of consciousness-raising, with the associated language of empowerment, liberation, and transformation. The early twentieth-century Italian political activist and philosopher Antonio Gramsci and later in the middle of the twentieth century, Paulo Freire, the Brazilian educator, among others, advocated an *educational* dimension to community development and emancipation, based on the premise that education can be transformative in enabling individuals and communities to resist and overcome oppression. In *Pedagogy of the Oppressed* (1970), Freire describes how education can inform action, and how through praxis (informed action), liberation and fulfilment can be achieved.

Systems theory (von Bertalanffy, 1971; Rapaport, 1986) and ecological systems theory (Bronfenbrenner, 1979) are two important building blocks in theories of change focused on the community dimension because they emphasize the continuous process of interaction between the person and the environment. Both theories offer a range of targets for change (the micro, meso, exo or macro systems in Bronfenbrenner's terminology); both emphasize that change in one element of a system can trigger changes in others; and different parts of a system are seen to be mutually interdependent and mutually shaping. The evolution of systems-based theories of change have had a profound impact on the helping professions in offering choices regarding targets for change, in emphasizing the person–environment dynamic, and in moving the focus away from intrapersonal and/or individual-focused theories of change.

More recently, concepts such as social capital, social inclusion, and capacity-building have been linked to newer paradigms based on concerns about the fragmentation of traditional community life, particularly in large urban settings, and the need to re-integrate communities seen as marginalized and socially excluded (and consequently a threat to the established order). Ledwith (2005) advocates a critical approach to modern community development work with the emphasis not on improvement but the *transformation* of communities. The concept of transformation links both to Freire's pedagogy of the oppressed and to empowerment theory originally relating to the work of Solomon (1976) and more recently Gutierrez et al. (1995) in the USA and Adams (1996, 2003) in the UK. To summarize, social policy-makers across the developed world are once more amenable to a role for projects that organize self-help, rather than provide direct care (Payne, 2005). Central to this policy shift is increased recognition of the value of user-led movements, self-help, advocacy groups, and peer support. In addition, the philosophy of health and social care services now emphasizes concepts of partnership between professionals and service-users and a tacit acceptance that the experience of the service-user is a central element of how a service is to be judged.

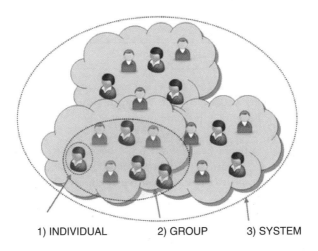

1) INDIVIDUAL   2) GROUP   3) SYSTEM

Figure 8.1   Nested systems within social systems.
Source: The Bumble Bee (www.bioteams.com/2007/07/01/design-better-html)

Definitions and concepts

Community development can refer to a range of initiatives and approaches, some sponsored at governmental level and consisting of national strategies; others at regional level; some centred on communities of interest or identity; others emerging at local level focused on local or interest-group specific concerns; some with very ambitious aspirations; others more pragmatic and conservative in aim. In considering contemporary approaches to community development and their ethical application in health and social care settings, several additional concepts need to be defined.

Social capital refers to the value of social relationships and networks. Although popularized in more recent times by French sociologist Bourdieu (who described different forms of capital – social, cultural, and symbolic, articulated through social relations in a multidimensional social space) and American sociologist Putnam (2000), the concept is seen to have had currency for over a century. Ascribed by some (Sheldon and McDonald, 2009) to Hanifan (1916) and originally defined with reference to social intercourse, mutual sympathy, friendship, and goodwill, social capital not only benefits the individual but also: 'The community as a whole will benefit by the co-operation of all its parts, while the individual will find in his associations the advantages of the help, the sympathy, and the fellowship of his neighbors' (Hanifan, 1916: 130–131). A more recent definition of social capital relates primarily to useful social networks: 'social capital is the sum of the resources, actual or virtual, that accrue to an individual or a group by virtue of possessing a durable network of more or less institutionalized relationships of mutual acquaintance and recognition' (Bourdieu and Wacquant, 1992: 119). Similarly, Saleebey

---

Box 8.1 Definitions and concepts

Community development is described in the social care/social work literature as 'a form of community work which seeks to engage people with shared interests usually in a particular locality to come together, identify shared concerns and work jointly to overcome them' (Payne, 2005: 208).

Alternatively, in public health terms it has been defined as 'collaborative work to improve the capacity of less powerful groups to address their social, economic and political needs, many of which play a role in determining health' (Teahan et al., 2002: 33).

Common to both definitions are: concepts of collective/collaborative work; a community group identity based on geographical/spatial boundaries or shared interests/ characteristics; an emphasis on capacity-building; and an action-based focus.

(2005) defines the concept in relation to potential resources: 'the human, economic, spiritual, and social stock of a community – those "funds" available for community development and action, and the confronting of conflict and trouble' (p. 244). Putnam's (2000) definition of the term is more directly related to a perceived collapse in civic community and in public trust across westernized societies. Similar to Hanifan and Bourdieu, Putnam focuses on the importance of social networks but he ties it more explicitly to the concept of a 'good society' built on civic virtue:

> social capital refers to connections among individuals – social net-
> works and the norms of reciprocity and trustworthiness that arise
> from them. In that sense social capital is closely related to what
> some have called 'civic virtue'. The difference is that 'social capital'
> calls attention to the fact that civic virtue is most powerful when
> embedded in a sense network of reciprocal social relations.
>
> (Putnam, 2000: 19)

Putnam's description of civic virtue reminds us of another relevant concept, that of 'civil society'.

Civil society is generally defined as collective groupings, outside of formal governmental or institutional arrangements, with shared purposes, values or interests, that can act as additional and/or alternative resources or voices to those groupings and institutions granted official status. Pinkerton and Campbell (2002) relate it specifically to choice – voluntary relationships for-med outside of 'the sphere of direct State control'; they suggest that some groups of helpers, such as social workers, with a central focus on issues of social justice, need to re-engage with the energy within civil society and strive to shift 'its practice ideology away from the controlling and technocratic, to that of an engaging empowerment' (p. 735).

Capacity-building is a relatively new concept that emerged from initia-tives in developing countries and was subsequently adopted within both the environmental and international aid arenas. Lately, it has become a favoured concept in public health promotion and in work with migrant populations. Capacity-building is

> an approach to development that builds independence . . . [and]
> increases the range of people, organisations and communities who
> are able to address problems, and in particular, problems that arise out
> of social inequity and social exclusion.
>
> (www.health.nsw.gov.au/public-health/health-promotion/
> capacity-building; accessed November 2009)

Linked to the notion of capacity-building is the role that education can play, as emphasized in different forms of social pedagogy, where it can be used 'to combat social exclusion and develop social identity, aiming at personal and social growth through problem-solving' (Payne, 2005: 214). Other forms of capacity-building can include coaching and mentoring on individual or group levels.

Skills for community development

Despite the re-emergence of community development and public health approaches in our health and social services, there is some evidence that professionals working in these fields worry that they do not have the necessary knowledge or skills to develop such approaches in their work. One study involving nearly three hundred health and social service professionals found that while most had a positive interest in community development, many thought they needed additional input on methods and techniques, values and principles of community development (Teahan et al., 2002). Is it true that social and health care professionals lack the necessary skills to expand their work to include groupwork and community development dimensions as Teahan et al. (2002) feared? Or, is it that the language and concepts are somewhat different but the core skills remain the same?

The skills associated with community development/groupwork initiatives are built on a foundation of participatory practice – engaging, involving, elicit-ing, and managing collective interactions. Interpersonal and group communi-cation skills are central tools for such work. In addition, a worker needs to be a clear thinker and be organized and able to plan and follow through on collective decisions in collaboration with the community group. Most of all, a worker needs to be clear about the values and process of community work: 'Effective participation requires partnership which offers ownership of activities and outcomes for local particpants' (Payne, 2005: 213). For health and social care workers, the starting point is to review one's own practice, role, and function to consider whether it is possible to incorporate a community work dimension to it.

In addition to moving from a focus on individual need to actively seek-ing opportunities for group or collective initiatives, it is important to make the shift from thinking *for* people to a position of thinking *with* people; to change your formulation from a role of direct helping to a role of enabling and facilitating collective action. To do this means combining your professional skills (such as advocacy, accessing resources, acting as a social broker) with the community or group's skills as 'experts through experience' (such as knowing what needs to be tackled, the range of ways these issues might be tackled, and the ability to make use of existing connections within the community). The example in Box 8.3 describes how a joint piece of work between a social worker and a health visitor in an inner-city area might unfold.

Box 8.2 Exercise: identifying exceptions to build on

Consider your current role and function:

1 Do you see any patterns in your world that point to collective needs? For example, are you doing individual work with a number of patients all with the same health issues?
2 Are you working with relatives/carers who might benefit from meeting together?
3 What other professionals that you work with might have the time and interest in working together to plan a joint group/community initiative?
4 How might you plan this to give the group an empowering experience?

Box 8.3 Practice example: moving from an individual to a collective focus

---

A social worker in central London becomes aware of a growing number of Bangladeshi families being referred for 'support' and 'child welfare concerns'. Most often it is mothers and children who are the focus of concern of GPs, school welfare officers, and health visitors. The most common problems are poor school attendance due to poor children's health, and maternal depression and isolation. A community development approach to meeting these local clustered needs is proposed and a partnership developed between local social workers and health visitors. Visits to the twenty plus Bangladeshi families living on this estate are made, first to the women with an interpreter, when they were asked what would help. English classes, access to sewing machines, and a place for Balgladeshi mothers to meet came top of the wish-list. Once it becomes clear that the women are really keen to meet together, it is decided to respect the traditional family hierarchy and revisit with a male interpreter to talk to the women's partners (invariably their husbands) to get their support for this project. A modest amount of funding to establish a local project and to cover running costs is obtained. Free use of a local meeting room is secured (part of a planned primary care centre, not yet operational). The Bangladeshi Mothers and Toddlers Group is established and runs successfully for many years every Friday morning; activities include English classes, Bangladeshi film shows, visits in and outside London, and health promotion talks.

Questions:
1 Can you identify community resources (including colleagues) that you could draw on to offer such an intervention in your work?
2 Can you identify any ethical issues that might arise in groupwork like this?

3   Can you think of any other situations you are struggling with, where that simple question – what would help? – could be used?

Commentary:
The benefits of this group intervention are clear to see: the women grew in confidence; they became proficient in English; the children's school attendance improved; the families received targeted help on common health problems and medical advice; both women and children became active citizens of London as they became more familiar with it through the regular trips; the men in the families became more trusting of local social and health services as they observed the benefits to their families. For the professionals, there is a more efficient use of time and energy in addition to the satisfaction of working in a way that focuses on capacity-building within the community as opposed to fostering dependency on individual professional helpers.

Values and ethical dimensions

Most mission statements for community development initiatives or organizations specify values that relate to respect, partnership, reciprocity, empowerment, and social justice. One in particular refers to the importance of hope:

> We value hope. We believe that community development and change begins with individual people and that they must have hope that things change through collective actions. We believe that community development is an on-going dynamic process of social change that can lead to sustained improvements in people's lives.
> (Winnipeg Regional Health Authority, www.wrha.communityhealth/ communitydevelopment; accessed October 2009)

Although it is debatable as to whether hope is exactly a value as opposed to a belief, this Canadian commentary does point to the need for community development to be seen as a positive approach with achievable, desirable outcomes, and not as a hollow exercise that sets out to tick the box marked 'consultation with community', without any genuine intention of real collaboration and partnership. Respect, partnership, and empowerment are values that underpin most, if not all, health and social care professional codes of ethics. Other values, traditionally associated with individual approaches, such as confidentiality and self-determination, may have quite different meanings in community development, and consequently may need to be explicitly addressed by a worker, particularly if it is the case that individual and groupwork/community interventions are conducted in tandem. Let us now look at some examples where expectations and practices may differ from more traditional helper–patient/client relationships.

Banks (1995) notes how some of the more traditional values of social work are altered when community development approaches are practised. In particular, she highlights how *confidentiality* is viewed differently (from individualized helping) when the focus of the work is collective action and empowerment, similar to how a professional helper working on a multi-disciplinary team, such as in a hospital or on a primary care team, might view the limits of confidentiality to stretch to a team. Ethical practice should involve making these limits of confidentiality explicit, particularly in an era when reporting of possible risk or harm is an overt requirement on many health and social care professionals.

Self-determination is another core principle in many helping professions, which, if exercised, may conflict with other principles. In community development work, a worker's role might focus primarily on the common good rather than promoting individual self-determination, in which case expectations regarding role and priorities need to be openly discussed.

Although across all forms of intervention the primary concern should be a client's/patient's well-being not the worker's interests, there is plenty of room for ethical dilemmas to develop in community development due to the strong emphasis placed on *participation* and *empowerment*. What if the worker feels that the community is choosing the wrong goal after conducting a process of empowerment and particpation? What if the worker's own interests point in a different direction? The overall principle is that it should be the group's well-being not the worker's interests that direct you to the right path. But in politically informed community development work, where a radical agenda may involve unsettling established orthodoxies or power groups, there may be quite a struggle between this principle and a worker's interests and no easy formula with which to resolve such a struggle.

Finally, there is empowerment itself, a central value, process, and aspiration in community work. *Empowerment* is a natural element to community development work, given that it is essentially related to developing skills, strengths, and abilities on an individual or collective basis for people to have more confidence and capacity to shape their own lives. It can be viewed as a process that focuses on one or more of the following levels: intrapersonal, interpersonal or collective (political), and can also address power dynamics in and between these three levels. Adams (1996) suggests that as a concept it is closely related to both self-help and user-led activities, although it is also a term that causes much confusion as it can be used in many different ways. It can mean giving clients/patients some limited choices (consumerist approach), power-sharing (citizenship approach), or encouraging individuals and groups to take charge of their own destinies (a radical approach) (Banks, 1995). It also has an important contextual element, in that the potential for any form of empowering practice may be powerfully influenced by the context of the helping encounter. There is also the danger that empowerment practices can be misused to manipulate people to alter their behaviours to comply with agency requirements or societal expectations, and it could cause difficulties if one group of people is empowered in a context of restricted political and social resources and so pitted against others (Payne, 2005).

Adams (1996) reminds us that empowerment as a concept is not derived from individually based or problem-centred approaches to practice, but that its antecedents are 'a combination of mutual aid, self-help and, more recently, movements of liberation, rights and social activism' (p. 2), buttressed by critical discourses such as feminism and anti-racism. Fundamental to the practice of empowerment is the notion of addressing the needs of marginalized, oppressed, and socially excluded members of a society; and of helping groups and individuals to overcome effects of racism, discrimination and oppression, individually and collectively. For Fook (2002), the concept of empowerment can mask as many conflicts and difficulties as it seeks to resolve. She advocates a form of empowerment practice that rests on a Foucauldian analysis of power (in the generative sense – as something used and created rather than simply possessed). Hence empowerment practice is not about giving power to the people, but of *working with* people so that they can empower themselves and combining this with a critical reflection on yourself as a helper and how in your practice as a professional you can disempower, as well as offer opportunities for empowerment.

Links between community development and solution-focused helping

The beliefs underpinning community development centre on: (i) the potential and capacity within communities to help themselves; (ii) that communities themselves know what is best for them; (iii) that ownership of any process of change should rest with the community; (iv) that partnerships harnessing a range of strategies and expertise are a preferred way of working; and (v) that collective action in one area of a community's functioning can generate changes in other areas too. Similarly, in solution-focused theory, core beliefs include: the individual's capacity for change; the belief that the client is expert on his or her own life; that the client needs to be in charge of the process, both in identifying goals and in deciding how to reach them; and the systemic idea that one small change can generate more changes in a person's life.

The main distinction between the two is that in the original theory of solution-focused therapy (SFT; de Shazer et al., 1986), the focus is firmly on the individual or familial interpersonal dynamic. No reference in the early work is made to extending these principles to group or community work, although Berg did subsequently engage in whole-programme and -organization change initiatives in child welfare (Berg, 1994; Berg and Kelly, 2000) and de Shazer developed whole-organization initiatives in addiction services with colleagues in Belgium (de Shazer and Isebaert, 2003). One significant adjustment that needs to be made in practice if one wants to combine a solution-focused approach with a community development perspective is that the assessment of need has to be holistic and incorporate a systemic analysis of problems (and resources) at different levels – individual, family, group, community, and environment (Coady and Lehman, 2008) – and hence it needs to reject the solution-focused assertion that one does not need to carry out a full assessment prior to action.

Sullivan and Rapp (2005) also note strong links between asset-based community development models (they draw on that of Kretzmann and McKnight, 1993) and the strengths perspective in social work (Saleebey, 1994, 2005) in relation to starting with what you have; starting with the problems identified by community members in the here and now; and a theory of change that emphasizes relational aspects of helping and developing individual and community resilience.

Social constructionist approaches such as solution-focused helping (and narrative work) advocate a position of actively working with people to help them identify their own issues and concerns and co-construct their own solutions to these in collaboration with a facilitator/helper (McNamee and Gergen, 1992). Underlying this is a belief in strengths and resources. Strengths-based approaches also start from the premise that in each individual and environment there are inherent resources:

> The reciprocal relationship between people and the environment, however construed, is a fundamental precept in . . . most professions concerned with the health and well-being of people . . . important gains are made in direct practice, community capacity, and public policy when efforts are extended to match and develop the inherent strengths of people *and* the social environment.
>
> (Sullivan and Rapp, 2005: 262–263, original emphasis)

A greater emphasis needs to be placed on locating resources in the community and environment, but Sullivan and Rapp also point out that too often the people that the helping professions engage with are viewed as burdens of society, not as resources in themselves but as liabilities, and that 'Recognizing the talents of those pushed to the margins is a vital first-step in the enhancement of community capacity' (p. 264).

The co-construction of solutions is an integral part of the process both for solution-focused helpers and for community development practitioners.

Explicitly a distinction is made between worker/agency goals and client goals, and power is shared with the professional helper taking the role of facilitator, assisting the community or group members to achieve their self-identified aims. Solution-focused helpers aim to use their expertise and knowledge to help clients have more control over their own lives. Solution-focused helpers can also be particularly well versed in the development of well-formed (and hence more achievable) goals (de Shazer, 1991). They recognize and actively construct bridges between broad hopes/aspirations for a preferred future and small steps of change that lead towards these goals.

Hope is a central element to be engendered in the process of empowerment, and relates directly to work by Freire (2004) and others on the pedagogy of hope, and its importance in counteracting the impacts of oppression, negativity, and discrimination on people. Solution-focused helping is inherently hopeful and through its belief in people's abilities to make positive changes in their lives and the specific techniques of future-focused, goal-focused, and exception-finding questions, aims to engender hopefulness in those who have lost it. Saleebey (2005: 255) describes such work as teaching 'the power of hope'.

The cornerstone is empowerment in both community development theory and solution-focused theory. Payne (2005), among others, argues for the need for a combination of approaches in the helping professions, as the more generic empowerment theory may be restricted in its usefulness for 'very damaged, oppressed or institutionalised people' for whom it may work in helping them achieve 'greater degrees of self-control and power' but that an adherence to empowerment principles 'should not exclude therapeutic work for their benefit as well' (Payne, 2005: 314). In addition, it should not be used to mask real needs for services and interventions or be confused with an expectation that an oppressed or marginalized community can empower itself without access to resources and power. It should also be grounded in realistic expectations so as to avoid the risk of being 'Pollyannish'.

Some of the roles that a helper undertakes in empowerment practice, including *coach* (helping people identify their own strengths and goals and make links with others), *educator* (where the helper structures learning experiences aimed at helping people identify their own solutions to their particular situations), and *social broker* to link people together (with common histories, experiences, issues, and concerns), are also common features of solution-focused groupwork and community development initiatives, as will be outlined below.

Bliss and Bray (2009) describe, in the spirit of a minimalist tradition (in line with de Shazer's use of the concept of Ockam's Razor), the smallest solution-focused particles that distinguish solution-focused work from other types of helping. They define it in terms of the worker 'using the client's language and frames of reference to co-construct the client's preferred future, discover the parts of that future that are already happening, and contruct signs that both are moving in the right direction' (p. 71). They consider that the absolute minimum for uniquely solution-focused work is that the worker takes the position of co-constructor, requiring that the worker 'learn from the client' (p. 72). While their definition is rooted in the area of individual/family therapy, perhaps such a definition might also be useful when considering how solution-focused community development might be operationalized; 'the client' in this formulation being the community.

In developing further the extension of solution-focused helping into community development, Saleebey's work on the strengths perspective provides a useful bridge to straddle both knowledge bases, as outlined in Box 8.4.

Solution-focused helping with communities and groups: the literature

Despite the links in the values and concepts of solution-focused helping and community development, the bulk of the literature on solution-focused work concentrates on individual and family work, followed by that on solution-focused groupwork. To a certain extent this is unsurprising given the roots of the approach in clinic-based individual and family therapy. Where the cross-over into community development initiatives initially occurred was primarily in education, and there are a range of papers and publications outlining its use

---

Box 8.4   Practice principles for community development

Saleebey (2005) outlines a strengths-based approach to community development that can be useful for those wanting to move their solution-focused practice in this direction.

The first step is to set out to establish the assets, resources, and strengths available in the community, potentially for the community. These can include problem-solving and leadership capacities.

The second element is to see yourself as a worker focused on releasing the potential in a community through your relational bonds within the community: positive, mutually respectful relationships are vehicles for change. The aims of community initiatives include those of fostering a sense of belonging and participating, of raising hopes, of developing appropriate expectations of achievement rather than failure.

A third element is to offer opportunities for people to make a contribution to their own community; to give something back, to make an investment in the future of the community.

with groups, classes, and schools (Metcalf, 1955; Murphy, 1994; Kral, 1995; Ajmal and Rees, 2001; Franklin et al., 2001). The literature on its use with groups relate primarily to treatment or psycho-educational support groups (akin to Payne's delineation of therapeutic or reformist) from within specialist service settings (Quick and Gizzo, 2007; Sharry, 2007; Thorslund, 2007; Smock et al., 2008; Froerer et al., 2009; Shin, 2009). There are few true community development initiatives with a solution-focused dimension in the literature (these will be summarized and described below). However, two areas of practice in particular where solution-focused helping has crossed over into genuine collective empowerment-based practice are family-centres/family support services and work with migrant communities. Both of these will be described in greater detail.

Solution-focused schools

As already noted, the education sector was probably the first to appreciate the potential of solution-focused groupwork, not only for children with specific difficulties, but also parents, teachers, and the school community itself. Kral (1995), Metcalf (1955), Murphy (1994), Ajmal and Rees (2001), and Franklin et al. (2001) were some of the earliest pioneers of its use in school settings.

Kim and Franklin (2009) recently reviewed the outcome literature on solution-focused work in schools. They highlight solution-focused behavioural therapy's (SFBT) particular appeal to school-based helpers as a short-term, goal-focused, and flexible approach, especially well suited because of its emphasis on specific behavioural goals. In addition, it is thought to be particularly appropriate for vulnerable/marginalized students in American public school settings. Overall, the review reported mixed results from the seven studies that met the criteria for inclusion in their analysis. At least three of the studies were groupwork interventions. Solution-focused behavioural therapy was not successful in raising grade levels or improving attendance rates in schools; nor was it found to improve the self-esteem of students. Where it was found to be beneficial was

> in helping students reduce the intensity of their negative feelings, manage their conduct problems, improve academic outcomes like credits earned, and positively impact externalizing behaviour problems and substance use ... In one study SFBT had equivalent results for impacting behavioural change as cognitive-behavioral therapy and had *better* outcomes for engaging clients and retaining them in the therapy process.
>
> (Kim and Franklin, 2009: 468, my emphasis)

In relation to self-esteem, the authors note that there is growing concern in the research community about the generalizability of using self-esteem as a dependent variable in studies. They conclude that their review 'shows that SFBT is achieving respectable outcomes when compared to other treatments that are being delivered in a community setting' (p. 469).

A range of recent publications has focused on projects and programmes centred on specific at-risk groups. Harris and Franklin (2008) created a schools-based life skills programme for adolescent mothers in the USA, called the 'Taking Charge' curriculum. Delivered through groups, the programme sets out to be a strengths-based approach to adolescent motherhood, with an eight-session goal-oriented, task-centred programme within a solution-focused groupwork framework. Newsome (2004) describes a specific groupwork programme for 'at-risk' junior high school students that showed promise as a group intervention. Cooley (2009) developed a form of school-based group counselling using solution-focused concepts, which claims to be adaptable for any topic, curriculum or age group.

Ajmal and Rees (2001) cover a range of examples of how SFBT can be used in British school settings – from individuals to groups to whole-school approaches – and also refer to using it as a basis for specific campaigns (such as anti-bullying). Harker (2001) describes how to build solutions at meetings of local authority education psychologists in Scotland in which he talks about moving away from the role of psychologist as 'expert scientist' to one of 'co-creator and facilitator' (p. 44). Mall and Stringer (2001) describe their experience of running a solution-focused group for students labelled disruptive in a Birmingham education support service. They opted for a groupwork approach, for a combination of pragmatic and therapeutic reasons: they could cope with a high rate of referrals, but also recognized that 'the power of peer group influence could be used to stimulate and motivate troubled young people in a group setting' (p. 62). Feedback from participants indicated that they liked the mix of pair, group, and individual activities involved, the focus on their successes, and how these were also elicited from peers in the groups. Young (2001) outlines a sophisticated group intervention for victims of bullying in the school setting. The purpose is to recreate a community of support around the individual target of the bullying, which may well include those named as being part of the problem, as well as possible bystanders or past friends. One value in the type of highly charged situation that occurs when a bullying allegation is made in a school setting is the future focus of the intervention. The facilitator invites the selected pupils to join with him or her to create a future focus of happiness for the child target.

Mall and Stringer (2001) identify one dilemma that arises when working in family or peer groups as that relating to different preferred futures or goals, and their example demonstrates the need for explicit negotiation around such differences to overcome the risk of disempowering one or more members of a group while empowering one other. The consensus goal has to be constructed with some skill to be 'face-saving' and respectful to all. Linked to this is the real possibility that individual members in a group may progress at different rates; especially when dealing with people who have many adversities in their lives, the differences can be stark. This too will have to be actively managed by the group facilitators. Aficionados of the cult TV series, *The Wire*, will remember in series four how a group of children in a Baltimore school identified as disruptive and labelled as 'corner kids' were taught in a pilot project as a separate group where many made significant progress. While several were successfully reintegrated into the mainstream classes, one was moved back into a group home facility, a move that was regressive for him and may have further reinforced his marginalized status.

Hillel and Smith (2001) describe a scheme called the ABC Peer Support Scheme in an inner-London comprehensive school, which sets out to empower students to empower others through training in solution-focused thinking. Their account, including case examples, demonstrates how children aged twelve to fifteen years were able quickly to grasp and use the central concepts of the approach with a training input of eight two-hour sessions. They found that scaling questions were particularly popular with these teenagers, and that they adopted enthusiastically specific questions such as 'What will be different when . . .?' The Miracle Question was not so popular and was replaced by an alternative formulation of 'an ideal day'. This ABC Peer Support Scheme also fits into the category of empowerment-based community development, given that it challenges the traditional hierarchies of educators and pupils and seeks to empower the student group from within to find their own (peer) solutions to difficulties and in the process also strengthens contact and community within the student group.

Solution-focused groupwork – therapeutic/reformist examples

The leading text on solution-focused groupwork is Sharry's (2001, 2007) *Solution-focused Groupwork*, although some other standard texts do include chapters on or references to groupwork dimensions (O'Connell and Palmer, 2003). Sharry, a principal social worker in a Dublin child and family mental health service, draws on an extensive experience base, including pioneering work on a parenting skills programme, which unlike many of the behavioural courses, is explicitly underpinned by solution-focused thinking. He views groupwork and solution-focused thinking as synergistic, where the power of the group is harnessed to create a constructive and supportive group culture. Located firmly within the field of therapeutic endeavour, Sharry's examples of solution-focused groupwork fit most closely within a category of therapeutic/reformist, meaning that it 'seeks the development of relatively small groups within the present social order . . . or improvement in the present social order'

(Payne, 2005: 208), rather than aiming for empowerment-based practice in a collective sense.

This observation is not intended to diminish the many very effective and positive models described by Sharry and others below; rather, it is to remind readers of the distinction between therapeutic/reformist groups and community development groups based on a more radical capacity-building philosophy, which also draws on historic attempts at empowerment, 'a combination of mutual aid, self-help and, more recently, movements of liberation, rights and social activism' (Adams, 1996: 2). These are broad distinctions rather than binary opposites. Sharry, for example, also draws on Saleebey's strengths-based social work model to develop his model and he also sets out to articulate the specific therapeutic factors of solution-focused groupwork (as including group support, group learning, group optimism, the opportunity to help others, and group empowerment). Most usefully, Sharry outlines practical suggestions for overcoming some of the practical challenges faced in groupwork (including the 'visiting' or 'complaining' group participant versus the fully engaged customer for change; the over-enthusiastic participant who may monopolize; withdrawn and quiet group members).

Other literature on solution-focused groupwork sourced for this chapter likewise falls into the therapeutic/reformist range but with some interesting nuggets of information contained within. Hoskisson's (2003) chapter on groupwork is written from the therapeutic/reformist perspective. It identifies benefits for the employer in relation to cost-effectiveness and an ability to absorb high numbers of referrals; for clients, its usefulness is outlined in relation to normalizing difficulties and providing group strength and membership, learning from peers, and being offered a greater choice of possible solutions.

Banks (2005) outlines a six-session model for group therapy, where through reframing and carefully constructed questions participants are helped to see the problem in a more hopeful light and work towards resolving their issues.

Burns (2005) runs through a range of options for health care professionals wishing to use a group format with patients. These range from single-session groups to planned short-term and topic-focused groups, integrated solution-focused groups, consultancy/team-building and teaching/training groups. Specific to the health care setting, she identifies the value of groupwork as helping to normalize symptoms and creating a sense of universality, as well as encouraging patients to generate their own solutions. Burns provides examples of groups for stroke sufferers, Parkinson disease education groups (reframed through the programme as 'Managing Parkinson's Disease Successfully'), and the exercises she suggests make full use of the group process, including pair exercises focused on specific challenges and less emphasis on specific techniques such as the Miracle Question.

Quick and Gizzo (2007) implemented 'Doing what Works', a five-session solution-focused therapy group for adult psychiatric patients, blended with a psycho-educational focus and actively using the group process. In their study, which evaluated outcomes for 108 participants, they found that self-rated 'control of the problem' increased after participation. Participants who attended more of the five sessions reported more change. Aspects of the programme identified as particularly useful were the amplification of small changes, the benefits of social interaction, acceptance, and the 'doing what works' philosophy.

Also within the therapeutic/reformist forms of groupwork are accounts of work by Shin (2009) using a solution-focused group treatment with Korean youth probationers aimed at reducing their aggressiveness and increasing their social adjustment. The results of a randomized controlled study involving pre- and post-test ratings indicate that solution-focused group treatment led to positive change. After the six-week programme, 'the experimental group's aggressiveness score showed a significant decrease compared to that of the control group'; in addition, 'the solution-focused approach was proven effective regarding social adjustment abilities' and was also seen to enhance group participant motivation and achievement motivation (Shin, 2009: 283).

Walker (2008) describes Waikiki Youth Circles, a project based in Hawaii in which homeless youths participate in a group process where they find ways to identify their specific needs and work with peer group members to find ways to resolve their difficulties. Walker reports that the project assisted the youths in learning goal-setting skills, and that 'As both a restorative justice and solution-focused intervention, the process invites and motivates youth to deal with their situation and does not blame or ask them why they are in their particular situation' (p. 85).

Smock et al. (2008) compared solution-focused group therapy (SFGT) with a traditional problem-focused treatment for Level One substance abusers, defined as meeting the criteria for a substance abuse problem but not requiring inpatient treatment. With a group of 38 participants and using pre- and post-test scores, the six-week programme was evaluated using a range of standardized instruments. Participants who received the SFGT intervention showed significant improvements in a depression score (Beck Depression Inventory) as well as a measure for progress in client outcomes (OQ®) compared with the control group. Smock et al. (2008) suggest that solution-focused groupwork interventions are particularly appropriate for substance abusers, not only because they are more efficient than individual treatment approaches but also because the group setting has the 'ability to create a milieu for solution-building to help ameliorate substance abuse' (p. 108).

Froerer et al. (2009) outline the potential use of solution-focused groupwork for clients diagnosed with HIV/AIDS who face the specific challenges of managing ongoing symptoms, daily life functions and life decisions, stigmatization and marginalization, possible internalized shame, and experiences of grief, loss and hopelessness. They view the future focus and working towards desired goals, the emphasis on existing strengths, and the encouragement of small changes as being particularly appropriate for this client group. Reviewing existing literature, they suggest that a six-session format, preceded by individual pre-screening, and concentrating on particular solution-focused questions could be useful. However, they warn of limitations, including the issue of confidentiality, the risk of exacerbating experiences of grief and loss through group participation, and the fact that groupwork may not suit everyone. For those who do not wish to participate in a group process, the principle of individual choice should ensure that other options are available.

Thorslund (2007) describes a study carried out in Sweden to determine whether solution-focused group therapy, consisting of eight sessions in total, had an effect on the psychological health and return-to-work rates of people on long-term sick leave. Using a randomized controlled group design (albeit with a small number of participants totalling 30), and both pre- and post-test standardized instruments, Thorslund found that more members of the treatment group returned to work than the control group, worked more days, and that their psychological health had improved at the end of treatment. The difference in work status increased at a follow-up assessment three months later.

Klingman (2002) describes a solution-focused group intervention used with school counsellors during the Intifada in Israel in the last months of 2000. Following the failure of a standard supportive-listening, debriefing-focused group intervention, group meetings were modified and then evaluated through participant feedback and self-ratings. A standardized programme was developed consisting of a two-session (ninety minutes each) group programme: 'The main components of the final version . . . were process debriefing, cognitive adaptation to a threatening situation with an emphasis on threat-devaluation coping, and a solution-oriented approach within an indicated preventive intervention frame of reference' (p. 253). Specific changes to the group process related to normalizing the crisis event, moving on quickly from catharsis and internal affect towards resilience, effects on other people (students), and external tasks; problems presented were rephrased and re-evaluated 'to promote an attitude of multiple options and solutions that are rich in opportunities and choices' (p. 255). Reviewing the new intervention, the author concludes that the solution-focused approach was most helpful in moving participants to adopt more optimistic and self-confident expectations, and

> The intervention as a whole proactively (a) helped participants see themselves as normal persons with normal difficulties in abnormal times, (b) enabled them to have a more flexible view of the current situation, and eventually to develop more realistic and optimistic expectations about the situation and their professional role in it,

(c) helped them to identify effective behaviours, (d) enhanced a sense of personal control, and (e) strengthened their self-confidence in handling their tasks at school . . . In borrowing and adapting solution-focused techniques, we have helped counsellors to become more attentive to positive aspects, to talk about strengths, and change their perspective.

(Klingman, 2002: 257)

Milner and Singleton (2008) review the progress of sixty-eight adults on a solution-focused programme aimed at reducing domestic violence. Citing the already substantial literature on the use of the approach with cases of domestic violence, Milner and Singleton describe the programme as neither denying nor minimizing accountability, but instead avoiding blame and confrontation: 'The solution-focused practitioner holds violent offenders responsible for finding their own solutions to their behaviour, particularly [asking] what their futures will be like when they are violence-free' (p. 32). The programme they designed followed a child welfare model developed by Turnell and Edwards (1999) in Australia: the Signs of Safety approach. Of their sixty-eight participants (fifty-two men and sixteen women), thirty-four men completed the programme and all were found to be still violence-free on review; all sixteen women who completed the programme were also violence-free when reviewed. The programme in this case consisted of a case-by-case specific programme including group interventions supplemented by individual and couple work. The review of progress consisted of self-report, partner's reports, and checks with police and other professionals such as health visitors and hospitals.

Love et al. (2008) developed a project in California for young mothers with mental health or sobriety issues, which offers a range of interventions depending on need with the main approach being solution-focused brief coaching of the mothers (Berg and Szabo, 2005), supplemented by solution-focused family therapy to address issues within the family context. Entitled The Young Mothers and Babies Wellness Program, and directed at young mothers and their infants or toddlers referred by probation or child welfare services, it aims to not only give them comprehensive mental health services, but also to 'create an environment of active support and education, dedicated at establishing safe, nurturing and responsive relationships between mothers and their young children' (p. 1437). Still in its pilot stage and consequently not yet evaluated, it is an ambitious project and the outcome data will be important in establishing its usefulness.

In conclusion, many solution-focused groupwork interventions fit most aptly within the expert helper or medical model, in which the group organizer decides what is wrong, how to name it, and then proceeds to decide how to treat it. These are of course valid interventions to make, especially when people come actively looking for help to change some element of their lives, as in the examples cited above but it means that work remains within the therapeutic/reformist domain, as defined by Payne (2005). For solution-focused groupwork that fits within this frame of practice, Sharry's (2007) principles (outlined below) are apt. For other forms of groupwork that fit more comfortably with a community-development philosophy, some additional elements are required.

Being solution-focused in programme design

A step in the right direction towards a more community-development approach is developing a programme design for an agency, residential service or other organizational level according to solution-focused principles. It may be that the impact is at a professional community-wide or organization-wide level, in a way that can influence the culture of the organization, and so change the dynamic of the relationship between workers and clients/patients. This in itself can be a powerful intervention. (The literature on building solution-focused organizations and using elements of the approach in business and management consultancy has expanded rapidly in recent years but is outside the remit of this chapter, which is specifically concerned with community-development and capacity-building from within non-profit-making health and social care contexts.)

One approach to residential treatment for children and youth encompasses an entire collaborative, competency-based approach to programme design (Durrant, 1993), starting from the premise that residential treatment should not be about fixing young people or families, but 'about finding ways to help them build a picture of themselves as potentially successful and competent and able to build upon the strengths and resources they already have' (p. xi). Some of the innovations that Durrant suggests for residential settings include: the concept that the young person's admission to the unit

---

Box 8.5 Solution-focused principles for reflexive-therapeutic groups

1 Focusing on change and possibilities
2 Creating goals and preferred futures
3 Building on strengths, skills, and resources
4 Looking for 'what's right' and 'what's working'
5 Being respectfully curious
6 Creating cooperation and collaboration
7 Using humour and creativity

(Sharry, 2007: 21)

might be considered as a 'rite of passage', a time to practise being different; building on the notion of the admission being a ritual, using the metaphor of the rite of passage, ending the stay with a celebration of graduation, and establishing a unique theme for each resident (related to the specific challenges or issues for that young person) but a theme focused on success; day-to-day work by staff concentrates on the goal of helping residents to 'practise having good days', and emphasizing exceptions, small steps and successes. An insight of some significance that he makes relating to the need to incorporate a hopeful solution-focused approach at institution level is the extent to which pessimism can be institutionalized in agencies and teams, ensuring no momentum for change will come from staff and thereby failing the resident children and young people.

A state-wide programme was adopted in child welfare services in Kentucky that consisted of a solution-based casework model (Christensen and Todahl, 1998). Antle et al. (2009) evaluated the effectiveness of this innovation, primarily focusing on the question of whether those families treated by workers using this model fared any better in terms of repeat referrals for child maltreatment than families that received help from workers not using the model. The methodology and results are impressive: 760 cases were tracked over a six-month period and the results pointed to a positive impact of the model on child maltreatment re-referrals. These results consolidate previous research studies that had demonstrated the effectiveness of this approach for intermediate outcomes such as family engagement and achievement of goals from the case plan (Antle et al., 2009). Given the plethora of previous literature advocating its use in child welfare settings (e.g. Berg, 1994; Walsh, 1997; Berg and Kelly, 2000), these research findings confirm its potential for this difficult area of practice, especially when designed and implemented on a whole-organization level with support and training embedded at that level. Further research is needed into the specific effects of such region- or state-wide initiatives not only on objective outcomes for clients, but also on specific effects on staff to determine whether there are discernible capacity-building effects evident that can be sustained over time.

Empowerment-based groupwork

To move from a therapeutic/reformist perspective towards one that meets more of the conditions necessary to be a genuine community-development initiative, the project needs to be successful in building capacity at the community as well as the individual level with some possibility of future self-generated activity involved. As already noted, Adams (1996) relates empowerment theory to the work of mutual aid, self-help, and liberation movements and social activism, in particular with oppressed or marginalized communities, where capacity-building relates to the community having a greater ability to over-come the effects of discrimination and oppression.

The concept of mutual aid groups will be well known to readers familiar with the American social work literature, where websites and contemporary literature continue to advocate its relevance (mutualaidbasedgroupwork. blogspot.com; Gitterman and Shulman, 2005). Mutual aid groups are seen to help individuals overcome social and emotional trauma in contemporary society by reducing isolation, universalizing individual problems, and mitigating stigma; there is also an emphasis on the benefits of group service – of the helped also being a helper (Gitterman and Shulman, 2005). One distinction between a therapeutic/reformist group and a mutual aid group relates to the notion that the group and worker fulfil different functions, using the concept of 'parallel processes' of being interdependent but different; another is that group members are actively encouraged to offer and receive help from each other and to learn from each other's experiences, opinions, and suggestions (similar to the philosophy and operation of self-help twelve-step programmes such as Alcoholics Anonymous and Narcotics Anonymous). One distinction between self-help and mutual aid groups is the presence of a facilitator, often a professional helper such as a social worker. Other characteristic features of mutual aid groups that distinguish them from self-help groups include a closed membership, a fixed duration, and an absence of advocacy activities (Hernandez-Plaza et al., 2006).

In some models, common interest groups (such as those of mental health service-users) may start with a facilitator following a mutual-aid approach, and then graduate to a self-directed group model with no facilitator present (Yip, 2002). In a more radical formulation, service-user groups have formed both in the USA and UK around advocacy and empowerment themes. In mental health in particular, the impact of the consumer/survivor/ex-patient movement has been significant. The National Empowerment Center (NEC) in the USA pursues an agenda of offering alternatives to people pressurized to accept hospitalization for mental health conditions. Instead, the NEC offers support and respite care as alternatives to hospitalization but also advocates strongly for the adoption of a recovery model in mental health services: 'that a diagnosis of mental illness is not for life, and that people can recover completely' (www.power2u.org).

Cohen and Graybeal (2007) argue that a strong link exists between solution-focused concepts and values and the ethos and aims of mutual aid groups. Relating mutual aid to an interactionist approach, they emphasize how the model can 'provide the opportunity for group members to identify common struggles and gain the realization that they are not alone' (p. 42), and by actively using a 'strengths in numbers' philosophy work to recognize and use the strengths that individual members bring to the group and also that the group can bring to individual members. While recognizing the inherent tension in bringing theory-driven interventions into the mutual aid group process, Cohen and Graybeal make a strong case for the inclusion of solution-focused techniques by facilitators, always with a view to modelling and/or explicitly teaching such techniques to group members themselves, illustrated by specific examples from groups.

> As members use specific skills in their unique ways, they can help each other to choose to focus on solutions instead of problems, envision a future for them, clarify manageable steps towards the vision, identify the shared purpose of the group, highlight areas of competence, identify exceptions, evaluate progress, and maintain change.
>
> (Cohen and Graybeal, 2007: 45–46)

Springer et al. (2000) applied solution-focused techniques to a groupwork initiative based in a school for Hispanic children of incarcerated parents in Texas. The project itself was small, involved only five children over six sessions, and the results were not conclusive, indicating that further work needs to be done on developing and evaluating a combined solution-focused mutual aid framework before its potential can be truly assessed.

Working with migrant communities

> People in the helping professions can easily get a biased picture of people from other cultures. They usually see people in despair or in the 'one down' position.
>
> (Aambo, 1997: 67)

Given the low rates at which migrant communities are reported to access formal services and supports (relating to factors of inaccessibility as much as choice), the structural nature of many of the difficulties members of migrant communities face, and the increasingly transnational nature of migration flows identified in Chapter 4, many argue for the value of community interventions (following detailed local needs assessments). Aims can include the strengthening of existing informal support networks, developing capacity within migrant communities themselves and enhancing community empowerment, while also bearing in mind the structural nature of many migrants' problems (Hernandez-Plaza et al., 2006). Mutual aid groupwork is one of the approaches advocated, with the helper taking a particular role:

> The social intervention professional's role becomes one of collaborator and facilitator of social change, rather than expert and counsellor.

As collaborators, professionals learn about the participants through their cultures, their worldviews, and their life struggles. Social workers and other intervention professionals collaborate with immigrants instead of advocating for them. The professional's skills, interests or plans are not imposed on the community; rather, professionals become a resource for migrant populations.

(Hernandez-Plaza et al., 2006: 1164)

One can see how a template for solution-focused mutual aid groupwork (such as that of Cohen and Graybeal above) could be adapted for a range of interventions with migrant communities. Aambo (1997) describes a Norwegian public health initiative with a migrant Pakistani population that encompasses both solution-focused work and Freire's concept of liberation through education. His example is outlined in Box 8.6.

Family-centred services and community parenting programmes as exercises in empowerment

An especially strong form of solution-focused work with children and families was developed in Australia. In addition to the seminal work of Turnell and Edwards (1999) on the Signs of Safety programme for assessments in child welfare, and that of Durrant (1993) on residential care for young people, Elliott (2000) describes optimistic family-centred practice for use in community-based local family services (a parallel to the thousands of Sure Start Centres now in evidence across Britain). Community-building and solution-focused helping are explicitly linked in Elliott's work; two other relevant knowledge bases are cognitive work and narrative therapy. The bridge between the four is viewed as 'the optimism factor': 'the belief that change is possible, and that the starting point for change is the strength and capacities of family members' (xvi). The stance of the worker is one of actively looking for possibilities for change, even when the outlook is bleak – the worker's role being to mobilize capacity in the family. The importance of the worker genuinely holding a belief in a family's capacity for change is, for Elliott, essential. But it is also acknowledged that with families who are experiencing difficulties, the process of change can be a challenging experience, and progress may not necessarily be a linear process. Concentrating on what is going well is seen to foster confidence and hope. Elliott also usefully discusses a range of challenges that family workers may face when being solution-focused in their work. These are centred around:

- believing that the family has the strength and capability to solve problems;

Box 8.6   Case study: tasteful solutions through natural helpers (Aambo, 1997)

A request is made from a migrant women's group in Oslo for some input on health information. Instead of presuming an expert-driven model of 'imparting knowledge', the local health department decides to treat it as a community development project, driven by solution-focused principles.

1   The focus was on what these women already knew and what they already did to master their own lives. 'We presupposed that they already had the resources needed to initiate change . . . we would listen to their experiences, point out what seemed useful . . . reinforce and amplify this' (p. 67).

2   The women identified what types of health information they were most interested in. These types were grouped as specific topics, and framed as future focused and how to highlight exceptions to difficulties.

3   One topic was around 'Coping with Grief'. The facilitator began by asking the women what rituals were conducted in their country of origin when someone passed away. They described the customs they already knew, which helped them to cope with grief; the facilitator showed how much of their wisdom fitted in with Western ideas about grieving. Much was shared in this group process and the capacity within the group to support each other became more obvious.

4   A focus on diet. Identifying what they wanted to change once they had an input on 'healthy eating' led to a request for cooking classes using local ingredients. This gave the women more choice in relation to what they cooked for themselves and their families and more knowledge about healthy diets and foods.

5   The women trained in the first six-month project took responsibility for forming their own health information groups, which then cascaded as a model for imparting health information to this migrant population in Oslo.

Aambo concludes: 'An arena for mutual learning between immigrant women and health workers has been established . . . Information can be understood as knowledge communicated and communication as a social event' (p. 73).

- making discoveries, not telling people what they do well;
- respecting diverse solutions and strategies; and
- accepting that solution-focused work may not be brief (Elliott, 2000).

In this model of family work, internal capacity-building work within a family is complemented by an explicit focus on community links, both to provide a network of support and to offer opportunities to family members to participate

in community-building activities. Isolation is identified as one particular problem that marginalized families under stress encounter that can be actively
counteracted through community-building activities:

> The community-building approach assists family workers to recognise
> why it is valuable for families in vulnerable circumstances to parti-
> cipate in activities that build networks . . . the probability of people
> participating in such activities is much greater when potential parti-
> cipants are involved in their planning . . . The community-building
> approach recognises the need to work on strategies that build links
> between people so trust and a sense of mutual concern and reciprocity
> can develop.
>
> (Elliott, 2000: 104)

An American model for family-centred services combines solution-
focused, narrative, appreciative inquiry and motivational interviewing elements in a form entitled 'collaborative helping' (Madsen, 2009). This framework
emphasizes culturally sensitive practice and is based around the principles of:

1 Striving for cultural curiosity and honouring family wisdom
2 Believing in possibilities and building on family resourcefulness
3 Working in partnership with families and fitting services around
   them
4 Engaging in empowering processes and making our work more
   accountable to clients.

(Madsen, 2009: 104)

The stance of the helper is that of an appreciative ally helping families develop
and articulate goals for a preferred future and then move towards that future,

---

Box 8.7 Principles for community-building in the context of family services
(Elliott, 2000)

- Developing human capital – self-esteem and communication skills
- Increasing the material well-being of families
- Developing physical infrastructure
- Promoting family-friendly practices
- Providing opportunities for people to connect
- Encouraging diversity
- Using natural networkers
- Promoting connections with decision-makers

with the active support of their local communities. It is a partnership approach, and while it emphasizes links outside the family with community resources and supports, the focus of the model is therapeutic work with individual families.

Practice example: an Irish community development programme for parents

Six Steps to Successful Parenting is a solution-focused parenting programme devised by Andrew Duggan, a UK-based educator and family therapist, and adapted for use in both Ireland and Finland. An Irish Six Steps Programme was developed by a solution-focused community worker (who acted as coordinator of the Project), based in a suburban area of Dublin with high indices of need and few parenting supports services available but with a range of energetic formal helping agencies and a positive community spirit. This is how they set about developing the project:

Developing a 'radical' idea

Previous research showed that over 70 percent of families self-identified the need for more support in parenting than was then available. In addition, all of the agencies involved

> shared a fundamental experience of having large numbers of families on their caseloads. Families who experience a range of difficulties and stresses in their lives, many of whom are receiving support from a number of agencies. With this in mind, the Organising Committee had a 'radical' idea: 'Wouldn't it be interesting if all of the professional agencies involved with this family had a similar solution-focused and strengths-based approach as opposed to the more usual problem-oriented one?'
>
> (Cullinane et al., 2005: 9)

Proposals for a pilot project were devised and despite a lack of designated funding, the community worker was persuasive in enlisting helpers from other agencies and schools to join her in developing this project.

Articulating a shared vision for the project

A shared vision was developed as a philosophy for the project, so all agencies involved came together with certain shared beliefs:

- Parents are the real experts on parenting their children
- Addressing problems facing families would prove most effective if parents were centrally involved in the generation of the solutions
- A coherent, inter-agency, strengths-based parenting approach, as opposed to a multiplicity of services with possible variations in style and approach would be most helpful to parents seeking support
- Parents, as a resource, could then be partnered with other professional 'expertise' and placed, in partnership, at the service of children and families experiencing difficulties.

(Cullinane et al., 2005: 10)

Inviting participation and training the facilitators

Thirty trainee helpers (including workers from agencies and parent-helpers) participated in a two-day course on the Six Steps to Successful Parenting Programme. The programme itself is built on the six steps as follows:

1 Locating and developing strengths and building competence
2 Noticing small changes – 'sparkling moments'
3 Building on what is already working
4 Unique children and parents require unique strategies
5 Keep change happening
6 Celebration (Cullinane et al., 2005)

Following the initial training, an adapted six-step programme for local use was devised and protocols developed to provide a structure and process for dealing with issues and concerns that might arise (for example, around confidentiality, record-keeping, complaints procedures, and child protection concerns).

Running the pilot projects

Five pilot parenting groups were run in the region (by combinations of local workers and parents) attended by forty-two different local parents. Referrals began with a home visit by facilitators:

> The facilitators were given a detailed referral form to complete with the participating parents and a 'Sparkling Moment Diary'. This form and diary were used to elicit examples of existing strengths and resources and to identify broad goals. The diary gave the parents a framework to begin to notice what was already working for them with their children.

(Cullinane et al., 2005: 13)

The project itself ran from June 2003 to February 2005, with the five parenting groups running from March to May 2004 in different locations in the area. Forty-two parents participated in the pilot project; between them they were responsible for over 120 children.

During the six-month project, weekly peer support meetings were offered to pilot group facilitators. This was subsequently identified as a critical component of the project's success, where the stance of the facilitator was that of a non-expert and where stories of success were shared and creative solutions generated by other parents/helpers.

Evaluation results from the project

A process-oriented qualitative evaluation was carried out with feedback collected from parents who participated, facilitators (both formal helpers and parents), and referrers. For parents, the evaluation methodology consisted of pre- and post-intervention questionnaires, plus an in-depth interview three to six months after the programme ended; for facilitators, an independently run feedback session and post-intervention questionnaire; and for referrers a questionnaire after the programme ended. In addition, the organizing committee itself reviewed the project. All instruments for the evaluation were solution-focused. For the parents who participated in the pilot groups, there were significant improvements in self-reported confidence (in parenting), parenting skills, motivation, and sense of support. There was also a significant reduction in reported stress relating to parenting. The follow-up interviews (three to six months later) found that parents were still positive and enthusiastic; special mention was made of the approach valuing them as 'experts' on their own parenting. All stakeholders identified what was most useful about the programme:

For parents: finding exceptions; doing something different; keeping a 'sparkling moment' diary; valuing small steps of change; appreciating own strengths; hearing other parents' stories; not feeling alone with difficulties; getting ideas from other parents; inclusivity.

For facilitators: underlying premise of belief in parents' skills and strengths; parents having ownership of the process; parents being linked in for ongoing support; the opportunity to co-facilitate with a local parent; the solution-focused ethos of the programme; the programme's flexibility – it could be adapted to individual need.

For referrers: relaxed, parent-focused approach; focused on positives/strengths; adaptability of programme to individual need; parents' expertise recognized; builds parents' confidence and self-esteem; very practical; no jargon and not theory-laden; parents confident in using it at home from the start.

The organizers who developed and ran this programme identified four specific ways in which the parents were helped: increased confidence as parents; better relationships with their children; doing things differently; greater self-awareness.

Finally, all three stake-holder groups (parents, facilitators, and referrers) made practical suggestions for change; some of which were incorporated into subsequent programmes.

The follow-on

Following evaluation, the Tallaght Six-Steps Programme has been adopted as a continuous programme in this area of high need. Parents who have been trained using this programme are recruited to run the programme in their own communities.

Conclusions

> One of the impossible tasks that social workers [and I add, other help-ing professions] have accepted is to make sure that no one is ever left behind . . . one fruitful strategy is to change the rules of engagement by linking the best of strengths-based practice with cutting edge models in community development with a single goal in mind – to enhance the capacity of individuals and society by recognizing and

---

Box 8.8   Practice principles for solution-focused group/community initiatives

- Community work principles (such as these) need to be articulated and form a value-base from which the project is then developed: (i) promotion of equality; (ii) participation; (iii) respect; (iv) balance of task and process; (v) holistic; (vi) empowerment; (vii) collaboration; (viii) develop the community/group.
- In applying the solution-focused approach to community work: (i) look for exceptions; (ii) identify what's working; (iii) recognize strengths and resources; (iv) acknowledge and utilize expertise; (v) focus on solutions; (vi) actively use constructive feedback; (vii) note and amplify change.
- Use the **'simple'** steps: **s**olutions, not problems; **i**n-between – the action is in the interaction; **m**ake use of what's there; **p**ossibilities – past, present, and future; **l**anguage – simply said; **e**very case is different.

(Cullinane, 2006)

> tapping the talents and gifts of marginalized citizens and to nourish the generative tendencies in the social environment.
>
> (Sullivan and Rapp, 2005: 277)

The case can be made that to create an effective bridge between solution-focused helping and empowerment-based community development, the strengths perspective is required as a midway strut, to underpin the transfer of solution-focused ideas and concepts from their origins in individual and family therapy into one well suited to group and community work settings. Saleebey (2005) notes that 'A more just and equitable distribution system is at the heart of the development and expression of individual and collective powers and capacities' (p. 281). The fit between the philosophy and practice of the strengths perspective and SFT has already been recognized in the context of individual interviewing (de Jong and Miller, 1995). To this I add the fit between empowerment-based community development and the philosophy of the strengths perspective. This bridge may enable helpers to move from individual, patient or client-focused practice into capacity-building on a community or group level while still using solution-focused concepts and strategies.

In both the UK and Ireland, there are an increasing number of examples of creative, radical practice combining solution-focused concepts and strategies with principles of capacity-building, empowerment, and community development. In Ireland, the community-based national youth mental health service Headstrong has adopted solution-focused practice as its approach of choice, 'utilising the knowledge and skills of the young person, with the emphasis on finding a solution rather than focusing on the problem that a person may present with' (Headstrong, 2009: 2). Community parenting support programmes, such as the Six Steps Project, demonstrate how the merger can take place in practice. For migrant communities, solution-focused helping at the group and community levels can help to develop the social supports and practical elements needed to make a successful transition to an unfamiliar society in a culturally responsive manner.

One significant adjustment to the solution-focused therapy model that needs to be made if one wants to combine a solution-focused approach with a community development perspective is that the assessment of need has to be holistic and incorporate a systemic analysis of problems (and resources) at different levels: individual, family, group, community, and environment (Coady and Lehman, 2008), and hence it needs to reject the solution-focused assertion that one does not need to carry out a full assessment prior to action.

References

Aambo, A. (1997) Tasteful solutions: solution-focused work with groups of immigrants, *Contemporary Family Therapy*, 19 (1), 63–79.

Abbott, A. (1988) *The System of Professions: An Essay on the Division of Expert Labour*. Chicago, IL: University of Chicago Press.

Abery, B. (2006) Family adjustment and adaptation with children with Down's syndrome, *Focus on Exceptional Children*, 38 (6), 1–18.

Adams, R. (1996) *Social Work and Empowerment*, 2nd edn. London: BASW/Macmillan.

Adams, R. (2003) *Social Work and Empowerment*, 3rd edn. London: BASW/Macmillan.

Ainsworth, M. and Bowlby, J. (1967) *Child Care and the Growth of Love*. London: Penguin.

Ajmal, Y. and Rees, I. (2001) *Solutions in Schools: Creative Applications of Solution Focused Brief Thinking with Young People and Adults*. London: BT Press.

Angelou, M. (1990) *Poems by Maya Angelou: I shall not be moved*. London: Virago.

Anscombe, G.E.M. (1958) Modern moral philosophy, *Philosophy*, 33, 1–19.

Antle, B.F., Barbee, A.P., Christensen, D.N. and Sullivan, D.J. (2009) The prevention of child maltreatment recidivism through the Solution-Based Casework model of child welfare practice, *Children and Youth Services Review*, 31, 1346–1351.

Azary, M. (2006) *The application of solution-focused brief therapy to the Iranian immigrant client*. Dissertation Abstracts International, Section B, p. 2213. Alliant International University, San Diego, CA.

Bachman, D. and Lind, R. (1997) Perinatal social work and the high-risk obstetrics patient, in R.F. Lind and D.H. Bachman (eds.) *Fundamentals of Perinatal Social Work*. New York: Haworth Press.

Baker, M. and Steiner, J. (1995) Solution focused social work: metamessages to students in higher education opportunity programs, *Social Work*, 40 (2), 225–232.

Banks, R. (2005) Solution-focused group therapy, *Journal of Family Psychotherapy*, 16 (1–2), 17–21.

Banks, S. (1995) *Ethics and Values in Social Work*. London: BASW/Macmillan.

Banks, S. (2006) *Ethics and Values in Social Work*, 3rd edn. Basingstoke: Palgrave Macmillan.

Barker, J. (1995) *Brief Solution Based Therapy and its Application in Childcare Services*. Norwich: University of East Anglia.

Baruch, G., Fonagy, P. and Robins, D. (eds.) (2007) *Reaching the Hard to Reach: Evidence-based Funding Priorities for Intervention and Research*. Chichester: Wiley.

Bateson, G. (1972). *Steps to an Ecology of Mind*. Northvale, NJ: Jason Aronson.

Bauman, Z. (1998) *Globalization: The Human Consequences*. Cambridge: Polity.

Bawden, A. (2009, 8 July) Dream teams: who will care for older people in the future . . . experienced council-employed staff or poorly-paid migrants in cash-starved independent homes? *The Guardian, Society*, pp. 1–2.

Beacock, C. (2003) Mental health and learning disabilities, in A. Markwick and A. Parrish (eds.) *Learning Disabilities: Themes and Perspectives*. London: Butterworth-Heinemann.

Beauchamp, T. and Childress, J. (2001) *Principles of Biomedical Ethics*, 5th edn. Oxford: Oxford University Press.

Beauchamp, T. and Childress, J. (2008) *Principles of Biomedical Ethics*, 6th edn. Oxford: Oxford University Press.

Bennun, I. (1999) Intensive care units: a systemic perspective, *Journal of Family Therapy*, 21 (1), 96–112.

Berg, I.K. (1993) *Dying Well* (audiotape). Milwaukee, WI: BFTC Press.

Berg, I.K. (1994) *Family Based Services*. New York: Norton.

Berg, I.K. (2003) Interview with Yalom (retrieved from: www.psychotherapy.net/interview/Insoo_Kim_Berg).

Berg, I.K. and de Jong, P. (2002) *Interviewing for Solutions*, 2nd edn. Pacific Grove, CA: Brooks/Cole.

Berg, I.K. and Dolan, Y. (2001) *Tales of Solutions: A Collection of Hope-inspiring Stories*. New York: Norton.

Berg, I.K. and Gallagher, D. (1991) Solution focused brief treatment with adolescent substance abusers, in T.C. Todd and M.D. Selekman (eds.) *Family Therapy Approaches with Adolescent Substance Abusers*. New York: Allyn & Bacon.

Berg, I.K. and Kelly, S. (2000) *Building Solutions in Child Protective Services*. New York: Norton.

Berg, I.K. and Miller, S.D. (1992a) Working with Asian American clients: One person at a time, *Families in Society: The Journal of Contemporary Human Services*, 73 (6), 356–363.

Berg, I.K. and Miller, S.D. (1992b) *Working with the Problem Drinker: A Solution-focused Approach*. New York: Norton.

Berg, I.K. and Miller, S.D. (1995) *The Miracle Method: A Radically New Approach to Problem Drinking*. New York: Norton.

Berg, I.K. and Steiner, T. (2003) *Children's Solution Work*. New York: Norton.

Berg, I.K. and Szabo, P. (2005) *Brief Coaching for Lasting Solutions*. New York: Norton.

Berliner, P., Jacobsen, L., Ianev, P. and Mikkelsen, N. (2004) Solution-focused methods in psychotherapy with survivors of torture, *Psyke & Logos*, 25 (1), 169–2002.

Bessant, J. (2009) Aristotle meets youth work: a case for virtue ethics, *Journal of Youth Studies*, 12 (4), 423–438.

Beyebach, M. and Carranza, V.E. (1997) Therapeutic interaction and dropout: measuring relational communication in solution-focused therapy, *Journal of Family Therapy*, 19, 173–212.

Biestek, F. (1961) *The Casework Relationship*. London: Allen & Unwin.

Blaschke, C., Freddolino, P. and Mullen, E. (2009) Ageing and technology: a review of the research literature, *British Journal of Social Work*, 39 (4), 641–656.

Bliss, E.V. and Bray, D. (2009) The smallest solution-focused particles: towards a minimalist definition of when therapy is solution-focused, *Journal of Systemic Therapies*, 28 (2), 62–74.

Bonanno, G.A., Wortman, C.B. and Nesse, R.M. (2004) Prospective patterns of resilience and maladjustment during widowhood, *Psychology and Aging*, 19 (2), 260–271.

Bonjean, M. (1989) Solution-focused psychotherapy with families caring for an Alzheimer's patient, *Journal of Psychotherapy and the Family*, 5 (1–2), 197–210.

Bonjean, M. (1997) Solution-focused brief therapy with aging families, in T. Hargrave and S.M. Hanna (eds.) *The Aging Family: New Visions in Theory, Practice and Reality*. Philadelphia, PA: Brunner/Mazel.

Bonjean, M. (2003) Solution-focused therapy: elders enhancing solutions, in J. Ronch and J. Goldfield (eds.) *Mental Wellness in Aging: Strengths-based Approaches*. Baltimore, MD: Health Professions Press.

Booth, C. (1992) Brief therapy in HIV counselling: recreating hope, *Family Therapy Case Studies*, 7 (2), 37–52.

Boscolo, L., Cecchin, G., Hoffman, L. and Penn, P. (1987) *Milan Systemic Family Therapy: Theoretical and Practical Aspects*. New York: Harper & Row.

Bourdieu, P. and Wacquant, L.J.D. (1992) *An Invitation to Reflexive Sociology*. Chicago, IL: University of Chicago Press.

Bowlby, J. (1999) *Attachment and Loss*, Vol. 1, 2nd edn. New York: Basic Books.

Braddock, D., Hemp, R. and Rizzolo, M. (2008) *State of the States in Developmental Disabilities*. Washington, DC: American Association on Intellectual and Developmental Disabilities.

Bradley, V.J. (2000) Changes in services and supports for people with developmental disabilities: new challenges to established practice, *Health and Social Work*, 25 (3), 191–200.

Bronfenbrenner, U. (1979) *The Ecology of Human Development: Experiments by Nature and Design*. London: Harvard University Press.

Brown, S.A. and Dillenburger, K. (2004) An evaluation of the effectiveness of intervention in families with children with behavioral problems within the context of a Sure Start Programme, *Child Care in Practice*, 10 (1), 63–77.

Browne, M., O'Mahony, A. and MacEochaidh. G. (2005) *Focus Group Discussions with Staff of Our Lady of Lourdes Hospital, Drogheda: A Report Prepared for the Care of People Dying in Hospitals Project*. Ireland: IHF/HSE North East.

Bucknell, D. (2000) Practice teaching: problem to solution, *Social Work Education*, 19 (2), 125–144.

Budman, S.H. (2002) *Theory and Practice of Brief Therapy*. New York: Guilford Press.

Budman, S. and Gurman, A. (1988) *Theory and Practice of Brief Therapy*. New York: Hutchinson.

Bullis, R.K. (1996) *Spirituality in Social Work Practice*. New York: Taylor & Francis.

Burck, C. and Daniel, G. (1995) *Gender and Family Therapy*. London: Karnac.

Burnham, J. (1986) *Family Therapy: First Steps Towards a Systemic Approach*. London: Tavistock.

Burns, K. (2005) *Focus on Solutions: A Health Professional's Guide*. London: Whurr.

Butler, W.R. and Powers, K.V. (1996) Solution-focused grief therapy, in S. Miller, M. Hubble and B. Duncan (eds.) *Handbook of Solution-Focused Brief Therapy*. San Francisco, CA: Jossey-Bass.

Cade, B. and O'Hanlon, W.H. (1993) *A Brief Guide to Brief Therapy*. New York: Norton.

Campbell, A.V. (2003) The virtues (and vices) of the four principles. *Journal of Medical Ethics*, 29, 292–296.

Carpenter, J. (1997) Editorial: investigating brief solution-focused therapy, *Journal of Family Therapy*, 19, 117–120.

Carr, A. (1995) *Positive Practice: A Step-by-step Guide to Family Therapy*. Chur, Switzerland: Harwood.

Carter, B. and McGoldrick, M. (eds.) (2005) *The Expanded Family Life Cycle: Individual, Family and Social Perspectives*, 3rd edn. Boston, MA: Allyn & Bacon.

Castles, S. and Miller, M.J. (1993) *The Age of Migration: International Population Movements in the Modern World*. New York: Guilford Press.

Castles, S. and Miller, M. (2009) *The Age of Migration: International Population Movements in the Modern World*, 4th edn. London: Palgrave/Macmillan.

Center for the Advancement of Healthcare (2003) *Report on Bereavement and Grief Research*. Washington, DC: CAH (retrieved from: www.cfah.org).

Central Statistics Office (2006) Central Statistics Office website (retrieved December 2008 from: www.cso.ie).

Chau, K. (1990) A model for teaching cross-cultural practice in social work, *Journal of Social Work Education*, 26 (2), 124–133.

Christensen, D.N. and Todahl, J. (1998) Solution based casework, *Family Social Work Journal*, 6 (1), 31–47.

Clark, S., Burgess, T., Laven, G., Bull, M., Marker, J. and Browne, E. (2004) Developing and evaluating the Grieflink web site: processes, protocols, dilemmas and lessons learned, *Death Studies*, 28, 955–970.

Coady, L. and Lehman, P. (2008) *Theoretical Perspectives for Direct Social Work Practice: A Generalist-eclectic Approach*. New York: Springer.

Cockburn, J.T., Thomas, F.N. and Cockburn, O.J. (1997) Solution-focused therapy and psychosocial adjustment to orthopedic rehabilitation in a work hardening program, *Journal of Occupational Rehabilitation*, 7 (2), 97–106.

Cohen, M.B. and Graybeal, C.T. (2007) Using solution-oriented techniques in mutual aid groups, *Social Work with Groups*, 30 (4), 41–58.

Commission for Social Care Inspection and Healthcare Commission (2006) *Joint Investigation into the Provision of Services for People with Learning Disabilities at*

Cornwall Partnership NHS Trust. London: Commission for Healthcare Audit and Inspection.

Compton, B. and Galaway, B. (1994) *Social Work Processes*, 5th edn. Pacific Grove, CA: Brooks/Cole.

Compton, B. and Galaway, B. (1999) *Social Work Processes*, 6th edn. Belmont, CA: Wadsworth.

Conway, S. (2007) The changing face of death: implications for public health, *Critical Public Health*, 17 (3), 195–202.

Cooley, L. (2009) *The Power of Groups: Solution-focused Group Counseling in Schools*. Thousand Oaks, CA: Corwin Press.

Corcoran, J. (2000) Solution-focused family therapy with ethnic minority clients, *Crisis Intervention and Time-limited Treatment*, 6 (1), 5–12.

Corcoran, J. and Pillai, V. (2009) A review of the research on solution-focused therapy, *British Journal of Social Work*, 39 (2), 234–242.

Cree, V. and Myers, S. (2008) *Social Work: Making a difference*. Bristol: The Policy Press.

Cribb, A. (2008) *Health and the Good Society: Setting Healthcare Ethics in Social Context*. Oxford: Clarendon.

Cullinane, B. (2006) *Lecture Notes from Module on Solution-Focused Therapy for Masters in Social Work Students*, Trinity College, Dublin, Ireland.

Cullinane, B., Martin, F., Peelo, W. and Duggan, A. (2005) *Making it Happen: Six Steps to Successful Parenting, a Pilot Project*. Dublin: HSE Area Four Community Work Service.

Curnock, K. and Hardiker, P. (1979) *Towards Practice Theory: Skills and Methods in Social Assessments*. London: Routledge & Kegan Paul.

Cutcliffe, J. (2004) *The Inspiration of Hope in Bereavement Counselling*. London: Jessica Kingsley.

Cuthbertson, S., Margetts, M.A. and Streat, S.J. (2000) Bereavement follow-up after critical illness, *Critical Care Medicine*, 28 (4), 1196–1201.

Dahl, R., Bathel, D. and Carreon, C. (2000) The use of solution-focused therapy with an elderly population, *Journal of Systemic Therapies*, 19 (4), 45–55.

Dalrymple, J. and Burke, B. (1995) *Anti-oppressive Practice: Social Care and the Law*. Buckingham: Open University Press.

Dalrymple, J. and Burke, B. (2007) *Anti-oppressive Practice: Social Care and the Law*, 2nd edn. Buckingham: Open University Press.

De Castro, S. and Guterman, J. (2008) Solution-focused therapy for families coping with suicide, *Journal of Marital and Family Therapy*, 34 (1), 93–106.

De Chesnay, M. (2007) Solution-focused nursing with survivors of sexual violence: a cultural context, in M. McAllister (ed.) *Solution-focused Nursing*. London: Palgrave.

De Jong, P. and Berg, I.K. (2001) Co-constructing cooperation with mandated clients, *Social Work*, 46 (4), 361–374.

De Jong, P. and Berg, I.K. (2008) *Interviewing for Solutions*, 3rd edn. Belmont, CA: Thomson/Brooks Cole.

De Jong, P. and Miller, S. (1995) How to interview for client strengths, *Social Work*, 40 (6), 729–736.

Department of Health (2001) *Valuing People: A New Strategy for Learning Disability for the 21st Century* (retrieved from: www.publications.doh.gov.uk/learning-disabilities/access).

Department of Health (2009) *Valuing People: A New Three Year Strategy for People with Learning Disabilities* (retrieved from: www.dh.gov.uk/en/policyandguidance/socialcare/deliveringadultsocialcare/learningdisabilities/index.htm).

Department of Health and Social Security (1978) *Social Services Area Teams: The Practitioners' View*. London: The Stationery Office.

Dermer, S.B., Hermeseth, C.W. and Russell, C.S. (1998) A feminist critique of solution-focused therapy, *American Journal of Family Therapy*, 26 (3), 239–250.

de Shazer, S. (1982) *Patterns of Brief Therapy: An Ecosystemic Approach*. New York: Norton.

de Shazer, S. (1985) *Keys to Solution in Brief Therapy*. New York: Norton.

de Shazer, S. (1988) *Clues: Investigating Solutions in Brief Therapy*. New York: Norton.

de Shazer, S. (1991) *Putting Difference to Work*. New York: Norton.

de Shazer, S. (1994) *Words were Originally Magic*. New York: Norton.

de Shazer, S. and Berg, I.K. (1997) What works? Remarks on research aspects of solution-focused brief therapy, *Journal of Family Therapy*, 19, 121–124.

de Shazer, S. and Isebaert, L. (2003) The Bruges Model: a solution-focused approach to problem drinking, *Journal of Family Psychotherapy*, 14 (1), 43–52.

de Shazer, S., Berg, I.K., Lipchik, E., Nunnally, E., Molnar, A., Gingerich W. et al. (1986) Brief therapy: focused solution development, *Family Process*, 25, 207–221.

de Shazer, S., Dolan, Y., Korman, H., Trepper, T., McCollum, E. and Berg, I.K. (2007) *More than Miracles: The State of the Art of Solution-Focused Brief Therapy*. London: Routledge.

Dolan, Y. (1991) *Resolving Sexual Abuse: Solution-focused Therapy and Ericksonian Hypnosis for Adult Survivors*. New York: Norton.

Dominelli, L. (1988) *Anti-racist Social Work*. London: BASW/Macmillan.

Dominelli, L. (1998) Multiculturalism, anti-racism and social work, in C. Williams, H. Soydan and M.R.D. Johnson (eds.) *Social Work and Minorities: European Perspectives*. London: Routledge.

Drury-Hudson, J. (1999) Decision-making in child protection: the use of theoretical, empirical and procedural knowledge by novices and experts and implications for fieldwork placement, *British Journal of Social Work*, 29, 147–169.

Durrant, M. (1993) *Residential Treatment: A Cooperative Competency Based Approach to Residential Care*. New York: Norton.

Eakes, G., Walsh, S., Markowski, M., Cain, H. and Swanson, M. (1997) Family centred brief solution-focused therapy with chronic schizophrenia: a pilot study, *Journal of Family Therapy*, 19, 145–158.

Edwards, G. (2000) Addiction treatment and the making of large claims, *Addiction*, 95, 1749–1750.

Edwards, L.M. and Pedrotti, J. (2004) Utilizing the strengths of our cultures: therapy with biracial women and girls, in A. Gillem and C. Thompson (eds.) *Biracial Women in Therapy: Between the Rock of Gender and the Hard Place of Race*. New York: Haworth Press.

Efran, J., Lukens, R. and Lukens, M. (1988, September/October) Constructivism: what's in it for you?, *Family Therapy Networker*, pp. 27–30.

Ehrenreich, B. (2010) *Smile or Die: How Positive Thinking Fooled America and the World*. London: Granta.

Eliott, J.A. (2005) *Interdisciplinary Perspectives on Hope*. New York: Nova Science.

Elliott, B. (2000) *Promoting Family Change: The Optimism Factor*. St. Leonards, NSW: Allen & Unwin.

Emerson, E. and Hatton, C. (2004) *Estimating Future Need/Demand for Supports for Adults with Learning Disabilities in England*. Lancaster: Institute for Health Research at Lancaster University.

Eraut, M. (1994) *Developing Professional Knowledge and Competence*. London: Falmer Press.

Erickson, M.H. (1954) Special techniques of brief hypnotherapy, *Journal of Clinical and Experimental Hypnosis*, 2, 109–129.

Erickson, M.H. and Rossi, E. (1979) *Hypnotherapy: An Exploratory Casebook*. New York: Irvington.

Falicov, C.J. (2007) Working with transnational immigrants: expanding meanings of family, community and culture, *Family Process*, 46 (2), 157–171.

Fauri, D.P., Ettner, B. and Kovacs, P.J. (2000) Bereavement services in acute care settings, *Death Studies*, 24 (1), 51–64.

Field, D., Reid, D., Payne, S. and Relf, M. (2005) *Adult Bereavement Support in Five Hospices in England*. Sheffield: University of Sheffield.

Field, N.P. and Friedrichs, M. (2004) Continuing bonds in coping with the death of a husband, *Death Studies*, 28, 597–620.

Finucane, T. E., Christman, C. and Travis, K. (1999) Tube feeding in patients with advanced dementia: A review of the evidence, *Journal of the American Medical Association*, 282, 1365–1370.

Fisher, S. (1984) Time limited brief therapy with families: a one year follow up study, *Family Process*, 23, 101–106.

Fitzgerald, M. (2005) *The Genius of Artistic Creativity: Asperger's Syndrome and the Arts*. London: Jessica Kingsley.

Flaskas, C., McCarthy, I. and Sheehan, J. (eds.) (2007) *Hope and Despair in Narrative and Family Therapy: Adversity, Forgiveness and Reconciliation*. London: Routledge.

Fong, R. (2004) Contexts and environments for culturally competent practice, in R. Fong, (ed.) *Culturally Competent Practice with Immigrant and Refugee Children and Families*. New York: Guilford Press.

Fontes, L.A. (2008) *Interviewing Clients Across Cultures: A Practitioner's Guide.* New York: Guilford Press.

Fook, J. (2000) Deconstructing and reconstructing professional expertise, in B. Fawcett, B. Featherstone, J. Fook and A. Rossiter (eds.) *Practice Research in Social Work: Postmodern Feminist Perspectives.* London: Routledge.

Fook, J. (2002) *Social Work: Critical Theory and Practice.* London: Sage.

Franklin, C., Biever, J., Moore, K., Clemons, D. and Scamardo, M. (2001) The effectiveness of solution-focused therapy with children in a school setting, *Research on Social Work Practice*, 11 (4), 411–434.

Freire, P. (1970) *Pedagogy of the Oppressed.* Harmondsworth: Penguin.

Freire, P. (2004) *Pedagogy of Hope.* New York: Continuum.

Friedson, E. (1986) *Professional Powers: A Study of the Institutionalization of Formal Knowledge.* Chicago, IL: University of Chicago Press.

Friedson, E. (2003) Comments on *Journal of Health Politics, Policy and Law* Review Symposium, *Journal of Health Politics, Policy and Law*, 28 (10), 168–172.

Froerer, A.S., Smock, S.A. and Seedall, R.B. (2009) Solution-focused group work: collaborating with clients diagnosed with HIV/AIDS, *Journal of Family Psychotherapy*, 20 (1), 13–27.

Furedi, F. (2004) *Therapy Culture: Cultivating Vulnerability in an Uncertain Age.* London: Routledge.

Furman, B. and Ahola, T. (1992) *Solution Talk: Hosting Therapeutic Conversations.* New York: Norton.

Fyson, R. and Kitson, D. (2007) Independence or protection – does it have to be a choice? Reflections on the abuse of people with learning disabilities in Cornwall, *Critical Social Policy*, 27 (3), 426–436.

Galambos, C. (2004) Social work practice with people with disabilities: are we doing enough?, *Health and Social Work*, 29 (3), 163–165.

Gale, J. and Long, J. (1996) Theoretical foundations of family therapy, in F. Piercy, D. Sprenkle, J. Wetchler and Associates (eds.) *Family Therapy Sourcebook*, 2nd edn. New York: Guilford Press.

Garfield, S.L. and Bergin, A.E. (eds.) (1978) *Handbook of Psychotherapy and Behavior Change.* New York: Wiley.

George, E., Iveson, C. and Ratner, H. (1990) *Problem to Solution-Brief Therapy with Individuals and Families.* London: Brief Therapy Press.

Georgiades, S.D. (2008) A solution-focused intervention with a youth in a domestic violence situation: longitudinal evidence, *Contemporary Family Therapy*, 30, 141–151.

Gilligan, C. (1982) *In a Different Voice: Psychological Theory and Women's Development.* Cambridge, MA: Harvard University Press.

Gingerich, W.J. and Eisengart, S. (2000) Solution-focused brief therapy: a review of the outcome research, *Family Process*, 39, 477–498.

Gitterman, A. and Shulman, L. (eds.) (2005) *Mutual Aid Groups, Vulnerable and Resilient Populations, and the Life Cycle*, 3rd edn. New York: Columbia University Press.

Goffman, E. (1968) *Asylums*. Harmondsworth: Penguin.

Goldberg, D. and Szyndler, J. (1994) Debating solutions: a model for teaching about psychosocial issues, *Journal of Family Therapy*, 16, 209–217.

Goodkin, K., Feaster, D.J., Asthana, D., Blaney, N.T., Kumar, M., Baldewicz, T. et al. (1998) A bereavement support group intervention is longitudinally associated with salutary effects on the CD4 cell count and number of physician visits, *Clinical and Diagnostic Laboratory Immunology*, 5 (3), 382–391.

Gray, S., Zide, M. and Wilker, H. (2000) Using the solution-focused brief therapy model with bereavement groups in rural communities: resiliency at its best, *Hospice Journal*, 15 (3), 13–30.

Guerin, P.J. (ed.) (1976) *Family Therapy: Theory and Practice*. New York: Gardner Press.

Guterman, J. and Leite, N. (2006) Solution-focused counseling for clients with religious and spiritual concerns, *Counselling and Values*, 51, 39–52.

Guthiel, I. and Souza, M. (2006) Psychosocial services at the end of life, in B. Berkman (ed.) *Handbook of Social Work in Health and Aging*. New York: Oxford University Press.

Gutierrez, L.M., DeLois, K. and GlenMaye, L. (1995) Understanding empowerment practice: building on practitioner-based knowledge, *Families in Society*, 76 (9), 534–542.

Haley, J. (1973) *Uncommon Therapy: The Psychiatric Techniques of Milton H. Erickson M.D.* New York: Norton.

Hanifan, L.J. (1916) The rural school community center, *Annals of the American Academy of Political and Social Science*, 67, 130–138.

Harding, R. and Leam, C. (2005) Clinical notes for informal carers in palliative care: recommendations from a random patient file audit, *Palliative Medicine*, 19 (8), 639–642.

Hare-Mustin, R.T. (1978) A feminist approach to family therapy, *Family Process*, 17, 181–194.

Hare-Mustin, R.T. (1987) The problem of gender in family therapy theory, *Family Process*, 26, 15–27.

Harker, M. (2001) Building solutions at meetings, in Y. Ajmal and I. Rees (eds.) *Solutions in Schools: Creative Applications of Solution-focused Brief Thinking with Young People and Adults*. London: BT Press.

Harlow, E. and Hearn, J. (1996) Educating for anti-oppressive and anti-discriminatory social work, *Journal of Social Work Education*, 15 (1), 5–17.

Harris, M.B. and Franklin, C. (2008) *Taking Charge: A School-based Life Skills Program for Adolescent Mothers*. New York: Oxford University Press.

Harrison, W.D. (1991) *Seeking Common Ground: A Theory of Social Work in Social Care*. Aldershot: Avebury.

Harvey, J.H. (2000) *Give Sorrow Words: Perspectives on Loss and Trauma*. London: Psychology Press.

Headstrong (2009) *Spring Newsletter*. Dublin: Headstrong, The National Centre for Youth Mental Health.

Health Service Excutive (2005) *National Service Plan for 2006*. Dublin: HSE.

Held, V. (2006) *The Ethics of Care: Personal, Political and Global*. Oxford: Oxford University Press.

Helmeke, K.B. and Sori, C.F. (2006) *The Therapist's Notebook for Integrating Spirituality in Counselling*, Vol. 2. New York: Routledge.

Hernandez-Plaza, S., Alonso-Morillejo, E. and Pozo-Munoz, C. (2006) Social support interventions in migrant populations, *British Journal of Social Work*, 36 (8), 1151–1169.

Hillel, V. and Smith, E. (2001) Empowering students to empower others, in Y. Ajmal and I. Rees (eds.) *Solutions in Schools*. London: BT Press.

Hinman, L. (2008) *Ethics: A Pluralist Approach to Moral Theory*. Belmont, CA: Thomson Wadworth.

Ho, W.-S., Tsui, M.-S., Chu, C.-K. and Chan, C.C. (2003) Towards culturally sensitive EAP counselling for Chinese in Hong Kong, *Journal of Workplace Behavioral Health*, 18 (4), 73–83.

Hoffman, L. (1990) Constructing realities: an art of lenses, *Family Process*, 29, 1–12.

Holland, S. (2009) Looked after children and the ethic of care, *British Journal of Social Work* (DOI: 10.1093/bjsw/bcp086).

Holloway, W. (2006) *The Capacity to Care: Gender and Ethical Subjectivity*. London: Routledge.

Horwarth, J. and Morrison, T. (1999) *Effective Staff Training in Social Care: From Theory to Practice*. London: Routledge.

Hoskisson, P. (2003) Solution-focused groupwork, in B. O'Connell and S. Palmer (eds.) *Handbook of Solution-focused Therapy*. London: Sage

Houston, S. (2000) Pathways to change: the application of solution-focused brief therapy to foster care, in G. Kelly and R. Gilligan (eds.) *Issues in Foster Care: Policy, Practice and Research*. London: Jessica Kingsley.

Houston, S. (2003) Establishing virtue in social work: a response to McBeath & Webb. *British Journal of Social Work*, 33 (6), 819–824.

Howe, D. (1986) *Social Workers and their Practice in Welfare Bureaucracies*. Aldershot: Gower.

Howe, D. (1989) *The Consumers' View of Family Therapy*. Aldershot: Gower.

Howe, D. (1991) Knowledge, power and the shape of social work practice, in M. Davies (ed.) *The Sociology of Social Work*. London: Routledge.

Howe, D. (1992) Child abuse and the bureaucratisation of social work, *Sociological Review*, 40 (3), 491–508.

Howe, D. (1996) Surface and depth in social work practice, in N. Parton (ed.) *Social Theory, Social Change and Social Work*. London: Routledge.

Hubble, M., Duncan, B. and Miller, S.D. (1999) *The Heart and Soul of Change: What Works in Therapy*. Washington, DC: American Psychological Association.

Hugman, R. (2006) Professional values and ethics in social work: reconsidering postmodernism?, *British Journal of Social Work*, 33, 1025–1041.

Hugman, R. (2008) An ethical perspective on social work, in M. Davies (ed.) *The Blackwell Companion to Social Work*, 3rd edn. London: Blackwell.

Husain, F. (2006) Cultural competence, cultural sensitivity and family support, in P. Dolan, J. Canavan and J. Pinkerton (eds.) *Family Support as Reflective Practice*. London: Jessica Kingsley.

Inclusion Ireland (2009) *Intellectual Disability: Causes and Prevention* (retrieved from: www.inclusionireland.ie/downloads/intellectualdisability).

Ingersoll-Dayton, B. and Rader, J. (1993) Searching for solutions: mental health consultation in nursing homes, *Clinical Gerontologist*, 13 (1), 33–50.

Ingersoll-Dayton, B., Schroepfer, T. and Pryce, J. (1999) The effectiveness of a solution-focused approach for problem behaviors among nursing home residents, *Journal of Gerontological Social Work*, 32 (3), 49–64.

International Federation of Social Workers (2008) *Code of Ethics* (retrieved from: www.ifsw.org).

International Work Group on Death, Dying and Bereavement (2005) Charter for the normalisation of dying, death and loss, *Mortality*, 10 (2), 157–161.

Irish Hospice Foundation (2006) *A Baseline Study on the Provision of Hospice/Specialist Palliative Care Services in Ireland*. Dublin: IHF.

Itzhaky, H. and Lipschitz-Elhawi, R. (2004) Hope as a strategy in supervising social workers of terminally ill patients, *Health and Social Work*, 29 (1), 46–54.

Jones, D. (2009) *What can we learn from research on outcome?*, paper delivered at BASPCAN (British Association for the Study and Prevention of Child Abuse and Neglect) 7th National Congress, Swansea, September.

Jones, M. and Jordan, B. (1996) Knowledge and practice in social work, in M. Preston-Shoot and S. Jackson (eds.) *Educating Social Workers in a Changing Practice Context*. London: Whiting & Birch.

Jordan, J.R. and Neimeyer, R.A. (2003) Does grief counselling work?, *Death Studies*, 27 (9), 765–786.

Juhila, K. (2009) From care to fellowship and back: interpretative repertoires used by social welfare workers when describing their relationship with homeless women, *British Journal of Social Work*, 39, 128–143.

Kasiram, M. (2009) The emigration of South African social workers: using social work education to address gaps in provision, *Social Work Education*, 28 (6), 646–654.

Kay, B. (2003) Changing philosophy in learning disabilities, in A. Markwick and A. Parrish (eds.) *Learning Disabilities: Themes and Perspectives*. London: Butterworth-Heinemann

Keeney, B.P. (1979) Ecosystemic epistemology: an alternative paradigm for diagnosis, *Family Process*, 18 (2), 117–129.

Keeney, B.P. and Sprenkle, D.H. (1982) Ecosystemic epistemology: critical implications for the aesthetics and pragmatics of family therapy, *Family Process*, 21 (1), 1–19.

Keigher, S. (2000) Emerging issues in mental retardation: self-determination versus self-interest, *Health and Social Work*, 25 (3), 163–168.

Kim, J.S. (2006) *Examining the effectiveness of solution-focused brief therapy: Meta-analysis using random effects modelling.* Unpublished doctoral dissertation, University of Michigan.

Kim, J.S. and Franklin, C. (2008) Solution-focused brief therapy in schools: a review of the outcome literature, *Children and Youth Services Review*, 31 (4), 464–470.

Kiser, D. (1988) *A follow up study conducted at the Brief Family Therapy Center.* Unpublished manuscript (cited in de Shazer, 1991).

Kiser D. and Nunally, E. (1990) *The relationship between treatment length and goal achievement in solution-focused therapy.* Unpublished manuscript (cited in de Shazer, 1991).

Kissane, D.W. and Bloch, S. (2002) *Family Focused Grief Therapy: A Model of Family-centred Care During Palliative Care and Bereavement.* Philadelphia, PA: Open University Press.

Kissane, D., Bloch, S., McKenzie, M., McDowall, A. and Nitzan, R. (1998) Family grief therapy: a preliminary account of a new model to promote healthy family functioning during palliative care and bereavement, *Psycho-Oncology*, 7 (1), 14–25.

Kitwood, T. (1997) *Dementia Reconsidered.* Buckingham: Open University Press.

Klass, D., Silverman, P.R. and Nickman, S.L. (eds.) (1996) *Continuing Bonds: New Understanding of Grief.* Philadelphia, PA: Taylor & Francis.

Klingman, A. (2002) From supportive-listening to a solution-focused intervention for counsellors dealing with political trauma, *British Journal of Guidance and Counselling*, 30 (3), 247–259.

Kolb, D.A. (1984) *Experiential Learning.* Englewood Cliffs, NJ: Prentice-Hall.

Koss, M. (1979) Length of psychotherapy for clients seen in private practice, *Journal of Consulting and Clinical Psychotherapy*, 47, 210–212.

Kral, R. (1995) *Strategies that Work: Techniques for Solutions in Schools.* Milwaukee, WI: Brief Family Therapy Press.

Kretzmann, J. and McKnight, J. (1993) *Building Communities from the Inside Out: A Path Towards Finding and Mobilizing Community Assets.* Evanston, IL: Centre for Urban Affairs and Policy Research, Northwestern University.

Krings, T., Bobek, A., Moriarty, E., Salamonska, J. and Wickham, J. (2009) Migration and recession: Polish migrants in post-Celtic tiger Ireland, *Sociological Research Online*, 14 (2/3) (www.socresonline.org.uk/14/2/9).

Kubler-Ross, E. (1973) *On Death and Dying.* London: Routledge.

Kuhn, T.S. (1970) *The Structure of Scientific Revolutions*, 2nd edn. Chicago, IL: University of Chicago Press.

Lambert, L. (2008) A counselling model for young women in the United Arab Emirates: cultural considerations, *Canadian Journal of Counselling*, 42 (3), 101–116.

Laming, The Lord (2009) *The Protection of Children in England: A Progress Report.* London: The Stationery Office.

Landau, J. (2007) Enhancing resilience of families and communities as agents for change. *Family Process*, 46 (3), 35–365.

Lazarus, R. (1999) Hope: an emotion and a vital coping resource against despair, *Social Research*, 66 (2), 653–678.

Lazarus, R.S. and Folkman, S. (1984) *Stress, Appraisal, and Coping*. New York: Springer.

Leathard, A. and McLaren, S. (2007) *Ethics: Contemporary Challenges in Health and Social Care*. Bristol: The Policy Press.

Ledwith, M. (2005) *Community Development: A Critical Approach*, 2nd edn. Bristol: Policy Press.

Lee, M.-Y. (1997) A study of solution-focused brief family therapy: outcomes and issues, *American Journal of Family Therapy*, 25 (1), 3–17.

Lee, M.Y. (2003) A solution-focused approach to cross-cultural clinical social work practice: utilizing cultural strengths, *Families in Society: The Journal of Contemporary Human Services*, 84 (3), 385–395.

Lee, M.Y. and Mjelde-Massey, L. (2004) Cultural dissonance among generations: a solution-focused approach with East Asian elders and their families, *Journal of Marital and Family Therapy*, 30 (4), 497–513.

Lee, V., Cohin, S.R., Edgar, L., Laizner, A. and Gagnon, A. (2006) Meaning-making intervention during breast or colorectal cancer treatment improves self-esteem, optimism and self-efficacy, *Social Science and Medicine*, 62, 3133–3145.

Lethem J. (1994) *Moved to Tears, Moved to Action*. London: Brief Therapy Press.

Leupnitz, D.A. (1988) *The Family Interpreted: Psychoanalysis, Feminism and Family Therapy*. New York: Basic Books.

Lewis, C.S. (1961) *A Grief Observed*. London: Faber & Faber.

Lewis, T.F. and Osborn, C.J. (2004) Solution-focused counseling and motivational interviewing: a consideration of confluence, *Journal of Counseling and Development*, 82 (1), 38–48.

Lightfoot, C. (2003) Discovering the experts, *Canadian Journal of Dietetics Practice and Research*, 64 (2), 3–4.

Lipchik, E. (1991) Spouse abuse: challenging the party line, *Family Therapy Networker*, 15 (3), 59–63.

Lipchik, E. (1994) The rush to be brief, *Family Therapy Networker*, 18 (2), 35–39.

Lipchik, E. (2002) *Beyond Technique in Solution-focused Therapy: Working with Emotions and the Therapeutic Relationship*. New York: Guilford Press.

Littrell, J. (1998) *Brief Counselling in Action*. New York: Norton.

Lloyd, H. and Dallos, R. (2006) Solution-focused brief therapy with families who have a child with intellectual disabilities: a description of the content of initial sessions and the processes, *Clinical Child Psychology and Psychiatry*, 11 (3), 367–386.

Lloyd, H. and Dallos, R. (2008) First session solution-focused brief therapy with families who have a child with severe intellectual disabilities: mothers' experiences and views, *Journal of Family Therapy*, 30, 5–28.

Lloyd, L. (2006) A caring profession? The ethics of care and social work with older people, *British Journal of Social Work*, 36 (7), 1171–1185.

Love, S.M., Suarez, A.M. and Love, M.E. (2008) Young mothers and babies wellness program, *Children and Youth Services Review*, 30 (4), 1437–1446.

Lustig, D.C. (1999) Family caregiving of adults with mental retardation: key issues for rehabilitation counsellors, *Journal of Rehabilitation*, 6 (2), 26–36.

Luthar, S.S. (2000) The construct of resilience: a critical evaluation and guidelines for future work, *Child Development*, 71 (3), 543–562.

Lutz, H. (2008, July) *Gender in the migratory process.* Paper delivered at conference on Theories of Migration and Social Change, Oxford.

Macdonald, A.J. (1997) Brief therapy in adult psychiatry – further outcomes, *Journal of Family Therapy*, 19, 213–222.

Macdonald, A.J. (2007) *Solution-focused Therapy: Theory, Research and Practice.* London: Sage.

MacDonald, A. (2009) www.solutionsdoc.co.uk.

Madsen, W.C. (2009) Collaborative helping: a practice framework for family-centered services, *Family Process*, 48 (1), 103–116.

Mall, M. and Stringer, B. (2001) Brief therapy approaches with groups and families in an education support service, in Y. Ajmal and I. Rees (eds.) *Solutions in Schools: Creative Applications of Solution-focused Brief Thinking with Young People and Adults.* London: BT Press.

Maple, F.F. (1998) *Goal-focused Interviewing.* Thousand Oaks, CA: Sage.

Massey, D.S., Arango, J., Hugo, G., Kouaouci, A., Pellegrino, A. and Taylor, J.E. (1998) *Worlds in Motion: Understanding International Migration at the End of the Millennium.* Oxford: Clarendon Press.

Maturana, H. and Varela, F. (1987) *The Tree of Knowledge: Biological Roots of Human Understanding.* Boston, MA: Shambala Publications.

McAllister, M. (ed.) (2007) *Solution-focused Nursing: Rethinking Practice.* Basingstoke: Palgrave Macmillan.

McBeath, G. and Webb, S. (2002) Virtue ethics and social work: being lucky, realistic and not doing one's duty, *British Journal of Social Work*, 32 (8), 1015–1036.

McCallion, P., Janicki, M. and Grant-Griffin, L. (1997) Exploring the impact of culture and acculturation on older families caregiving for persons with developmental disabilities, *Family Relations*, 46, 347–357.

McCarthy, J.R. (2007) 'They look as if they're coping but I'm not': the relational power/lessness of 'youth' in responding to experiences of bereavement, *Journal of Youth Studies*, 10 (3), 285–303.

McCarthy, M. and Thompson, D. (1992) *Sex and the Three Rs, Rights, Responsibilities and Risks: A Sex Education Package for Working with People with Learning Difficulties.* Brighton: Pavilion.

McCubbin, H.I., Thompson, A. and Cubbin, M.A. (1996) *Family Assessment: Resiliency, Coping and Adaptation.* Madison, WI: University of Wisconsin.

McKeown, K., Haase, T. and Pratschke, J. (2001) *Distressed Relationships: Does Counselling Help?* Dublin: Marriage Relationship Counselling Service.

McNamee, S. and Gergen, K. (eds.) (1992) *Therapy as Social Construction*. London: Sage.

Meagher, G. and Parton, N. (2004) Modernising social work and the ethics of care, *Social Work and Society*, 2 (1), 10–27.

Menzies, I. (1960) Social systems as a defence against anxiety: an empirical study of the nursing service of a general hospital, *Human Relations*, 13, 95–121.

Metcalf, L. (1995) *Counseling Toward Solution: A Practical Solution-focused Program for Working with Students, Teachers and Parents*. New York: Simon & Schuster.

Miller, G. and de Shazer, S. (1998) Have you heard the latest about? Solution-focused therapy as a rumor, *Family Process*, 37 (3), 363–377.

Miller, S.D. and Berg, I.K. (1995) *The Miracle Method: A Radically New Approach to Problem Drinking*. New York: Norton.

Miller, S.D., Hubble, M.A. and Duncan, B.L. (eds.) (1996) *Handbook of Solution-focused Brief Therapy*. San Francisco, CA: Jossey-Bass.

Miller, W.R. (2000) Professional ethics and marketing of treatment, *Addiction*, 95 (12), 1764–1765.

Miller, W.R. and Rolnick, S. (2002) *Motivational Interviewing: Preparing People to Change Addictive Behavior*, 2nd edn. New York: Guilford Press.

Mills, S. & Sprenkle, D.H. (1995) Family therapy in the post-modern era, *Family Relations*, 44, 450–462.

Milner, J. and Singleton, T. (2008) Domestic violence: solution-focused practice with men and women who are violent, *Journal of Family Therapy*, 30 (1), 29–53.

Minichiello, V., Browne, J. and Kendig, H. (2000) Perceptions and consequences of ageism: views of older people, *Ageing and Society*, 20 (3), 253–278.

Mitchell, S.L., Teno, J.M., Miller, S.C. and Mor, V. (2005) A national study of the location of death for older persons with dementia, *Journal of the American Geriatrics Society*, 53 (2), 299–305.

Morrison, P. (2007) Facilitating family, friends and community transition through the experience of loss, in M. McAllister (ed.) *Solution-focused Nursing: Rethinking Practice*. Basingstoke: Palgrave/Macmillan.

Murphy, J.J. (1994) Working with what works: a solution-focused approach to school behavior, *The School Counselor*, 42, 59–65.

Murphy, J.J. and Davis, M.W. (2005) Video exceptions: an empirical case study involving a child with developmental disabilities, *Journal of Systemic Therapies*, 24 (4), 66–79.

Murray-Parkes, C. (1972) *Bereavement: Studies of Grief in Adult Life*. London: Pelican/ Tavistock Institute of Human Relations.

Murray-Parkes, C., Laungani, P. and Young, B. (eds.) (1996) *Death and Bereavement Across Cultures*. London: Routledge.

Musker, M. (2007) Learning disabilities and solution-focused nursing, in

M. McAllister (ed.) *Solution-focused Nursing: Rethinking Practice*. Basingstoke: Palgrave Macmillan.

Narabayashi, R. (2003) Helping families with 'Hikikomori', *Seishin Igaku (Clinical Psychiatry)*, 45 (3), 271–277.

National Institute for Health and Clinical Excellence (2004) *Improving Supportive and Palliative Care for Adults with Cancer: Research Evidence*. London: Kings College, University of London (retrieved from: http://www.nice.org.uk/page.aspx?o=110010).

National Institute of Social Work (1983) *Social Workers: Their Roles and Tasks*. London: NISW.

National Social Work Qualifications Board (2003) *Handbook of Accreditation Standards and Procedures for Courses Leading to the National Qualification in Social Work (NQSW) Award*, 3rd edn. Dublin: NSWQB.

Neilson-Clayton, H. and Brownlee, K. (2002) Solution-focused brief therapy with cancer patients and their families. *Journal of Psychosocial Oncology*, 20 (1), 1–14.

Neimeyer, R. (2000) Searching for the meaning of meaning: grief therapy and the process of reconstruction, *Death Studies*, 24 (6), 541–558.

Neimeyer, R. (2001) *Meaning Reconstruction and the Experience of Loss*. Washington, DC: American Psychological Association.

Neimeyer, R. (2005) Grief, loss and the quest for meaning: narrative contributions to bereavement care, *Bereavement Care*, 24 (2), 27–30.

Nestle, M. and Jacobson, M. (2000) Halting the obesity epidemic: a public health policy approach, *Public Health Reports*, 115 (1), 12–24.

Newsome, S. (2004) Solution-focused brief therapy groupwork with at-risk junior high school students: enhancing the bottom line, *Research on Social Work Practice*, 14 (5), 336–343.

Nirje, B. (1969) The normalization principle and its human management implications, in R. Kugel and W. Wolfensberger (eds.) *Changing Patterns in Residential Services for the Mentally Retarded*. Washington, DC: President's Committee on Mental Retardation.

Noddings, N. (1984) *Caring: A Feminine Approach to Ethics and Moral Education*. Berkeley, CA: University of California Press.

Noddings, N. (2002) *Starting at Home: Caring and Social Policy*. Berkeley, CA: University of California Press.

NSPCC (2003) *It Doesn't Happen to Disabled Children*. Report of the National Working Group on Child Protection and Disability. London: National Society for the Prevention of Cruelty to Children.

Nucleus Group (2004) *Review of Specific Grief and Bereavement Services: Final Report*. Melbourne, VIC: Department of Human Services (retrieved from: http://www.health.vic.gov.au/palliativecare/final report_grief).

O'Brien, J. (1987) A guide to life-style planning, in B. Wilcox & T. Bellamy (eds.) *A Comprehensive Guide to the Activities Catalogue*. Baltimore, MD: Paul H. Brookes.

O'Brien, J. and O'Brien, C.L. (2004) *Find Meaning in the Work: Direct Support Workers Consider the Meaning of their Jobs*. Lithonia, GA: Responsive Systems Associates.

O'Connell, B. and Palmer, S. (eds.) (2003) *Handbook of Solution-focused Therapy*. London: Sage.

O'Connell, J. (1994) *Reach Out*. Report by the DTEDG on the Poverty 3 Programme 1990–1994. Dublin: Pavee Point Publications.

O'Connor, C.A., Fauchald, S.K. and Patsdaughter, C.A. (2004) Remembering those who have gone before: the importance of AIDS memorial services for families and friends, *Illness, Crisis and Loss*, 12 (4), 307–318.

O'Connor, E. (2008) *The Beaumont Model for Bereavement Care in Acute Hospitals: practice and research*, Presentation to the 8th International Conference on Grief and Bereavement in Contemporary Society, Melbourne, VIC, Australia.

O'Daly, K. (2006) Project Leader, *Solas, Barnardo's Bereavement Counselling for Children*, Dublin (private correspondence).

O'Hanlon, B. and Weiner-Davis, M. (2003) *In Search of Solutions: A New Direction in Psychotherapy*. New York: Norton.

Oltjenbruns, K. and James, L. (2006) Adolescents' use of the Internet as a modality of grief support, *The Forum – Uses of the Internet and Death*, 32 (4), 5–6.

O'Reilly, J. (1990) The Hospital Memorial Service: a contemporary response to society's ritual needs, *Religious Education*, 85 (4), 536–547.

Ormandy, P. (1998) A memorial service for renal patients, *EDTNA ERCA Journal*, 24 (3), 22–24.

Orsulic-Jeras, S., Shepherd, J. and Britton, P. (2003) Counseling older adults with HIV/AIDS: a strengths-based model of treatment, *Journal of Mental Health Counseling*, 27 (3), 233–247.

Papadatou, D. (2006) Caregivers in death, dying and bereavement situations, *Death Studies*, 30 (7), 649–663.

Parkes, C.M., Stevenson-Hinde, J. and Morris, P. (1991) *Attachment Across the Life Cycle*. London: Tavistock/Routledge.

Parrenas, R.S. (2005) *Children of Global Migration: Transnational Families and Gendered Woes*. Stanford, CA: Stanford University Press.

Parton, N. (2003) Rethinking *professional* practice: the contributions of social constructionism and the feminist 'ethics of care', *British Journal of Social Work*, 33 (1), 1–16.

Parton, N. and O'Byrne, R. (2000) *Constructive Social Work: Towards a New Practice*. London: Macmillan.

Payne, M. (1997) *Modern Social Work Theory*, 2nd edn. Basingstoke: Macmillan.

Payne, M. (2005) *Modern Social Work Theory*, 3rd edn. London: Palgrave.

Peters, J., Parry, G., Van Cleemput, P., Moore, J. Cooper, C. and Walters, S. (2009) Health and use of health services: a comparison between Gypsies and Travellers and other ethnic groups, *Ethnicity and Health*, 14 (4), 359–377.

Pichot, T. and Dolan, Y. (2003) *Solution-focused Brief Therapy: Its Effective Use in Agency Settings*. London: Routledge.

Piercy, F., Sprenkle, D., Wetchler, J. and Associates (eds.) (1996) *Family Therapy Sourcebook*, 2nd edn. New York: Guilford Press.

Pilalis, J. and Anderton, J. (1986) Feminism and family therapy – a possible meeting point, *Journal of Family Therapy*, 8, 99–114.

Pinkerton, J. and Campbell, J. (2002) Social work and social justice in Northern Ireland: towards a new occupational space, *British Journal of Social Work*, 32 (3), 723–737.

Pollack, D. (2005) The capacity of a mentally challenged person to consent to abortion and sterilization, *Health and Social Work*, 30 (3), 253–257.

Pomeroy, E.C., Green, D.L. and Van Langingham, L. (2002) Couples who care: the effectiveness of a psychoeducational group intervention for HIV-serodiscordant couples, *Research on Social Work Practice*, 12 (2), 238–272.

Prigerson, H. (2005) Complicated grief when the path of adjustment leads to a dead end, *Healthcare Counselling and Psychotherapy Journal*, 5 (3) (adapted from article of same name in *Bereavement Care*, 2004, 23 (3), 38–40).

Pritchard, J. (2008) *Good Practice in Safeguarding Adults*. London: Jessica Kingsley.

Psychotherapy Networker (2002) Report on American Psychological Association Symposium on 'The (overlooked) virtues of negativity', *Psychotherapy Networker*, 1: 15.

Putnam, R.D. (2000) *Bowling Alone: The Collapse and Revival of American Community*. New York: Simon & Schuster.

Quick, E.K. and Gizzo, D.P. (2007) The 'Doing What Works' group: a quantitative and qualitative analysis of solution-focused group therapy, *Journal of Family Psychotherapy*, 18 (3), 65–84.

Quinones, M.A. (1997) Contextual influences on training effectiveness, in M.A. Quinones and A. Ehrenstein (eds.) *Training for a Rapidly Changing Workplace: Applications of Psychological Research*. Washington, DC: American Psychological Society.

Rachels, J. (1986) *The Elements of Moral Philosophy*. New York: Random House.

Rapaport, A. (1986) *General System Theory: Essential Concepts and Applications*. Cambridge, MA: Abacus.

Reamer, F. (2001) *Social Work Ethics Audit*. Washington, DC: National Association of Social Workers.

Reder, P., Duncan, S. and Gray, M. (1993) *Beyond Blame*. London: Routledge.

Reid, M.A. and Barrington, H. (1994) *Training Interventions: Managing Employee Development*, 5th edn. London: Institute of Personnel and Development.

Reid, W. and Epstein, L. (1972) *Task Centred Casework*. New York: Columbia University Press.

Reid, W.J. and Shyne, A.W. (1969) *Brief and Extended Casework*. New York: Columbia University Press.

Reimers, S. and Treacher, A. (1995) *Introducing User-friendly Family Therapy*. London: Routledge.

Rhodes, J. and Ajmal, Y. (1995) *Solution Focussed Thinking in Schools*. London: BT Press.

Rimon, E., Kagansky, N. and Levy, S. (2005) Percutaneous endoscopic gastronomy: evidence of different prognosis in various patient subgroups, *Age and Ageing*, 34 (4), 353–357.

Roberts, A. (2006) *Hospice-based bereavement support: assessing the effectiveness of service delivery*, Presentation to Research Forum of EAPC Congress, May 2006, Italy.

Robertson, J., Emerson, E., Hatton, C., Elliott, J., McIntosh, B., Swift, P. et al. (2005). *The Impact of Person Centred Planning*. Lancaster: Institute for Health Research, Lancaster University (available electronically at: Valuingpeople.gov.uk).

Rogers, E. (1995) *Diffusion of Innovations*, 4th edn. New York: Free Press.

Rollnick S. and Miller, W.R. (1997) What is motivational interviewing?, *Behavioural and Cognitive Psychotherapy*, 23, 327–334.

Rollnick, S., Miller, W.R. and Butler, C. (2007) *Motivational Interviewing in Health Care: Helping Patients Change Behavior*. New York: Guilford Press.

Ross, W.D. (1930, reprinted 2002) *The Right and the Good*. Oxford: Oxford University Press.

Rowan, T. and O'Hanlon, B. (1999) *Solution-oriented Therapy for Chronic and Severe Mental Illness*. New York: Wiley.

Rowson, R. (2006) *Working Ethics: How to be Fair in a Culturally Complex World*. London: Jessica Kingsley.

Rubak, S., Sandboek, A., Lauritzen, T. and Christensen, B. (2005) Motivational interviewing: a systematic review and meta-analysis, *British Journal of General Practice*, 55, 305–312.

Rutter, M. (1987) Psychosocial resilience and protective mechanisms, *American Journal of Orthopsychiatry*, 57 (3), 316–331.

Rutter, M. (1990) *Helping Troubled Children*. London: Penguin.

Rutter, M. (1999) Resilience concepts and findings: implications for family therapy, *Journal of Family Therapy*, 21 (2), 119–144.

Saleebey, D. (1992) *The Strengths Perspective in Social Work*. New York: Longman.

Saleebey, D. (1994) Culture, theory, and narrative: the intersection of meanings in practice, *Social Work*, 39, 351–359.

Saleebey, D. (1997) *The Strengths Perspective in Social Work*, 2nd edn. New York: Longman.

Saleebey, D. (2001) *The Strengths Perspective in Social Work*, 3rd edn. New York: Pearson/Allyn & Bacon.

Saleebey, D. (2005) *The Strengths Perspective in Social Work*, 4th edn. New York: Pearson/Allyn & Bacon.

Saleebey, D. (2008) *The Strengths Perspective in Social Work*, 5th edn. New York: Pearson/Allyn & Bacon.

Sandel, M. (2009) *Justice: What's the Right Thing to Do?* New York: Farrar, Straus & Giroux.

Schön, D. (1983) *The Reflective Practitioner*. New York: Basic Books.

Schön, D. (1987) *Educating the Reflective Practitioner: Towards a New Design for Teaching and Learning in the Professions*. San Francisco, CA: Jossey-Bass.

Schut, H., Stroebe, M., van den Bout, J. and Terheggen, M. (2002) The efficacy of bereavement interventions: determining who benefits, in M. Stroebe, R. Hansson, W. Stroebe and H. Schut (eds.) *Handbook of Bereavement Research: Consequences, Coping and Care*. Washington, DC: American Psychological Association.

Seidel, A. and Hedley, D. (2008) The use of solution-focused brief therapy with older adults in Mexico: a preliminary study, *American Journal of Family Therapy*, 36, 242–252.

Seligman, M.E.P. (1991) *Learned Optimism*. New York: Knopf.

Seligman, M. (1998) *Learned Optimism*, 2nd edn. New York: Pocket Books.

Sharry, J. (1996) Believing in miracles: applying solution focused therapy in a child and family clinic, *Feedback*, 6 (2), 22–25.

Sharry, J. (2001) *Solution-focused Groupwork*. London: Sage.

Sharry, J. (2007) *Solution-focused Groupwork*, 2nd edn. London: Sage.

Sheldon, B. and McDonald, G. (2009) *A Textbook of Social Work*. London: Routledge.

Shin, S.-K. (2009) Effects of a solution-focused program on the reduction of aggressiveness and the improvement of social readjustment for Korean youth probationers, *Journal of Social Services Research*, 35 (3), 274–284.

Shine, J. (1997) Isolated in Ireland, in T. Walsh (ed.) *Solution-focused Child Protection: Towards a Positive Frame for Social Work Practice*. Occasional Paper #6. Dublin: Trinity College, Department of Social Studies.

Shoham, V., Rohrbaugh, M. and Patterson, J. (1995) Problem- and solution-focused couple therapies: the MRI and Millwaukee models, in N.S. Jacobson and A.S. Gurman (eds.) *Clinical Handbook of Couple Therapy*. New York: Guilford Press.

Sidell, N. (1997) Easing transitions: solution-focused principles and the nursing home resident's family, *Clinical Gerontologist*, 18 (2), 21–41.

Sikkema, K., Hansen, N., Kochman, A., Tate D. and Difrancisco, W. (2004) Outcomes from randomized controlled trial of group intervention for HIV positive men and women coping with AIDS-related loss and bereavement, *Death Studies*, 28 (3), 187–209.

Simpson, J.A. and Rholes, W.S. (eds.) (1998) *Attachment Theory and Close Relationships*. New York: Guilford Press.

Smale, G. (1996) *Mapping Change and Innovation*. London: The Stationery Office.

Smale, G. (1998) *Managing Change through Innovation*. London: The Stationery Office.

Smith, I. (2005) Solution-focused brief therapy with people with learning disabilities: a case study, *British Journal of Learning Disabilities*, 33, 102–105.

Smock, S., Trepper, T.S., Wetchler, J.L., McCollum, E.E., Ray, R. and Pierce, K. (2008) Solution-focused group therapy for Level One substance abusers, *Journal of Marital and Family Therapy*, 34 (1), 107–120.

Snyder, C.R. (ed.) (2000) *Handbook of Hope: Theory, Measures and Applications*. London: Academic Press.

Snyder, C.R. and Lopez, S.J. (eds.) (2002) *Handbook of Positive Psychology*. New York: Oxford University Press.

Solomon, B. (1976) *Black Empowerment: Social Work in Oppressed Communities*. New York: Columbia University Press.

Song, S.J. (1999) Using solution-focused therapy with Korean families, in K. Ng (ed.) *Counseling Asian Families from a Systems Perspective*. Alexandria, VA: American Counseling Association.

Sontag, S. (1983) *Illness As Metaphor*. London: Penguin.

Souza, S. (2005) *Fostering solution-focused relationships with multicultural families: An in-service training for Child Protective Services*. Dissertation Abstracts International, Section B, p. 2317. San Francisco, CA: Alliant International University.

Soydan, H. and Williams, C. (1998) Exploring concepts, in C. Williams, H. Soydan and M. Johnson (eds.) *Social Work and Minorities: European Perspectives*. London: Routledge.

Springer, D., Lynch, C. and Rubin, A. (2000) Effects of a solution-focused mutual aid group for Hispanic children of incarcerated parents, *Child and Adolescent Social Work Journal*, 17, 431–442.

Sriskandarajah, D. and Road, F.H. (2005) *United Kingdon: Rising Numbers, Rising Anxieties* (retrieved July 2009 from: www.migrationinformation.org/Profiles/display.cfm).

Stalker, C.A., Levene, J.E. and Coady, N.F. (1999) Solution-focused brief therapy – one model fits all?, *Families in Society: The Journal of Contemporary Human Services*, 80 (5), 468–477.

Stams, G.J., Dekovic, M., Buist, K. and de Vries, L. (2006) Efficacy of solution-focused brief therapy: a meta-analysis, *Dutch Journal of Behavior Therapy (Gedragstherapie)*, 39 (2), 81–95.

Stephen, A.I., Wimpenny, P., Unwin, R., Work, F., Dempster, P., MacDuff, C. et al. (2009) Bereavement and bereavement care in health and social care: provision and practice in Scotland, *Death Studies*, 33, 239–261.

Stevenson, O. (1998) Neglect: where now? Some reflections, *Child Abuse Review*, 7, 111–115.

Stoddart, K., McDonnell, J., Temple, V. and Mustata, A. (2001) Is brief better? A modified brief solution-focused therapy approach for adults with a developmental delay, *Journal of Systemic Therapies*, 20 (2), 24–40.

Stroebe, M. and Schut, H. (1999) The dual process model of coping with bereavement: rationale and description, *Death Studies*, 23 (3), 197–213.

Stroebe, W. and Stroebe, M. (1987) *Bereavement and Health: Psychological and Physical Consequences of Partner Loss*. New York: Cambridge University Press.

Stroebe, W., Zech, E., Stroebe, M.S. and Abakoumkin, G. (2005) Does social support help in bereavement?, *Journal of Social and Clinical Psychology*, 24 (7), 1030–1050.

Styring, L. (2003) Community care: opportunities, challenges and dilemmas, in A. Markwick and A. Parrish (eds.) *Learning Disabilities: Themes and Perspectives*. London: Butterworth-Heinemann.

Suarez-Orozco, C. and Suarez-Orozco, M. (2001) *Children of Immigration*. Cambridge, MA: Harvard University Press.

Sullivan, W.P. and Rapp, C.A. (2006) Honoring philosophical traditions: the strengths model and the social environment, in D. Saleebey (ed.) *The Strengths Perspective in Social Work*, 4th edn. Boston, MA: Pearson Education.

Sun, A.-P. (2004) Principles of practice with substance-abusing pregnant women: a framework based on the five social work intervention roles, *Social Work*, 49 (3), 383–394.

Sundman, P. (1997) Solution-focused ideas in social work, *Journal of Family Therapy*, 19, 159–172.

Teahan, B., Gaffney, B. and Yarnell, J. (2002) Community development: knowledge, attitudes and training needs in Northern Ireland, *Health Education Journal*, 61 (1), 32–43.

Thomas, S. and Wolfensberger, W. (1999) An overview of social role valorization, in R.J. Flynn and R.A. Lemay (eds.) *A Quarter Century of Normalization and Social Role Valorization: Evolution and Impact*. Ottawa, ON: University of Ottawa Press.

Thompson, N. (1993) *Anti-discriminatory Practice*. London: Palgrave Macmillan.

Thompson, N. (1997) *Anti-discriminatory Practice*, 2nd edn. London: BASW/Macmillan.

Thompson, N. (1998) *Promoting Equality: Challenging Discrimination and Oppression*. London: Palgrave Macmillan.

Thompson, N. (2003) *Promoting Equality: Challenging Discrimination and Oppression*, 2nd edn. London: Palgrave Macmillan.

Thompson, N. (2006) *Anti-discriminatory Practice*, 4th edn. London: Palgrave Macmillan.

Thompson, R. and Littrell, J.M. (1998) Brief counseling for students with learning disabilities, *Professional School Counseling*, 2 (1), 60–67.

Thorslund, K.W. (2007) Solution-focused group therapy for patients on long-term sick leave, *Journal of Family Psychotherapy*, 18 (3), 11–24.

Tizard, B. and Phoenix, A. (2002) *Black, White or Mixed Race? Race and Racism in the Lives of Young People of Mixed Parentage*, 2nd edn. London: Routledge.

Tomori, C. and Bavelas, J.B. (2007) Using microanalysis of communication to compare solution-focused and client-centered therapies, *Journal of Family Psychotherapy*, 18 (3), 25–35.

Torode, R., Walsh, T. and Woods, M. (2001) *Working with Refugees and Asylum-Seekers: A Social Work Reference Book*. Dublin: Dept. of Social Studies, Trinity College Dublin.

Trice, E.D. and Prigerson, H.G. (2009) Communication in end-stage cancer: review of the literature and future research, *Journal of Health Communication*, 14, 95–108.

Tronto, J. (1993) *Moral Boundaries: A Political Argument for an Ethics of Care.* New York: Routledge.

Trute, B., Hiebert-Murphy, D. and Levine, K. (2007) Parental appraisal of the family impact of childhood developmental disability: times of sadness and times of joy, *Journal of Intellectual and Developmental Disability*, 32 (1), 1–9.

Turnell, A. and Edwards, S. (1999) *Signs of Safety: A Solution and Safety Oriented Approach to Child Protection Casework.* London: Norton.

Turnell, A. and Lipchik, E. (1999) The role of empathy in brief therapy: the overlooked but vital context, *Australian and New Zealand Journal of Family Therapy*, 2(4), 177–182.

United Nations Centre for Human Rights (1994) *Human Rights and Social Work: A Manual for Schools of Social Work and the Social Work Profession.* New York: UNCHR.

Van der Klis, M. and Karsten, L. (2009) The commuter family as a geographical adaptive strategy for the work–family balance, *Community, Work and Family*, 12 (3), 339–354.

Van der Kolk, B., McFarlane, A. and Weisaeth, L. (eds.) (1996) *Traumatic Stress Disorder: The Effects of Overwhelming Experience on Mind, Body, and Society.* New York: Guilford Press.

Van Doorslaer, O. and Keegan, O. (2001) *Contemporary Irish Attitudes towards Death, Dying and Bereavement.* Dublin: Royal College of Surgeons, Health Services Research Centre.

Vekic, K. (2003) *Unsettled Hope: Unaccompanied Minors in Ireland: From Understanding to Response.* Dublin: Marino Institute Centre for Education Services.

Von Bertalanffy, L. (1971) *General System Theory: Foundations, Developments, Applications.* London: Allen Lane.

Walker, L. (2008) Waikiki Youth Circles: homeless youth learn goal setting skills, *Journal of Family Psychotherapy*, 19 (1), 85–91.

Walsh, F. (2007) Traumatic loss and major disasters: strengthening family and community resilience, *Family Process*, 46 (2), 207–227.

Walsh, T. (1995) Brief solution focused therapy: miracle cure or quack medicine?, *The Irish Social Worker*, 13 (1), 4–7.

Walsh, T. (ed.) (1997) *Solution-focused Child Protection: Towards a Positive Frame for Social Work Practice.* Dublin: Trinity College School of Social Work and Social Policy.

Walsh, T. (2002) *The introduction of solution-focused therapy to Irish social workers: a case study of innovation diffusion*, Unpublished PhD thesis, Trinity College Dublin Library, Ireland.

Walsh, T. (2006) Two sides of the same coin: ambiguity and complexity in child protection work, *Journal of Systemic Therapies*, 25 (2), 38–49.

Walsh, T., Foreman, M. and Curry, P. (2007) *Bereavement Care in Acute Hospitals: An Evaluation of the Beaumont Hospital Bereavement Care Service*. Dublin: Beaumont Hospital/Trinity College Dublin.

Walsh, T., Foreman, M., Curry, P., O'Driscoll, S. and McCormack, M. (2008) Bereavement support in an acute hospital: an Irish model, *Death Studies*, 32 (8), 768–786.

Walter, T. (1994) *The Revival of Death*. London: Routledge.

Walter, T. (1999) *On Bereavement: The Culture of Grief*. Basingstoke: Open University Press.

Wampold, B.E. (2001) *The Great Psychotherapy Debate: Models, Methods and Findings*. Hillsdale, NJ: Lawrence Erlbaum Associates.

Warnock, M. (2009, 17 May) Comment and debate: don't call me vulnerable just because I am growing older, *Observer*, p. 31.

Warnock, M. (2010, 28 March) School of life: ideas for modern living, No. 5: Morality, *Observer Magazine*.

Watzlawick, P. (ed.) (1984) *The Invented Reality: How do we know what we believe we know? Contributions to Constructivism*. New York: Norton.

Watzlawick, P. (1990) *Munchausen's Pigtail or Psychotherapy and 'Reality'*. New York: Norton.

Watzlawick, P., Weakland, J. and Fisch, R. (1974) *Change: Principles of Problem Formation and Problem Resolution*. New York: Norton.

Weakland, J. (1991) Foreword, in S. de Shazer, *Putting Difference to Work*. New York: Norton.

Weakland, J. and Fisch, R. (1992) Brief therapy – MRI style, in S.H. Budman, M.F. Hoyt and S. Friedman (eds.) *The First Session in Brief Therapy*. New York: Guilford Press.

Weakland, J., Fisch, R., Watzlawick, P. and Bodin, A.M. (1974) Brief therapy: focused problem resolution, *Family Process*, 13, 141–168.

Westcott, H. (1991) The abuse of disabled children: a review of the literature. *Child: Care, Health and Development*, 17, 243–258.

Wetchler, J. (1996) Social constructionist family therapies, in F. Piercy, D. Sprenkle, J. Wetchler and Associates (eds.) *Family Therapy Sourcebook*, 2nd edn. New York: Guilford Press.

Wheeler, J. (1995) Believing in miracles: the implications and possibilities of using solution focused therapy in a child health setting, *ACPP Review*, 17 (5), 5–12.

White, M. and Epston, D. (1990) *Narrative Means to Therapeutic Ends*. Adelaide, SA: Dulwich Centre.

Williams, P. (2006) *Social Work with People with Learning Difficulties*. Exeter: Learning Matters Ltd.

Wilson, D.M., Truman, C.D., Thomas, R., Fainsinger, R., Kovacs-Burns, K., Froggatt, K. et al. (2009) The rapidly changing location of death in Canada, 1994–2004. *Social Science and Medicine*, 68, 1752–1758.

Wilson, K., Ruch, G., Lymbery, M. and Cooper, A. (2008) *Social Work: An Introduction to Contemporary Practice*. Harlow: Pearson Longman.

Witkin, S. (1998) Human rights and social work, *Social Work*, 43 (3), 197–201.

Witkin, S. and Saleebey, D. (eds.) (2007) *Social Work Dialogues: Transforming the Canon in Inquiry, Practice and Education*. Alexandria, VA: CSWE.

Wolfensberger, W. (1972) *The Principle of Normalisation in Human Services*. Toronto, ON: National Institute on Mental Retardation.

World Health Organization (2008) WHO website definition (retrieved from: www.who.int/cancer/palliative/definition).

Yeung, F. (1999) The adaptation of solution-focused therapy in Chinese culture: a linguistic perspective, *Transcultural Psychiatry*, 36 (4), 477–489.

Yip, K.-S. (2002) A mutual aid group for psychiatric rehabilitation of mental ex-patients in Hong Kong, *International Journal of Social Psychiatry*, 48 (4), 253–265.

Young, S. (2001) Solution-focused anti-bullying, in Y. Ajmal and I. Rees (eds.) *Solutions in Schools*. London: BT Press.

Zimmerman, T.S., Jacobsen, R.B., Macintyre, M. and Watson, C. (1996) Solution-focused parenting groups: an empirical study, *Journal of Systemic Therapies*, 15, 12–25.

Zimmerman, T.S., Prest, L.A. and Wetzel, B.E. (1997) Solution-focused couples therapy groups: an empirical study, *Journal of Family Therapy*, 19, 125–144.

Index

Index entries appear in word-by-word alphabetical order.

AN INTRODUCTION TO
Applying
Social Work
Theories and
Methods

BARBRA TEATER

**AN INTRODUCTION TO
APPLYING SOCIAL WORK
THEORIES AND METHODS**

Barbra Teater

9780335237784 (Paperback)
July 2010

eBook also available

This practical book provides a basic introduction to the most commonly used theories and methods in social work practice. The book explores the concept of a theory and a method, the difference between the two and the ways in which they are connected. Teater also discusses the social worker-client relationship and offers a handy overview of anti-oppressive practice.

Key features:

- Each chapter explores a single theory or method in depth
- Uses a variety of interactive tools to encourage exploration of thoughts and beliefs
- Step-by-step illustrations show how to apply the theory/method to a social work case

www.openup.co.uk

OPEN UNIVERSITY PRESS
McGraw - Hill Education

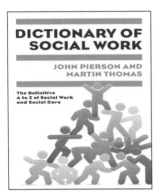

DICTIONARY OF SOCIAL WORK
The Definitive A to Z of Social
Work and Social Care

John Pierson and Martin Thomas

9780335238811 (Paperback)
September 2010

eBook also available

With over 1500 entries, this popular dictionary provides concise and up to date explanations of the theories, approaches and terminology that define front-line social work and social care. These entries explain, in jargon-free language, how key concepts can be used to improve practice. Clear explanations outline significant developments such as Every Child Matters and the personalization of adult services.

Key features:

- Entries are helpfully cross referenced and are evidence based
- Written by specialists in the field
- Specific focus on the most recent legislation and policy guidance from government

www.openup.co.uk   **OPEN UNIVERSITY PRESS**
McGraw - Hill Education